Securing Microsoft 365

Defending against the top cybersecurity threats in Microsoft 365

About the Author

Joe Stocker is the founder and CEO of Patriot Consulting, one of the top Microsoft Security partners in the United States. Patriot Consulting has completed more than 800 cybersecurity projects since 2015.

Joe's expertise and leadership have resulted in Patriot being invited into the Microsoft Elite Security Partner program and the Microsoft Security Partner Advisory Council (SECPAC). These two invite-only programs are limited to a small handful of Microsoft partners worldwide.

In 2020, Joe was awarded the Microsoft MVP award for his work in security (1 of 23 in the United States). Joe was invited by Microsoft to provide cybersecurity consulting services for Microsoft Defending Democracy, which helped to secure the US 2020 Elections. In 2021, this program was extended to provide services to 31 democracies around the world.

Joe started his career in 1999 as a system administrator and began public speaking in 2008. Joe writes a technology blog at www.TheCloudTechnologist.com and hosts a podcast on Spotify and iTunes called "Cybersecurity 101 with Joe and Larry."

Joe lives in California with his family and enjoys studying the Bible.

Contents

Introduction

Over the past decade, I've had the honor of speaking to more than 3,000 companies around the world about cybersecurity trends and listening to their top concerns. And as a consultant specializing in Microsoft Cybersecurity, I've helped hundreds of organizations deploy Microsoft solutions. There are three topics that have remained consistent, and I expect will continue to remain a focus:

1) Identity
2) Email
3) Devices

Did you know that more than 90% of the Fortune 500 and 500,000 businesses in the United States use Microsoft 365?[1] This book is for those IT Professionals or Security Analysts that are responsible for protecting these 250 million users of Microsoft 365. I will share with you the best practices I have used successfully to protect some of the world's largest organizations, including government institutions, banks, healthcare, retail, manufacturing, entertainment, and several other industries.

This book describes how to defend against attacks that I have observed first-hand while responding to security incidents. I have investigated the Tactics, Techniques, and Procedures that adversaries have used to hack and which countermeasures have been effective.

The Urgency of Security

My job as a security consultant is to listen to the threats that organizations are facing and then present effective solutions. Often, the problems are urgent. For example, as I write this introduction, I am thinking about how to best help three different organizations that I spoke with today.

The first was a local government agency that had their email compromised and needed to determine whether it was an insider attack or an external threat. (70% of all breaches in 2020 were caused by outsiders[2]). In Chapter Ten, "Incident Response," I will share the techniques I use when responding to account takeovers in Microsoft 365.

The second was a global logistics company under a massive bot-net attack that threatened to disrupt their shipments. In Chapter Four, "Preventing Data Breaches," I will explore Microsoft solutions that can detect and prevent data breaches.

The third was a humanitarian organization responsible for solving food insecurity in 100 countries. They found out that their Microsoft 365 configuration was spilling personally identifiable information for children in Africa who had been recently diagnosed with HIV. In Chapter Eight, "Preventing Sensitive Data Leaks," I will describe each Microsoft solution that can help with these types of issues.

These three conversations all happened in one day, and that is why I decided to write this book. I feel a sense of urgency to share my knowledge with as many people as possible because these problems are often preventable.

---

[1] https://www.linkedin.com/pulse/why-90-fortune-500-companies-now-using-microsoft-cloud-natasha-spurr/?articleId=6633338614921211904

[2] https://enterprise.verizon.com/resources/executivebriefs/2020-dbir-executive-brief.pdf

Chapter One – Securing the Identity in M365

Identity: The new security perimeter

Network Firewalls have been the de facto security perimeter since they were invented in the late 1980s[3]. If a firewall blocked all incoming traffic from the internet, then the level of difficulty for the hacker was significant. I remember a time when hacking incidents rarely made news headlines. For the first part of my career, between 1999 and 2014, none of the organizations I had worked for experienced a data breach. Fast forward to 2021, and cyberattacks are regularly in the news, with an average ranging from three data breaches per day to four hundred per day.[4] Many go unreported to avoid damaging public reputation, although this is changing due to new global, federal, and state regulations that impose fines for not reporting breaches to personally identifiable information.

So, what changed?

As organizations began adopting Cloud Computing in general, or Software as a Service (SaaS)[5] in particular, the security perimeter shifted to the credentials used to authenticate to internet-connected systems. More than 80% of breaches in the present era can be traced to a guessed or stolen password. Attacks have now shifted to target the identity of users, as there are now less than 5% breaches involving exploitation of a software vulnerability.[6] Ten years ago, an email address was typically different from the username, and so when organizations started moving to the cloud, they changed the username to equal the email address. This one change reduced the number of factors for an attacker to guess by 50%.

For Microsoft 365, the username is the email address[7], and for 90% of all M365 users, it is protected by a single factor (a password). This is a HUGE problem because anyone with an internet connection can attempt to guess the password of nearly any account. While Azure Active Directory has a configurable lockout policy (the default is to lock the account after 10 failed attempts), clever attackers are using global botnets to perform password sprays in parallel, at a rate of 4,000 guesses per hour. This is due to the *Githubification*[8] of security tools, where junior-level hackers can leverage code written by skilled programmers (in the 2000's they were called "script kiddies"). Various studies have found that users will click on around 20% to 50% of phishing emails designed to trick the user into giving away their username and password.

Another thing that changed was the aggregation of password dumps for sale in dark corners of the internet, making it simple for newbie hackers to perform more effective targeted attacks using

[3] For the history of the first network firewalls, read this interesting article https //www.darkreading.com/who-invented-the-firewall/d/d-id/1129238

[4] https://www.statista.com/statistics/273550/data-breaches-recorded-in-the-united-states-by-number-of-breaches-and-records-exposed/

[5] Early examples of SaaS applications include Salesforce in 1999 or Microsoft's "Business Productivity Online Services" (BPOS) in 2008. BPOS has evolved into what is now called Microsoft 365 which is used by more than 200 million people worldwide and generates more than 50 billion in annual revenue for Microsoft (2020).

[6] 2020 Verizon Data Breach Report https://enterprise.verizon.com/resources/executivebriefs/2020-dbir-executive-brief.pdf

[7] There is a new preview feature called Home Realm Discovery that allows a user to sign in using any proxy email address, which prevents IT from having to change the Active Directory User Principal Name (UPN). https://docs.microsoft.com/en-us/azure/active-directory/authentication/howto-authentication-use-email-signin

[8] The Githubification of InfoSec https://medium.com/@johnlatwc/the-githubification-of-infosec-afbdbfaad1d1

"credential stuffing tools[9]" such as *Snipr* or *Hydra*. These are automated credential verification tools that take some of the 11 billion passwords dumped[10] from all the hacked websites over the years and target a list of popular websites like Microsoft 365 or Google. These tools leverage a human weakness known as password recycling, where we often reuse the same password on sites like Netflix with other websites such as Spotify. If one of these sites is hacked and the credentials are obtained, hackers load these passwords into tools to see what other websites the email address and password combination will work on.

Are Network Firewalls still important? Absolutely! Researchers at the University of Maryland purposefully placed vulnerable computers on the Internet to see how often they would be attacked and observed one attack every 39 seconds. [11] Likewise, Identity information without additional security measures beyond a password is like plugging your most valuable server to the internet without a firewall. At one of the RSA Security Conferences I attended, Todd Inskeep of Booz Allen Hamilton stated that the Cyber Threat Alliance (CTA) discovered that Multi-Factor Authentication would have prevented each of the 159,700 cyber incidents tracked by CTA that year.[12]

For organizations that have adopted cloud technologies, their security perimeter is now the Identity of the user signing into the cloud service. Technically, this has been true for the past ten years and many organizations are just now realizing the need for additional layers of in-depth defense around identity.

> *"Identity without MFA is like plugging your most valuable server to the internet without a firewall."*

So how do we prevent unauthorized access to Microsoft 365?

It starts with securing an identity to use other factors besides the password. While some security vendors are limited to just two factors of authentication (sometimes referred to as "two-factor authentication" or 2FA), Microsoft provides multiple factors of authentication (MFA). However, not all MFA options are created equally. We will describe the available options and point out the pros and cons of each.

MFA Authentication Method #1: Text Message (SMS)

The most common 2nd factor of authentication[13] is the short message service (SMS). Chances are, you experience something like this when you sign into online banking (if not, you should go enable that

9 A non-complete list of tools such as SentryMBA, Vertex, STORM, Snipr, Account Reaper, Hydra, Cr3dOv3r, PrimeKiller, Joyn was published online https://medium.com/@jbron/list-of-credential-stuffing-tools-c42f972195ed

10 The website "Have I been Pwned" reports 11,145,906,797 pwned accounts as of April 10th, 2021, https://haveibeenpwned.com/

11 https://eng.umd.edu/news/story/study-hackers-attack-every-39-seconds

12 Page 6 https://published-prd.lanyonevents.com/published/rsaus18/sessionsFiles/8631/TECH-T10_TECH-T10-Evidence-based-Security-the-New-Top-5-Controls.pdf

13 The most common 2FA methods are text messages (44%), push notifications (4%) and voice calls (1%). https://techcommunity.microsoft.com/t5/azure-active-directory-identity/all-your-creds-are-belong-to-us/ba-p/855124

now). Microsoft has stated that enabling SMS will reduce the risk of compromise by 99.9%![14]. SMS has its limitations, as we will describe next, but it is certainly better than nothing at all because it blocks automated password spray attacks.

But research has found that nation-state-backed hacking groups or cybercrime syndicates have a 24% success rate at bypassing SMS 2FA using a variety of techniques such as SIM-Card Swapping, Phone Number Porting, Man-In-The-Middle, Signaling System No. 7 (SS7), or Social Engineering.

In March 2021, Vice reported a gaping flaw in SMS that allowed hackers to take over phone numbers in minutes simply by paying a company to reroute text messages. "A Hacker Got All My Texts for $16".[15]

Roger Grimes from KnowBe4 presented "12 Ways to Hack MFA" at the RSA Conference (this session is now on YouTube: https://www.youtube.com/watch?v=QJL63_LO6c8).

It's time to move away from SMS as a 2FA Factor.

The Payment Card Industry (PCI) does not recommend SMS for 2FA and has proposed to prohibit it for upcoming standards. A division of the US Department of Commerce known as the National Institute of Standards and Technology (NIST) has published guidance that prohibits using SMS as a form of 2FA (800-63). I highly recommend Alex Weinert's (Microsoft) article, which recommends discontinuation of telephony-based factors of authentication "It's Time to Hang Up on Phone Transports for Authentication."[16]

Some organizations have resisted deploying 2FA because the phones are not owned by the organization. They are often owned by the employee (this model of using a personal phone for work is known as bring-your-own-device or BYOD). Organizations are afraid that if they require their employees to use text messages as a 2nd factor, then they are liable to pay for the phone or the phone bill. California has regulations that do, in fact, make employers responsible for some of these payments.

Today you can globally disable SMS and Call to Phone to leave stronger authentication options available.

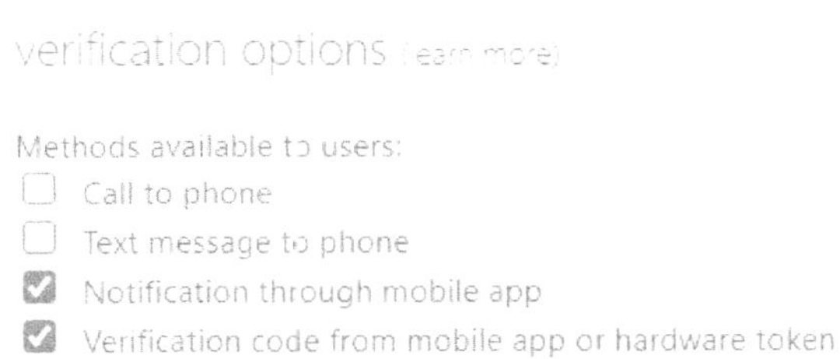

[14] "Based on [Microsoft] studies, your account is more than 99.9% less likely to be compromised if you use MFA" https://techcommunity.microsoft.com/t5/azure-active-directory-identity/your-pa-word-doesn-t-matter/ba-p/731984

[15] https://www.vice.com/en/article/y3g8wb/hacker-got-my-texts-16-dollars-sakari-netnumber

[16] https://techcommunity.microsoft.com/t5/azure-active-directory-identity/it-s-time-to-hang-up-on-phone-transports-for-authentication/ba-p/1751752

When this box is unchecked, the next time the user signs in, they will be required to register for the remaining factors of authentication if they have not yet enrolled in those other methods. Users can also enroll in the stronger methods manually at any time by browsing ***Myprofile.Microsoft.com***.

The registration of security factors can be controlled by Conditional Access Policy (An Azure AD Premium P1 license is required for this feature)[17]. For example, you can prevent users from registering factors of authentication from a personal computer or from any location outside of a corporate network. Microsoft announced Temporary Access Pass[18] at the Ignite 2021 Conference; this feature is handy because users can now register strong authentication methods for a limited period (for example, for new employees or for users who have lost or forgotten their other authentication factors).

Microsoft will soon allow organizations to limit the use of SMS to groups, roles, or administrative units. This will be helpful for large organizations that have lower-risk user populations, who will take time to transition to stronger authentication methods since retiring SMS will take time. For the same reason, organizations struggle to mandate SMS 2FA for personal devices. These same organizations have an even harder time mandating the use of the Microsoft Authenticator app since most BYOD devices are not enrolled into the Mobile Device Management Solutions (MDM), where the app is pushed out. Users must manually download the app before they can use it for authentication. Microsoft is planning on improving this experience using in-band authentication inside of some of their mobile applications. For example, in the Outlook Mobile app, users will be able to receive an authentication prompt without having to install the Authenticator app.

MFA Authentication Method #2: Mobile App Push Notification

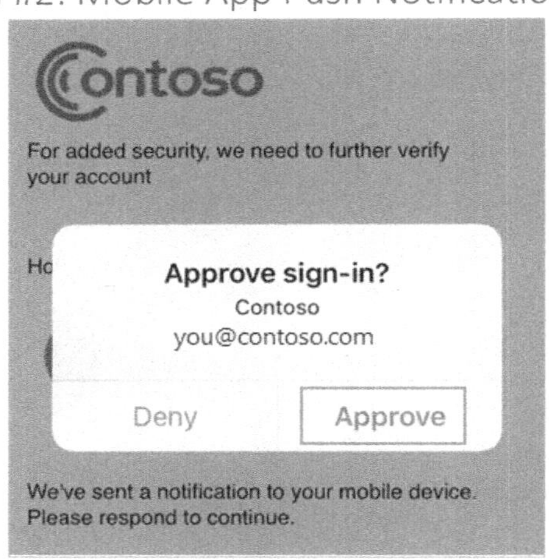

Pros: Perhaps the most convenient user authentication method next to Passwordless

Cons: (1) Android users can install auto-accept applications such as Tasker to accept any push notification.[19] (2) Some users made mistakes and accepted a push notification generated when a hacker guessed the password. (3) Requires the user to install the Authenticator Mobile App, which is

[17] https://docs.microsoft.com/en-us/azure/active-directory/conditional-access/howto-conditional-access-policy-registration

[18] https://docs.microsoft.com/en-us/azure/active-directory/authentication/howto-authentication-temporary-access-pass

[19] For examples of Android App Store apps that can auto approve push notifications see DUO Auto Approve, OKTA Auto Approve, Tasker (auto accept anything)

sometimes hard in BYOD environments when there is no MDM solution to push the app, or users and/or unions complain about company apps on personal devices (4) vulnerable to Man-in-the-middle.

MFA Authentication Method #3: Mobile App Verification Code

Also known as a one-time-passcode (OTP), this solves the problems with the push notification but at the expense of user convenience (users must type in the code they see rotating on their mobile app). Another benefit of this OTP method is that it does not rely upon cellular or Wi-Fi connectivity other than the first time the codes are synchronized during registration.

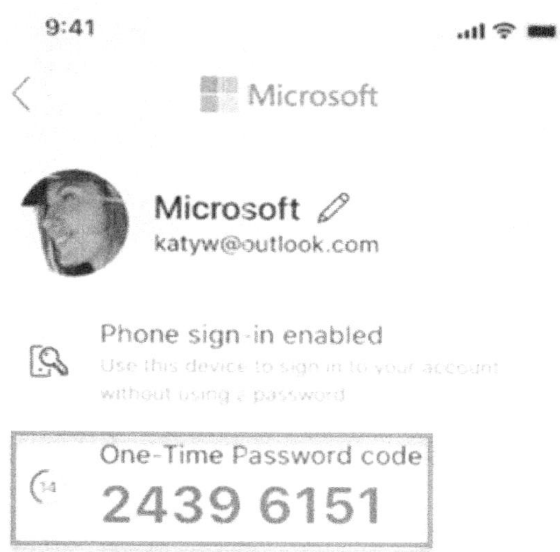

MFA Authentication Method #4: Hardware tokens

There are two manufacturers that make hardware tokens natively for Azure AD without any on-premises servers: DEEPNET[20] (England) and Token2[21] (Switzerland).

Why Hardware tokens? I recommend these when mobile devices are not an option for 2FA.

For example, you might offer these to employees who are reluctant to install the Microsoft Authenticator Mobile App.

MFA Authentication Method #5: Passwordless

The first factor by default is the password, but Microsoft provides the following three "Passwordless" authentication methods that can become the user's first factor for authentication, AND, all three satisfy the "Require MFA" Conditional Access policy in Azure Active Directory too.

1. Windows Hello for Business
2. Microsoft Authenticator for iOS or Android (Free)

---

[20] https://deepnetsecurity.com/authenticators/one-time-password/safeid/hardware-mfa-tokens-office-365-azure-multi-factor-authentication/

[21] https://www.token2.com/shop/page/hardware-tokens-for-azure-cloud-multi-factor-authentication

3. FIDO2 Hardware Security Keys (starting at $20 USD each)

Think of Passwordless as a convenient way for users to sign in. Hackers can still ignore Passwordless and select "other ways to sign in" (as shown below) to attack other authentication methods. Microsoft is planning on allowing organizations to disable Passwords entirely in the future.

FIDO2 is the latest generation of the U2F protocol. U2F ("Universal 2nd Factor") is an open authentication standard that enables internet users to securely access any number of online services with one single security key instantly and with no drivers or client software needed. FIDO stands for ("Fast Identity Online") and is an open industry association launched in February 2013 whose mission is to develop and promote authentication standards that help reduce the world's over-reliance on passwords.

The key advantage of FIDO2 keys over Windows Hello for Business (WH4B) is that FIDO2 can be used as a Passwordless sign-in option for shared workstations, whereas WH4B is limited to a single user per workstation. The 2nd advantage of FIDO2 is that it has a feature known as URL Binding that creates phishing-resistant authentication. We will discuss URL binding as an email security solution in Chapter Two.

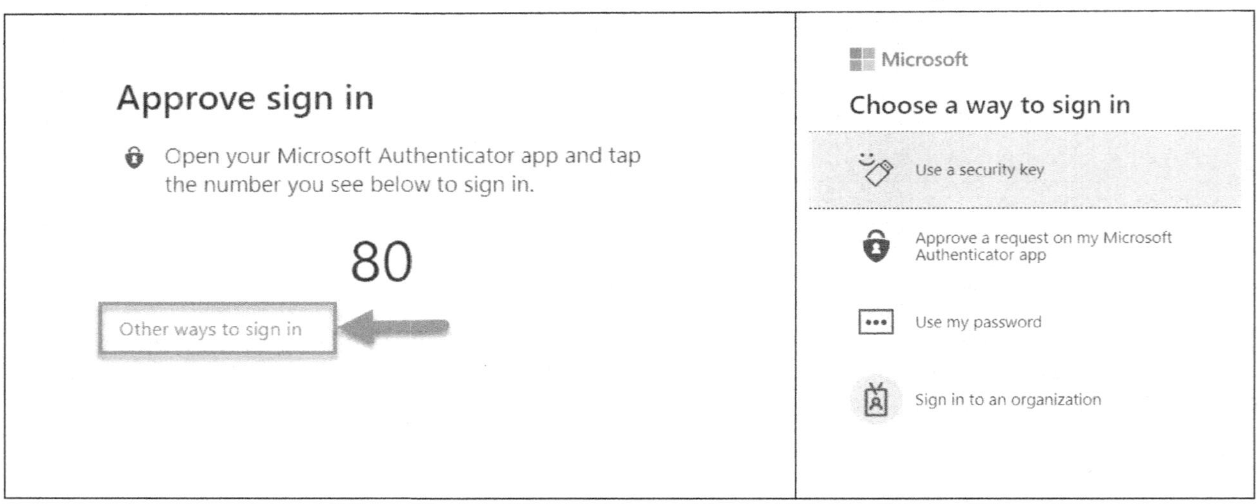

Figure 1 Passwordless Authentication dialog box with an option for the hacker to select other authentication methods.

Less than 10% of the 200 million users in Microsoft 365 are using MFA[22]. This makes 90% of the users in Microsoft 365 vulnerable to Password Spray and Spear Phishing. I'll cover Spear Phishing in Chapter Two.

Since Microsoft does not yet support the feature to eliminate passwords completely (to turn it off as an authentication method), to reduce the risk of a successful Password Spray, it is important that users don't use weak passwords. To help with this, Microsoft includes a feature called Password Protection.

Password Protection

Human beings have limited memory, and studies have shown that people will, at most, use four unique passwords across all the websites they use[23]; this is referred to as "password recycling." People are typically terrible at selecting strong passwords, often going with simple passwords such as "123456" or "password."[24]

The Microsoft solution for preventing users from choosing weak passwords is called Password Protection. It's free for cloud accounts, but if you have accounts syncing from an on-premises Active Directory, then you will need an Azure AD Premium P1 license to install the Password Protection solution on your Active Directory Domain Controllers.

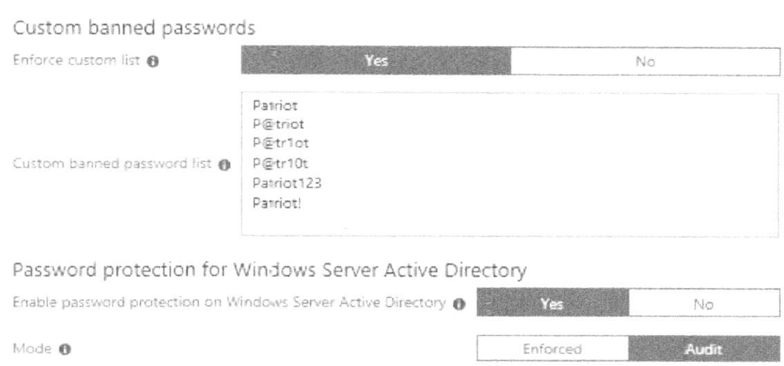

Figure 2 TIP: Microsoft will automatically substitute @ for A, 1 for I, etc., so there is no need to enter the variations as shown in this example.

You can specify your own list of banned words, such as your company name, and then Microsoft will merge that with its own list of custom banned passwords. Microsoft's list of banned passwords is dynamically generated anytime more than 5 people worldwide use the same password. So, when "Summer2022!" becomes a popular password, then it will become banned.

When the "Mode" is switched from Audit to Enforced (see screenshot above), then the next time users attempt to change their password using a weak password, they will see this new error message:

---

[22] https://techcommunity.microsoft.com/t5/azure-active-directory-identity/all-your-creds-are-belong-to-us/ba-p/855124

[23] Passwords Usage and Human Memory Limitations: A Survey across Age and Educational Background https://www.ncbi.nlm.nih.gov/pmc/articles/PMC3515440/

[24] Top 200 most common passwords https://nordpass.com/most-common-passwords-list/

"Unfortunately, your password contains a word, phrase, or pattern that makes your password easily guessable. Please try again with a different password."

Attack Simulator

Microsoft Attack Simulator is a solution that is included in the Microsoft Defender for Office 365 Plan 2 license. It can simulate password spray attacks or brute force attacks (and other attacks that I will cover in Chapter Two). For example, if you want to know how many users in your organization are using "Password1234!", then it will return a list of all users using that weak password. Or, if you have a dictionary that you want to upload to simulate a brute force attack, you can do that without locking out any accounts.

Navigate to Attack Simulator at https://protection.office.com/attacksimulator

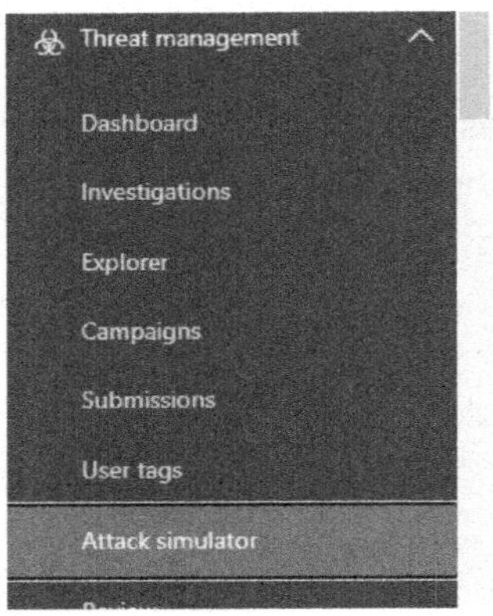

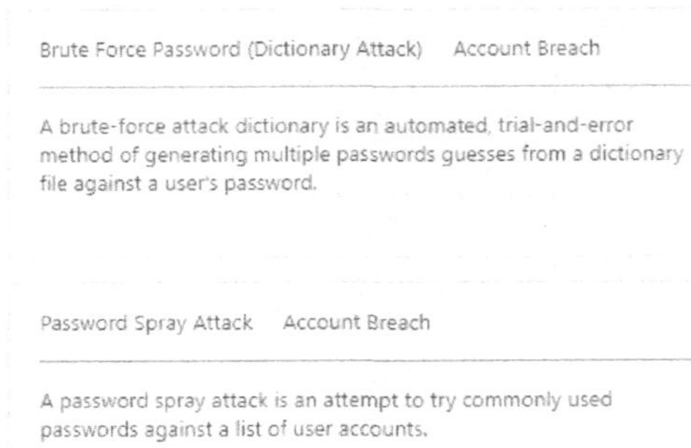

Note: I will discuss the new version of the Attack Simulator in Chapter Two.

Only Global Administrators can use this powerful tool for obvious reasons, and the Administrator sign-in is checked to see if it has been signed in using Microsoft's native 2FA methods. If a 3rd party 2FA was used, such as DUO, then a manual work-around must be used to trigger the authentication using the following hyperlink: https://protection.office.com/?mfa=1

Local Administrator Password Solution (LAPS)

When the local administrator account has been compromised, attackers can move laterally through the network. A common hacker technique is to use tools like NetSess[25] to identify workstations used by Domain Admins and then disable Antivirus and ASR rules so they can extract password hashes from the Local Security Authority Subsystem Service (LSASS.exe) using tools such as Mimikatz. LAPS is a free download[26] that randomizes local admin passwords. When combined with Windows Firewall, and Tamper Protection, this can increase the time and difficulty for adversaries to move laterally.[27]

There are two major components to LAPS: the first modifies the forest's schema to include two new fields to store the password generated on the client; the second is a Group Policy extension that runs on

[25] http://www.joeware.net/freetools/tools/netsess/

[26] https://www.microsoft.com/en-us/download/details.aspx?id=46899

[27] https://sid-500.com/2017/08/25/active-directory-installing-and-configuring-local-administrator-password-solution-laps/

the client to report the new password back to Active Directory. This requires modifying the Active Directory and every client in the environment.

It is recommended to deploy LAPS to any internet-connected server and all user workstations.

Blocking Legacy Authentication

Most of the IT Administrators I speak to do not realize that legacy authentication methods bypass Conditional Access Policies. Microsoft reported that less than 16% of organizations are blocking legacy authentication[28]. Microsoft had intended to block legacy authentication in the second half of 2021 but backed off in an announcement made in a February 2021 blog post[29]. Instead, Microsoft plans to only block legacy authentication protocols that are not used regularly. This includes EWS, ActiveSync (for older Apple devices running less than iOS v11), POP, IMAP, Remote PowerShell, MAPI, RPC, SMTP AUTH and OAB. AutoDiscover is a legacy protocol but is not slated for retirement because it doesn't provide access to user data, and as a tenant, has some EWS or Exchange ActiveSync (EAS) usage, AutoDiscover is necessary for client configuration. So, this means attackers will likely switch to using the AutoDiscover as their favorite password spray protocol for guessing passwords. Currently, SMTP, IMAP and POP are the most popular protocols used for account compromise in Microsoft 365.

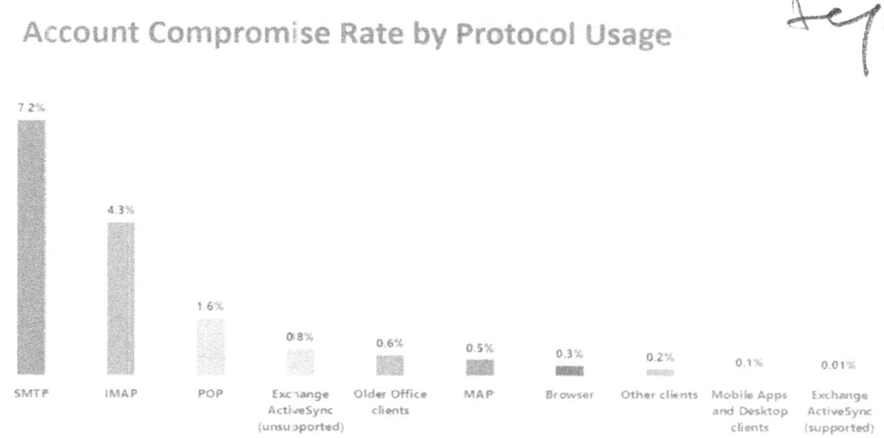

Figure 3 Microsoft reported the top legacy authentication protocols used to perform account takeovers in Microsoft 365

The concern many have with the new policy is that application vendors may use this as an excuse to not update their software.

In August of 2020, the default Conditional Access configuration for legacy authentication changed for any new policy created so that it applies to all client apps—including legacy authentication clients. Prior to August 2020, unless you explicitly selected "other clients," they were not automatically included in a CA policy. This change should help protect new tenants going forward, but there are hundreds of thousands of tenants that need to update their policies and block legacy authentication to protect themselves from password spray attacks.

---

[28] https://techcommunity.microsoft.com/t5/azure-active-directory-identity/conditional-access-policies-now-apply-to-all-client-applications/ba-p/1257371

[29] https://techcommunity.microsoft.com/t5/exchange-team-blog/basic-authentication-and-exchange-online-february-2021-update/ba-p/2111904

Report-only mode[30] is an effective way for clients to determine what the impact of blocking legacy authentication would be before turning it off. This is the default option when creating a new Conditional Access Policy.

REPORT-ONLY MODE GOTCHA

A REPORT-ONLY CA POLICY WITH "REQUIRE COMPLIANT DEVICES" MAY PROMPT USERS ON MAC, IOS, AND ANDROID TO SELECT A DEVICE CERTIFICATE.

The other option is to export the Azure AD sign-in logs, which record historical sign-ins using legacy authentication protocols.

Authentication Policies in Exchange Online[31] can be assigned to individual users. For example, you can assign the account used by the helpdesk application to connect with legacy IMAP and SMTP, whereas those protocols would be disabled for everyone else.

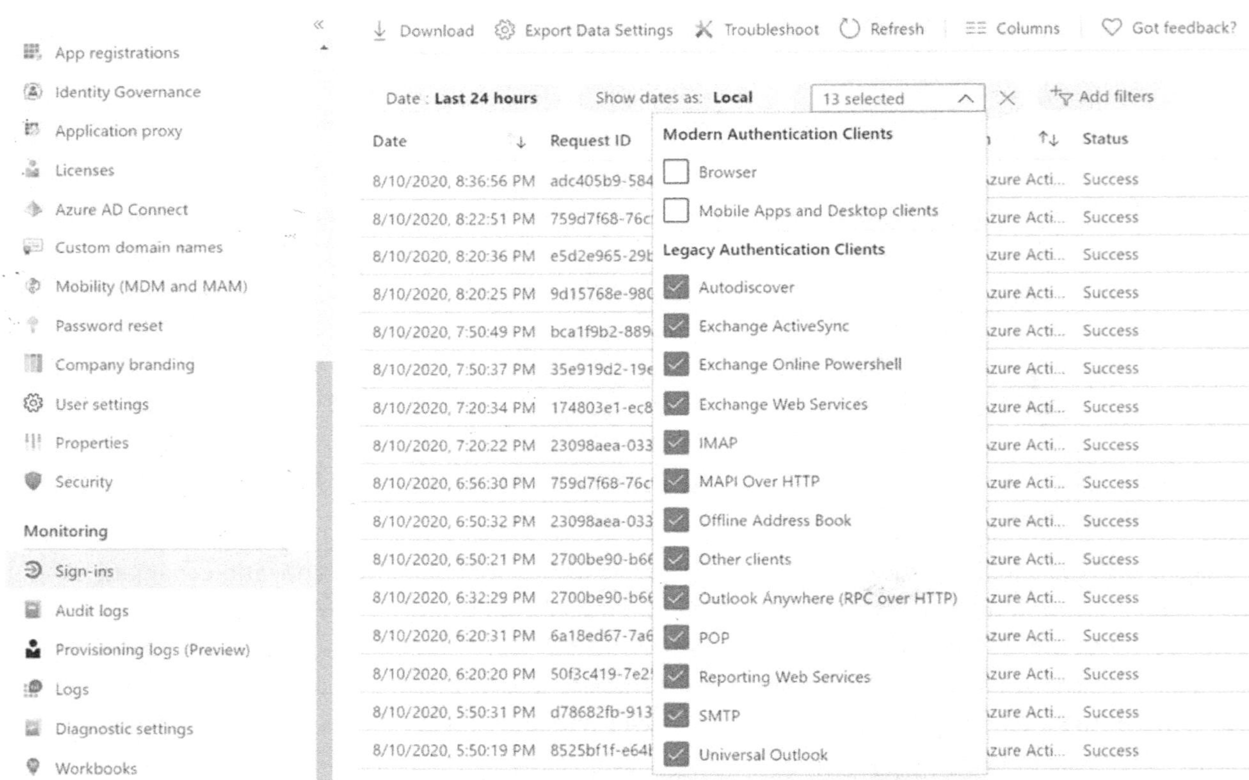

---

30 https://docs.microsoft.com/en-us/azure/active-directory/conditional-access/concept-conditional-access-report-only

31 https://docs.microsoft.com/en-us/exchange/clients-and-mobile-in-exchange-online/disable-basic-authentication-in-exchange-online

There are two types of MFA that can be enabled on a user account in Microsoft 365: Always-ON MFA or Conditional Access MFA. If you enable them both on the same user account, Always-ON MFA wins.

Always-ON MFA overrides Conditional MFA

A confusing thing that sometimes happens is that users start off with Always-ON MFA, and they forget to turn it off when moving to Conditional MFA, and they wonder why they are being prompted for MFA all the time, rather than on the conditions set in the policy. You must disable Always-ON MFA if you plan to use Conditional MFA; otherwise, Always-ON MFA will override conditional MFA.

Benefits of Always-ON MFA

1. Always-ON MFA is free with all Azure AD and M365 License Plans, whereas Conditional MFA requires an Azure AD Premium P1 license
2. Always-ON MFA automatically blocks legacy authentication, but conditional MFA requires an explicit Azure AD Conditional Access Policy to block legacy authentication protocols.

MFA App Password Gotcha

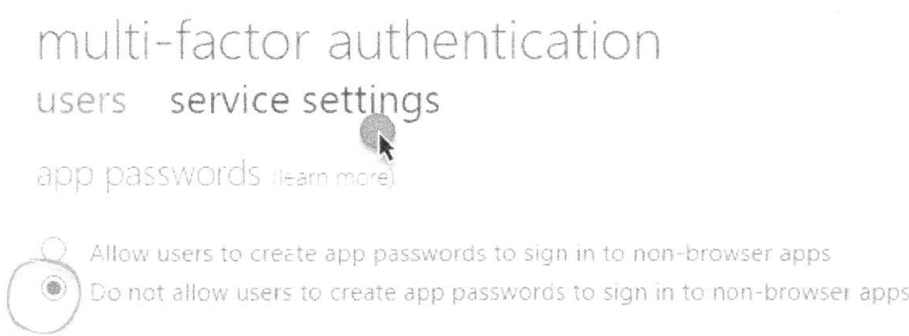

Figure 4 I recommend disabling MFA App Passwords

Up until Microsoft modernized the user enrollment interface for MFA, the older MFA enrollment wizard provided end-users with an MFA App password by default (although it was possible to disable it, the "service settings" did not look like a clickable link, so many of my clients told me they didn't realize there was a hidden series of configuration options there). This App Password was used for older applications such as Office 2010 that did not support MFA. The issue with the MFA App Password was that if the user held on to the password, say on a sticky note, and if they ever left the organization, they could still sign in using that app password even when IT reset the password on the user's account. This is because many IT organizations do not disable user accounts during the employee exit/termination procedure. They often reset the password and give it to team members or managers to access the user's account. They don't realize that the terminated user can still sign in using the MFA app password since it was, by design, used as an alternative means of authentication. Going forward, the new MFA enrollment wizard at Myprofile.Microsoft.com does not generate app passwords, but it is still encouraged to disable the App Password feature (just make sure you don't have any legacy applications like Office 2010 still laying around).

MFA App Passwords can be disabled here:
https://account.activedirectory.windowsazure.com/usermanagement/mfasettings.aspx

Redirecting oAuth for Administrator Approval

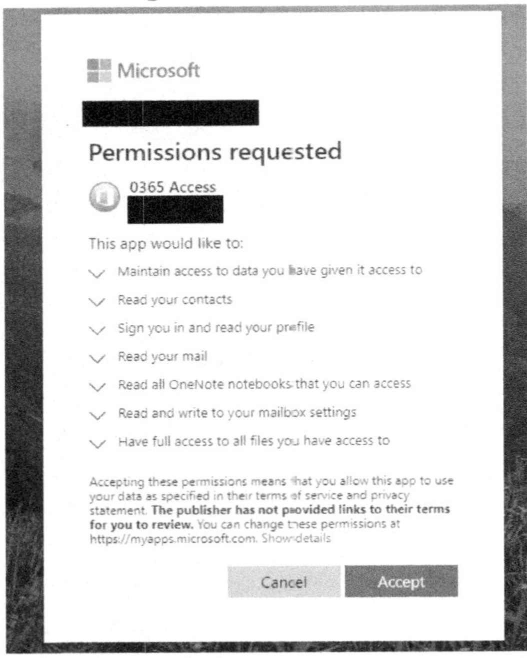

Would any of your users click on a pop-up that requests "Office 365 Access?" Seems innocent enough. It has an icon that looks like Microsoft, and who reads all the fine print anyway? Yes, chances are your users will eventually be tricked to click on an illicit oAuth application created by a hacker to gain persistent access to your user's data.

I've encountered these applications during incident response investigations. For example, the company that hired me said they had reset the user's password, and they couldn't understand why emails were still being sent out by the hacker. These illicit oAuth applications do not rely upon the user's credentials, so they remain persistent even after a password change.

The first step is to disable user consent:

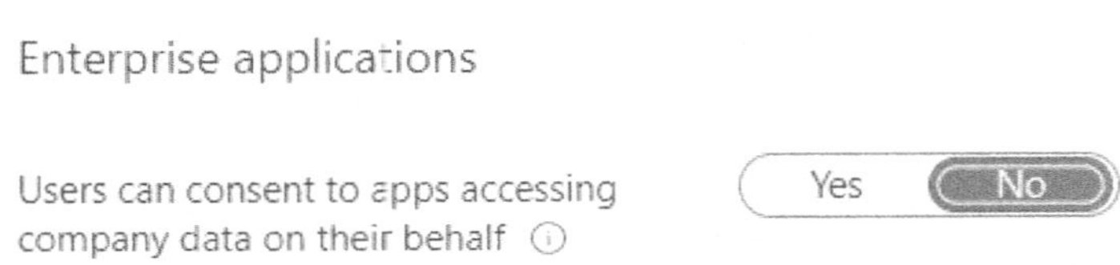

The second step is to enable Admin Consent Requests and select the user groups or roles that can approve the consents, as shown below.

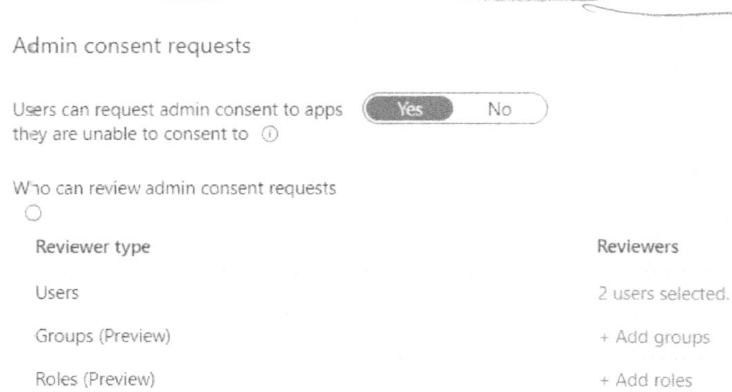

What about all the past illicit oAuth applications?

Go to Portal.Azure.com > Azure Active Directory > Enterprise Applications, inspect your applications, and disable suspicious applications as shown below: *Properties > Enable for users to sign-in? (No)*

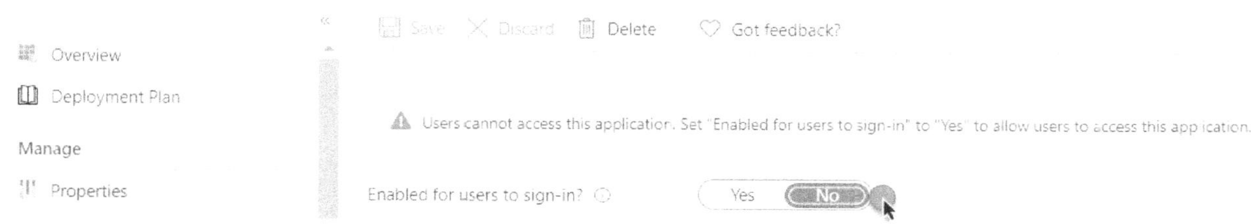

Continuous Access Evaluation (CAE)

CAE is off by default but can be enabled in Azure AD to enforce network location changes, disabled users, or password resets in near real-time. This is helpful because some clients do not check back for revoked tokens often.

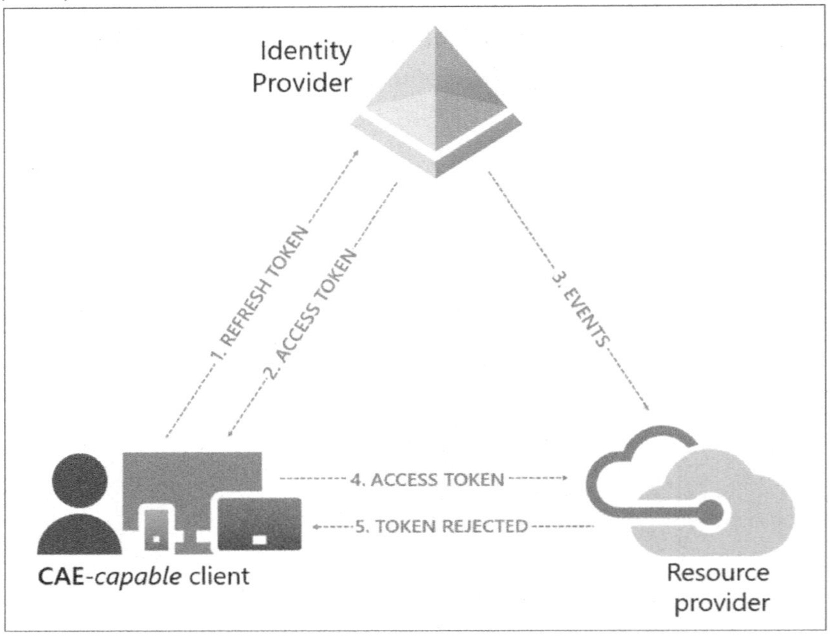

Supported Clients

- Outlook Windows
- Outlook iOS
- Outlook Android
- Outlook Mac
- Outlook Web App
- Teams for Windows (Only for Teams resource)
- Teams iOS (Only for Teams resource)
- Teams Android (Only for Teams resource)
- Teams Mac (Only for Teams resource)
- Word/Excel/PowerPoint for Windows
- Word/Excel/PowerPoint for iOS
- Word/Excel/PowerPoint for Android
- Word/Excel/PowerPoint for Mac

Security Defaults

Why can't Microsoft just make all these settings secure by default? Microsoft listened to that feedback and provided a toggle switch to enable several security settings in a simple toggle option called Security Defaults[32].

The setting is found in Portal.Azure.com > Azure Active Directory > Properties > Manage Security Defaults

The recommendation is to enable this for smaller organizations (small businesses) as larger enterprises will often require the flexibility of conditional access to gradually enable MFA over time. For example, if you have 20,000 users and only 10 people on the helpdesk, it could be quite disruptive to flip the switch to enable MFA overnight.

So, what happens when this switch is enabled?

- All users are required to register for Azure AD Multi-Factor Authentication.
    - This is a nice feature because normally, forced registration requires an Azure AD Premium P2 license and is enabled through the Azure Identity Protection feature.
- Requiring administrators to perform multi-factor authentication
- Blocking legacy authentication protocols.
- Requiring users to perform multi-factor authentication when necessary.
- The weakest forms of 2FA are blocked (No SMS, MFA App Passwords, or Call to Phone)
- Protecting privileged activities like access to the Azure portal.

Important: Exchange Online Tenants created before August 2017 will need to enable the Modern Authentication Toggle Switch in their tenant[33].

Privileged Identity Management (PIM)

Privileged Identity Management provides just-in-time administrative rights for roles or groups such as the Global Administrators. Microsoft recommends having less than 5 Global Admins in Microsoft 365. For large organizations, this is a major hurdle. I've seen an organization with 100,000 users that had 100 Global Admins, and I've seen organizations with 50,000 users with only 2 global administrators (so it can be done!). The trick is to implement role-based access control (RBAC) so that users are granted the least privilege possible to perform their job functions. Then, instead of always signing into an account with

---

[32] https://docs.microsoft.com/en-us/azure/active-directory/fundamentals/concept-fundamentals-security-defaults
[33] https://docs.microsoft.com/en-us/exchange/clients-and-mobile-in-exchange-online/enable-or-disable-modern-authentication-in-exchange-online

high privileges, or having to maintain a second account, check out the role to perform the activities for a short time. It will automatically demote the user to a standard user account when the time expires. PIM requires an Azure AD Premium P2 license. The most frequent question I get asked is whether it can extend to on-premises workloads such as Active Directory roles or local administrator elevation. PIM is limited to Office 365 and Azure roles and groups.

Microsoft recently retired the Enhanced Security Admin Environment (ESAE) architecture (often referred to as red forest, admin forest, or hardened forest). The environment was complex to administer and required Microsoft Identity Manager. The direction Microsoft is moving in is to help customers migrate to pure Azure AD environments. Most of my clients have had to deploy solutions from Thycotic or CyberArk to provide the equivalent features of PIM for their on-premises environments while using LAPS for workstations to reduce the license cost for these 3rd party solutions.

Risk-Based Authentication

Azure Identity Protection is a feature that requires the Azure AD Premium P2 license (which is also included in EMS E5, or M365 E5 Security). This feature can proactively block sign-ins when the risk level meets a threshold defined by administrators.

Think about Azure AD P1 as reactive, whereas Azure AD P2 provides proactive risk-based policies to block risky sign-ins at the front door, saving your SECOPS team from investigating dozens of alerts.

For example, if you set the policy to block sign-ins when the user risk is high, it would trigger under the following two conditions: 1) if the user's password has been found in a data breach or 2) if the combined aggregate of individual sign-in risk events has caused the overall user to be at high risk.

Many organizations are required to be compliant with NIST 800-63b[34], which includes the rule that verifiers SHALL cross-check passwords against previous data breaches.

Azure Identity Protection's risk-based policy allows Microsoft to check passwords to see if they have been found in previous data breaches, in compliance with NIST 800-63b.

> When processing requests to establish and change memorized secrets, verifiers SHALL compare the prospective secrets against a list that contains values known to be commonly-used, expected, or compromised. For example, the list MAY include, but is not limited to:
>
> - Passwords obtained from previous breach corpuses
> - Dictionary words.
> - Repetitive or sequential characters (e.g. 'aaaaaa', '1234abcd').
> - Context-specific words, such as the name of the service, the username, and derivatives thereof.

Figure 5 NIST 800-63b

Some organizations have not yet synced their passwords from Active Directory to Azure AD. There is still this concern about 'storing passwords in the cloud.' It's really a myth because the password is not actually stored in the cloud. The data stored in place of the password is several orders of magnitude more secure when compared to how organizations protect their on-premises Active Directory database.

---

[34] https://www.nist.gov/itl/tig/projects/special-publication-800-63 Many people remember this NIST guidance because it was made famous for the 180 U-Turn on password age. NIST basically said "stop making users arbitrarily changing their passwords every 90 days." The thinking is: if users have a strong 2nd factor, then the strength of the first factor doesn't matter if it has not been found on a data breach or doesn't use dictionary words or repetitive or sequential characters. Long Passphrases such as "MyCoffeeCup@MyHouse2020" is significantly stronger than an 8 character password that a user has to write down "*a{<$9ol" because they'll be more likely just to numerically increase the last digit by 1 number every time.

Myth: Passwords are synced to the Cloud

Technically the password is not really stored in the cloud. The actual process is much more complicated.

The PBKDF2 key is derived from a SHA256 hash of the MD4 hash, which is derived from crypto API per RFC 2898. This PBKDF2 key is then sent within an SSL encrypted session. The PBKDF2 key is stored on a Bitlocker encrypted disk.

How does this compare to an on-premises Active Directory NTDS.dit database?

The NTDS.dit can be brute-forced at about 418 million keys per second. An eight-character password can be cracked in about 20 hours.[35]

PBKDF2 slows password crackers to a crawl at just 74 keys per second.

Still not convinced? Use Azure AD Pass-Thru-Authentication. Still better than ADFS since it's not internet-facing.

Do you know what else is better than on-premises Active Directory security? Think about the typical VPN authentication today: at best, it asks for a password and perhaps a 2FA challenge. That's about all that stands between a hacker from a TCP connection to the Domain Controller, which holds the keys to the kingdom. On a bad day, where the Domain Controller has not been patched with the latest updates, this is a data breach waiting to happen. Compare that to Azure AD, which does not directly expose itself via NTLM, Kerberos, or other authentication methods, but instead acts more like a SaaS service and can be strengthened with multiple factors of authentication, as we described in this chapter with Device Auth, Compliance checking. This is substantially more secure than 99% of the on-premises AD networks I have seen.

[35] https://techcommunity.microsoft.com/t5/azure-active-directory-identity/your-pa-word-doesn-t-matter/ba-p/731984

Network Session hijacking proxy theft

I first learned about this hacking technique, which I refer to in this book as "Man-in-the-middle," from a KnowBe4 blog post[36] in May 2018. I then tested 13 different Microsoft methods for defending against this attack and wrote a blog article[37] describing how about 50% of them were effective.

To understand how Azure Conditional Access can block EvilGinx2, it's important to understand how EvilGinx2 works. First, the attacker must purchase a domain name, like "office-mfa.com," and convince an end-user to click on that link. The attacker's machine passes all traffic onto the actual Microsoft Office 365 sign-on page. Since all traffic is proxied, the end-user sees the *actual* Office 365 sign-in page. This means the attacker does not have to waste valuable time trying to make the page look identical. The authentication token is captured after the user performs user-based authentication (SMS or Authenticator App). The attacker can then import the cookie into their own browser to access Office 365.

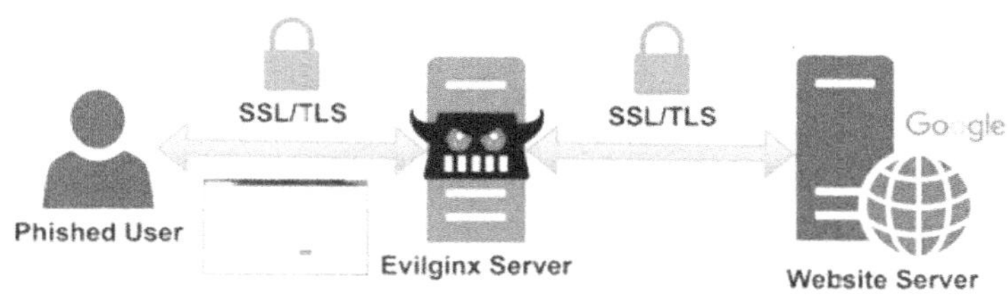

The attacker's EvilGinx2 server terminates the SSL session, and it then re-transmits a new SSL session against login.microsoftonline.com. This avoids all SSL errors in the browser since there is a valid SSL handshake to the attacker's machine. This is an advantage for the hacker, but it turns out to be the Achilles heel because Azure Conditional Access can perform additional checks that will all block EvilGinx, such as IP address, Domain Join Membership, Compliance (via Intune UEM), or Certificate (via CASB).

Kuba Gretzky (@mrgretzky) stated that it can defeat ***any form of 2FA***!

> ***"Be aware that:*** Every sign-in page, requiring the user to provide their password, with any form of 2FA implemented, can be phished using this technique!"
> **https://breakdev.org/evilginx-2-next-generation-of-phishing-2fa-tokens**

I will now describe several successful defenses using Microsoft technology to defend against this Man-in-the-middle technique: **IP Fencing, Hybrid Domain Join, FIDO2, and Intune Compliance.** There are other methods I wrote about in my blog[38], but these are my four top recommendations from the least to the greatest.

---

36 https://blog.knowbe4.com/heads-up-new-exploit-hacks-linkedin-2-factor-auth.-see-this-kevin-mitnick-video
37 https://www.thecloudtechnologist.com/defending-against-evilginx2-in-office-365/
38 https://www.thecloudtechnologist.com/defending-against-evilginx2-in-office-365/

MFA Authentication Method #6: IP Fencing

An IP Fence is a configuration design that forces all authentication to originate from a trusted network. All authentications to Azure AD that do not originate from this network would be prevented from signing in.

Pros

IP Fencing is an effective deterrent to Man-in-the-middle attacks because the attacker's machine that has the stolen authentication token cannot replay that token unless the attacker is inside the IP Fence. While because IP Fencing is effective against this attack, it has many disadvantages, and I've helped multiple organizations move towards a more mobile, work-from-anywhere design.

Cons

IP Fencing requires remote employees to connect to a VPN before authenticating to Microsoft 365. This is not a great experience for mobile users and is especially burdensome for iOS and Android devices, which are often personally owned devices. I encounter very few organizations that purchase phones for all their employees. To save expenses, organizations LOVE BYOD.

Split Tunneling breaks IP Fencing. In the year 2020, when the COVID19 pandemic hit, many businesses had to shift to a work from home model. Organizations that had IP Fencing setup saw a dramatic increase in their VPN traffic, and some could not handle the load. Many network administrators had to revert to a split-tunnel design so that heavy network protocols such as Teams or Zoom would flow through the local internet connection and avoid tying up the internet bandwidth at the corporate data center. The tradeoff to split tunneling was that the IP Fence broke because the user's authentication traffic appeared to originate from their home network. Some VPNs were augmented to support a partial split-tunnel where only the Microsoft traffic was backhauled through the corporate network.

IP Fencing is the opposite of Zero Trust. A major problem with IP Fencing is that it assumes everything inside your network is safe. The problem is: we know that is not the case. People can bring rogue devices into the network, which may contain malware or ransomware.

IP Fencing is not compatible with startups. Many born-in-the-cloud startups don't have traditional networks or data centers. Indeed, after COVID19, many businesses decided that their employees would no longer be required to come into a physical office again. So large organizations are beginning to have the same cloud-first model that startups have, and IP Fencing doesn't work in that model.

Device-Based Authentication

So, if IP Fencing is not the answer, how can we defeat the threat of Man-in-the-middle while still securely authenticating both users and devices? We'll cover two methods of Device Authentication: Intune and Hybrid Domain Join.

If the percentage of users worldwide using 2FA is small, I imagine that the number of organizations that require device authentication is an even smaller percentage. Thus, I think this book's recommendation to require Device authentication will stand the test of time for the next three years easily.

Since 70% of all attacks are from external attackers, often overseas, consider the threat model of device authentication. By requiring a device to authenticate to Office 365, we are saying that our threat model accepts the risk of a super hacker thief. I am willing to accept that a super hacker thief might break in and steal my laptop and that the laptop may be unlocked at the time of the theft. However, my threat model does not accept the risk of a remote attacker who does not have physical access to my device. This model allows the employee to never be bothered with nagging 2FA prompts unless a high confidence risk has been detected, such as an impossible journey from another country.

Figure 6 Scene from a popular movie where the thief happens to have hacking skills.

MFA Authentication Method #7: Intune Compliance

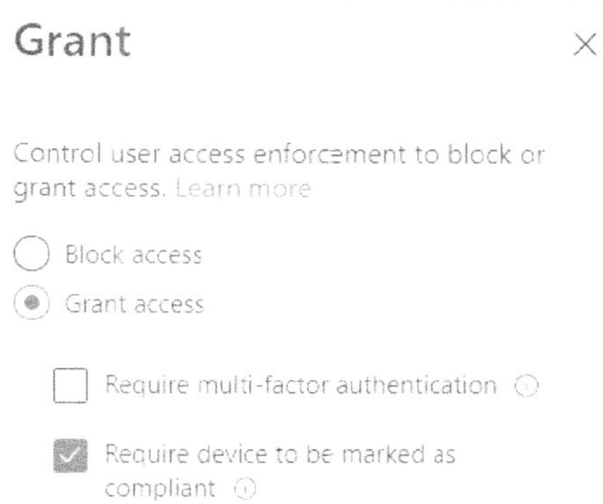

The process of enrolling a device into Intune establishes a certificate trust with the device, which is used to authenticate the device. Intune requires a stand-alone license or an EMS E3 or M365 E3 license. Intune Compliance uses certificate-based authentication and is an effective deterrent to a Man-in-the-middle proxy attack because the attacker's machine that has the stolen authentication token cannot replay that token unless the attacker's machine is enrolled into Intune.

Figure 7 Azure AD Conditional Access Policy requiring Devices to be Compliant with Intune Policy

The other benefit of Intune Compliance is that it is a true Zero Trust solution. It allows an organization to set policies to only allow healthy devices with low risk to connect to applications or data. For example, the screenshot below shows that a firewall has been disabled, and therefore, it is no longer a compliant device. The Azure AD Conditional Access Policy will block the device from connecting until the user enables the firewall.

SETTING	STATE
Windows Defender Antimalware	Compliant
Windows Defender Antimalware signature up-to-date	Compliant
Encryption of data storage on device.	Compliant
Firewall	Error
Real-time protection	Compliant
Require BitLocker	Compliant
Require a password to unlock mobile devices.	Compliant
Require the device to be at or under the machine risk score:	Compliant

Intune compliance supports all platforms other than Linux (See section "Linux Considerations" for more information).

TIP: Configure Intune to have enrollment restrictions, or associate the "Intune Enrollment Application[39]" with a conditional access policy to restrict enrollment to trusted locations or prompt for 2FA. Otherwise, an external attacker could theoretically enroll a device into Intune. A second device would be required to complete the MFA challenge for corporate devices like Android Enterprise or iOS/iPad Automated Device Enrollment because the primary device can't receive calls or text messages during the provisioning process.

MFA Authentication Method #8: Hybrid Domain Join

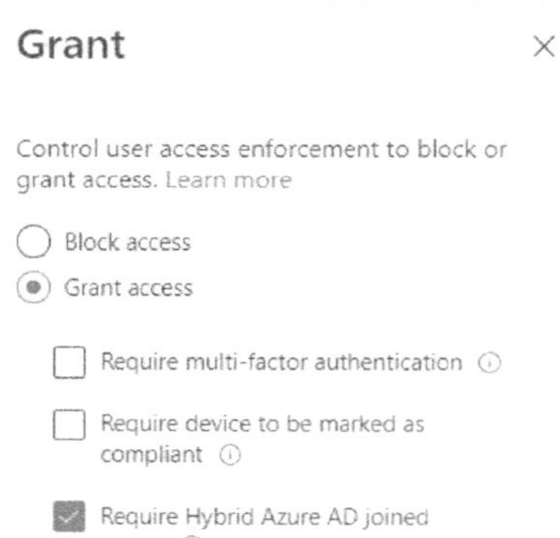

Hybrid Domain Join (HDJ) is an on-premises Active-Directory-joined computer that is synchronized to Azure AD using Azure AD Connect. It is enabled in the Azure AD Connect Configuration Wizard or with Microsoft Endpoint Manager Configuration Manager (MEM SCCM).

Figure 8 Azure AD Policy requiring Hybrid Azure AD Joined Device

Pros:

Like Intune, HDJ uses certificate-based authentication behind the scenes to authenticate a device. It's often used to prevent personal computers from connecting to Microsoft 365. HDJ is an effective deterrent to a Man-in-the-middle proxy attack because the attacker's machine that has the stolen authentication token cannot replay that token unless the attacker's machine is enrolled into Intune.

[39] https://docs.microsoft.com/en-us/mem/intune/enrollment/multi-factor-authentication

HDJ is a prerequisite for Windows 10 Endpoint DLP when the computer is joined to Active Directory.

Cons

HDJ is limited to Windows 7, Windows 8.1, and Windows 10, and therefore it is not compatible with Mac OSX, Android, iOS, or Linux. It's also not a fit for cloud-based startups that run pure Azure AD with no traditional Active Directory environments.

MFA Authentication Method #9 Certificate-Based Authentication (CBA)

As of this writing, there are two methods of performing explicit CBA to authenticate applications in M365 E5:

1. CBA using Microsoft Cloud App Security
   a. Pros: Allows you to bring your own root certificate (public key), issued from either Active Directory Certificate Authority (CA) or 3rd party CAs.
   b. Cons: Limited to web browsers only.
2. CBA using ADFS
   a. Pros: Allows sign-in using a certificate as the first factor of authentication (Passwordless)
   b. Cons:
      i. Requires ADFS
      ii. Cannot be used in combination with Intune Compliance[40]
      iii. Non-standard network firewall port 49443 to be opened from client to ADFS farm if older ADFS 2012 R2 or older are deployed. On ADFS 2016 and higher, you can configure it to use TCP 443.[41]

Linux Considerations

Since there is not yet a device authentication option for Linux, there are two recommendations:

1. Require Linux users to connect to a VPN with force tunnel enabled so that egress communication to Microsoft 365 will appear from the trusted network location. You can then rely upon the VPN vendor to perform device or certificate-based authentication. The next step is to target Linux users with a Conditional Access Policy through Conditions > Device platforms and exclude all other supported operating systems, leaving Linux as the only remaining option.

---

40 https://docs.microsoft.com/en-us/windows-server/identity/ad-fs/operations/configure-user-certificate-authentication

41 https://docs.microsoft.com/en-us/windows-server/identity/ad-fs/operations/ad-fs-support-for-alternate-hostname-binding-for-certificate-authentication

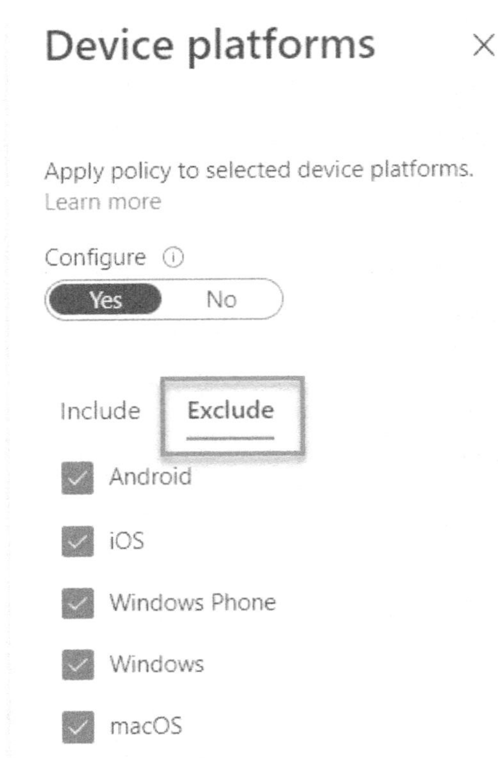

2. Linux Users (or any operating system) can change the user agent to evade conditional access policies. So, it's very important to have a device authentication option for each Device Platform. Otherwise, let's say you don't require a compliant app for mobile devices. The Linux user can change their user agent to iPhone and evade the device authentication restriction. For example, in Chromium Developer Tools, you can spoof the user agent as shown below:

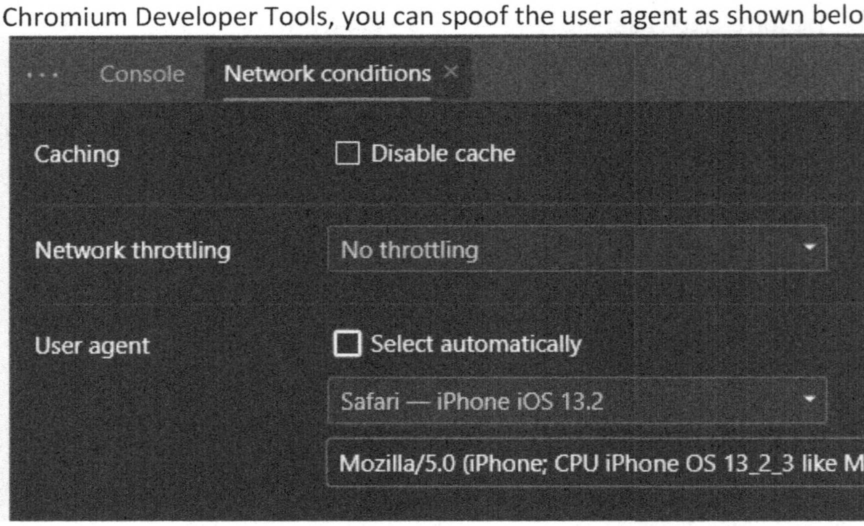

Figure 9 Spoofed User Agent String in Microsoft Chromium Edge Web Browser can evade loose conditional access policies

Zero Trust

Microsoft Zero Trust is a concept where we no longer assume the network perimeter is safe. We no longer assume the computer is compliant. We assume the network, device, and user are all compromised, and we check and continuously re-check to verify compliance with security policy. This thought process is known as Assume Breach, and it is a very realistic and practical way of protecting an organization. At the heart of it is the Azure Conditional Access, which applies policies based on user and device risk.

For example, many healthcare organizations need to make sure that Bitlocker encryption is enabled before a user attempts to gain access to applications containing ePHI (Electronic Protected Health Information). A conditional access policy can be configured to prevent unencrypted devices from connecting to SaaS applications that contain sensitive data. Or access can be allowed while encrypting downloads.

Not only can you check to make sure that devices are running antivirus, but you can also check to determine the risk level of the device (if Mimikatz is found on a device, the risk level would be Medium, and therefore, we can block that device from gaining access to other applications).

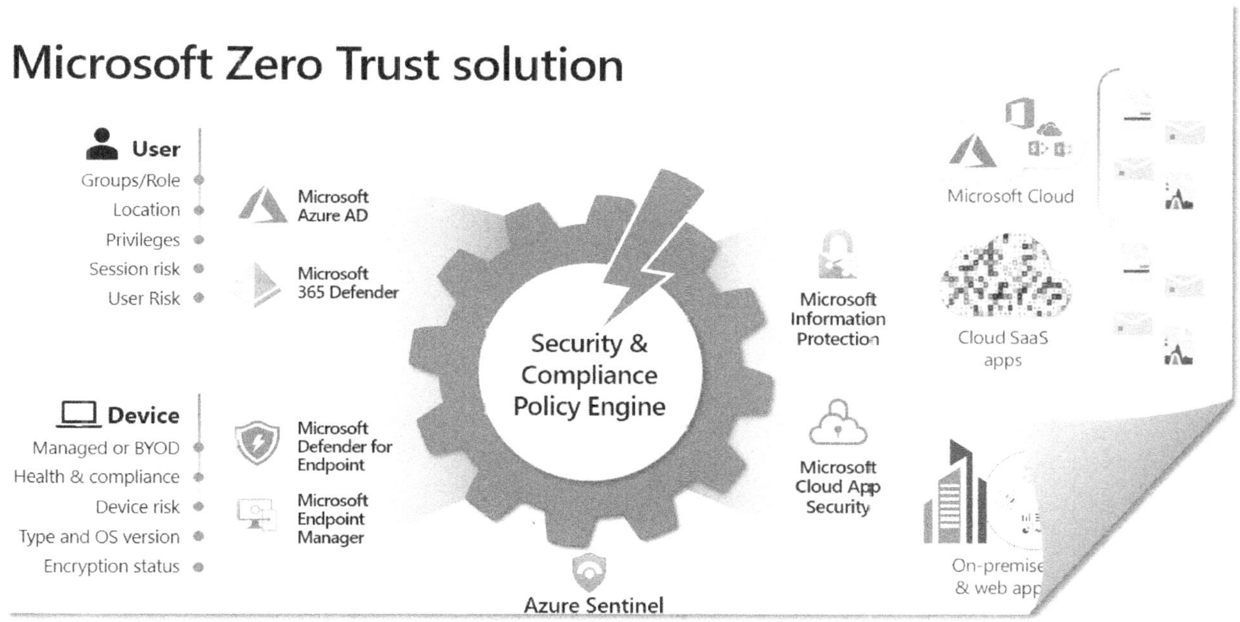

One of my customers put together this design to show their Zero Trust Policy, which shows how an unmanaged (personal device) brought into the corporate network is blocked from accessing anything other than Outlook on the Web and lacks download permissions. When the device is internal to the network, the user never receives 2FA prompts, but when they network the device externally, they will receive 2FA prompts. In this design, it would be important that this organization enables Continuous Access Evaluation (CAE) to detect the network location change. Otherwise, without CAE, only Exchange Client Access Rules (administered via PowerShell) can prevent network access changes after an authentication token is issued (and Client Access Rules are limited to Exchange Only, so CAE is better).

Application/Service	Corporate Network		Public Network	
	Managed Device	**Unmanaged Device**	**Managed Device**	**Unmanaged Device**
Exchange Online Full Outlook Client	Allow	Block All Access	Require MFA	Block All Access
Exchange Online Outlook on the Web	Allow	Require MFA Block Downloads	Require MFA	Require MFA Block Downloads
SharePoint Online	Allow	Block All Access	Require MFA	Block All Access
OneDrive	Allow	Block All Access	Require MFA	Block All Access
Teams	Allow	Require MFA	Require MFA	Require MFA

The issue with the diagram above is that it shows different enforcement actions depending on the workload. This is a problem for the Microsoft Teams app because it has service dependencies.

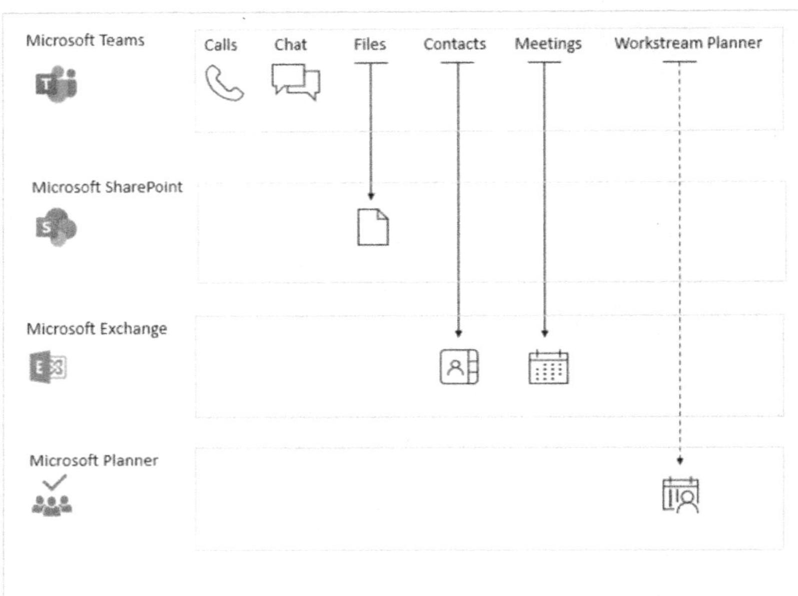

To fix this, Microsoft released a special app inside Conditional Access called "Office 365 App[42]" so that your policies will result in a more consistent user experience. Administrators can then exclude specific apps from the policy by including the Office 365 app and excluding specific apps.

[42] https://docs.microsoft.com/en-us/azure/active-directory/conditional-access/concept-conditional-access-cloud-apps#office-365

Identity Security Best Practices

Licensing

The following table presents a "Good, Better, Best... and Next Level!" approach based on the available licenses in your Microsoft 365 tenant. For those fortunate enough to have the full M365 E5 license, you can achieve next-level status with the most secure environment possible!

Best Practice	Microsoft License Requirement
Good: Enable User-based MFA (Always-ON MFA, or Conditional MFA)	Azure AD Free or Higher ("Always-ON MFA") Azure AD P1 for Conditional MFA
Better: Enable Device-Based Authentication	Azure AD P1 for Conditional Access requiring Hybrid Domain Join
Best: Passwordless + Device Compliance	Azure AD P1 and Intune (Or packages such as EMS E3 or M365 E3)
Next Level: Passwordless + Device Compliance + Only Prompt for 2FA when Risk Level is elevated using User Risk, Session Risk, or User Behavior Anomalies while blocking all forms of Legacy Authentication	Azure AD P2, Intune, and MCAS (Or Packages such as EMS E5, or M365 E5 Security)

Azure AD Conditional Access Policy Design

Create one policy for each unique operating system, for example, Windows, Mac, and Mobile. Set Windows and Mac to require Intune Compliant and Mobile BYOD to Intune App Compliant. Create a separate policy for Linux (see previous section "Linux Considerations")

- [ZERO TRUST] Company-Owned PC's must be Hybrid Azure AD domain joined and/or compliant (if enrolled in Intune)
  - Based on membership in O365_Intune_PC
  - Based on OS being Windows
  - Optional: exclude browser and allow from any Windows Device, then create a separate policy for Windows Browsers that restricts downloads and excludes Compliant Devices.
  - Note: The only known vulnerability with this is "Pass-the-PRT," which we blogged about (here). Therefore, you must protect the PRT on the local workstation (think EDR); otherwise, the PRT can be stolen and replayed on another device for up to 14 days.
- [ZERO TRUST] Company-Owned Mac OSX must be enrolled in Intune and marked as 'Healthy' and 'Compliant.'
  - Based on membership in O365_Intune_MacOSX
  - Based on OS being Mac OSX
- [ZERO TRUST] Company-Owned Mobile Devices must be enrolled into Intune and marked as 'Healthy' and 'Compliant' and only use Compliant Applications
  - Based on membership in "O365_InTune_COD_Devices."
  - Based on Mobile OS being Android, iOS, and Windows Mobile
  - Require only approved applications (this blocks ActiveSync)
- [ZERO TRUST] Personal Mobile Devices (BYOD)
  - Based on membership in "O365_InTune_Personal_Devices."
  - Require MFA
  - Require only approved applications (this blocks ActiveSync)
  - And we Apply an Intune MAM Policy
- [OPTIONAL] Block External Access for Some Users
  - Based on membership in "O365_Block."
  - Block all external access to O365 (you must be inside the corporate LAN)

- [ZERO TRUST] Block Unauthorized Mobile Devices
    - If you are not a member of "O365_InTune_COD_Devices" or "O365_InTune_Personal_Devices," then we block you if you are connecting from iOS, Android, or Windows Mobile
- [OPTIONAL] Block Untrusted Countries
    - If login is coming from a country in the "untrusted countries" named location, then we block access.
    - Make sure to *not* check the box for unknown countries; otherwise, IPv6 inside the USA may get blocked
    - Note: Skilled Attackers simply use TOR or NordVPN/similar clients to evade this
- [IMPORTANT] Block Legacy Authentication
    - In Conditions > Client Apps > Select "Other Clients" with an Access Control of Block.
      This will block legacy Exchange Web Services (EWS), ActiveSync (for example, for iOS clients older than version 11), POP, IMAP, Remote PowerShell, MAPI, RPC, SMTP AUTH, and OAB.
    - UPDATE August 11, 2020: Configuration change: Now, all new Conditional Access policies will apply to **all client app types** (including 'other' (legacy auth) **when the client apps condition is not configured).** Read more here:
      Conditional Access policies now apply to all client applications by default - Microsoft Tech Community
    - UPDATE February 25, 2021: Microsoft has postponed disabling Basic Auth for protocols in active use by tenants until further notice but will continue to disable Basic Auth for protocols, not in use. The overall scope of this change now covers EWS, EAS, POP, IMAP, Remote PowerShell, MAPI, RPC, SMTP AUTH, and OAB. Go here for the full announcement:
      Basic Authentication and Exchange Online – February 2021 Update - Microsoft Tech Community
- [IMPORTANT] Block ActiveSync
    - Block Exchange ActiveSync clients, which enforces the use of Compliant Apps. Why? So, you can do selective wipes and block copy/paste, etc.
    - NOTE: If you permit oAuth, users can grant access to 'iOS Apps,' and that will override conditional access block policies!
- Block registering of security information from untrusted devices or locations
    - Based on the user action of registering security information (MFA/SSPR)
    - UPDATE: You can now use Temporary Access Pass, which allows users to register security information without being blocked by CA policies (avoids new employees being caught in a catch22).
- Terms of Use
    - Require acceptance of Terms of Use prior to connecting to your O365 tenant (helpful for GDPR, etc.)
    - Note: Policies in Report-only mode requiring compliant devices may prompt users on macOS, iOS, and Android to select a device certificate.
- Block Roaming
    - Block Roaming from trusted to untrusted networks using Exchange Client Access Rules
    - UPDATE: Enable Continuous Access Evaluation to help with this too.
- Microsoft Cloud App Security Conditional Access App Control
    - Ability to block printing, copy/paste
    - Ability to block downloads or encrypt downloads
- [IMPORTANT] Exclude Break Glass Accounts from MFA Policies in case MSFT has another MFA outage
- [IMPORTANT] Exclude "On-Premises Directory Sync" services account from MFA, but then create a 2nd policy that restricts it to your IP ranges.
- [IMPORTANT] If you use IP Fencing Rules, make sure you understand the "include unknown areas" checkbox; otherwise, you could be blocking or allowing unmapped regions, including both IPv6 and IPv4 IPs.
- [IMPORTANT] If you don't exclude AIP from your policies, be aware that external users who attempt to access your files encrypted by AIP may be unable to open the documents you send to them.
- [IMPORTANT] If you don't exclude Guest accounts from your policies and you attempt to share documents with them in your SharePoint online, be aware that they may be unable to access things you share with them.

- [IMPORTANT] Block Access to Azure App
    - This prevents people from enumerating the Azure AD Privileged Roles and Directory

- Combine this with PowerShell command; otherwise, users can also enumerate directory with get-MsolUser

- TIP: Audit CA Policy User Exclusions Regularly
    - A "feature" in CA Policy causes highly privileged administrator users to often be excluded from important protection policies. This feature is designed to prevent administrators from locking themselves out. The problem is that Administrators often don't see the dialogue, and they end up accidentally adding themselves to the exclusion list and, thus, become unprotected by important policies. I've seen multiple cases where administrators were scratching their heads, wondering why so many global admins were not protected by MFA policies. This dialogue box may be obscured, depending on the web browser resolution and an administrator might click save without realizing that they are excluding their very important admin account from protection.

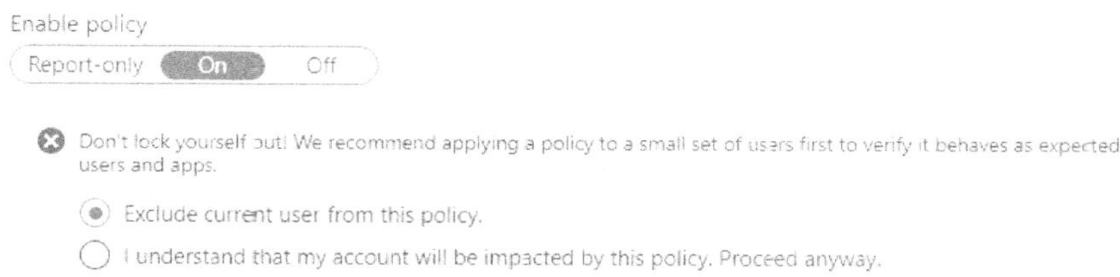

    - So, the solution is to have someone tasked with setting a recurring calendar invite and auditing user exclusions regularly to make sure that no global admins are excluded other than the authorized break glass account/s.

- Important
    - Azure AD P1 Licensed Tenants: Do not enable the checkbox for "Allow users to remember multi-factor authentication on devices they trust." This legacy setting has been replaced with a superior Azure AD Conditional Access session lifetime setting because it caused the rich clients to expire at the same time, leading to a LOT of MFA prompts for users (some IT Departments may want that, but it's not the best user experience).

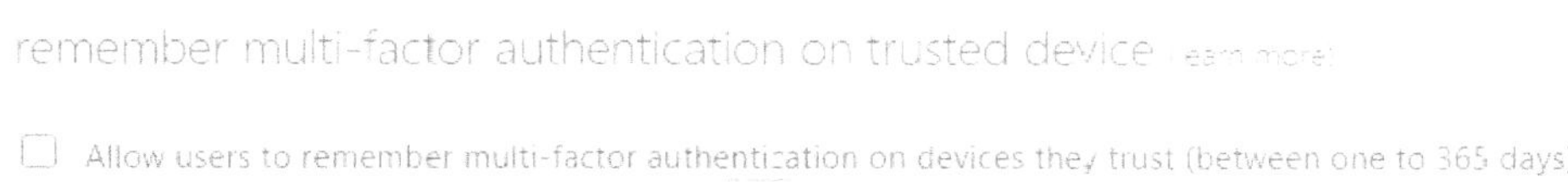

    - For M365 Tenants without any Azure AD P1 licensing, the recommendation is to leave the box above checked but set it to at least 90 days (which is the new default).
    - If necessary, use the Conditional Access Session token lifetime instead. For example, you can set a policy to reduce token lifetime for 8 hours for web access on unmanaged external devices. You can also block persistent browser cookies from unmanaged external devices.

Naming Convention

The conditional access policy naming standard helps you to find policies quickly while understanding their purpose at first glance. Here is a suggested naming convention:

- A Sequence Number
- The cloud app(s) it applies to
- The response
- Who it applies to
- When it applies (if applicable)

<SN>-	<Cloud app>:	<Response>	For	<Principal>	When	<Conditions>

Example: A policy to require MFA for marketing users accessing the Dynamics CRP app from external networks might be:

CA01 -	Dynamics CRP:	Require MFA	For	marketing	When	On external networks

A descriptive name helps you to keep an overview of your Conditional Access implementation. The Sequence Number is helpful if you need to reference a policy in a conversation. For example, when you talk to an administrator on the phone, you can ask them to open policy CA01 to solve an issue.

Combined Registration

For all tenants created before August 15th, 2020, users must register separately for Azure AD Multi-Factor Authentication and self-service password reset (SSPR). After this date, any new tenant created will automatically be enabled for a feature known as Combined Registration[43]. This allows users to register authentication methods once.

Combined Registration is also required for at least two other tenant features to function properly:

1. FIDO2 Security Keys require combined registration to be enabled
2. The Conditional Access "User Actions" setting requires combined registration to be enabled

To enable Combined Registration, browse to Portal.Azure.com > Azure Active Directory > User Settings > User Feature Previews > Users. The chosen users can use the combined security information registration experience.

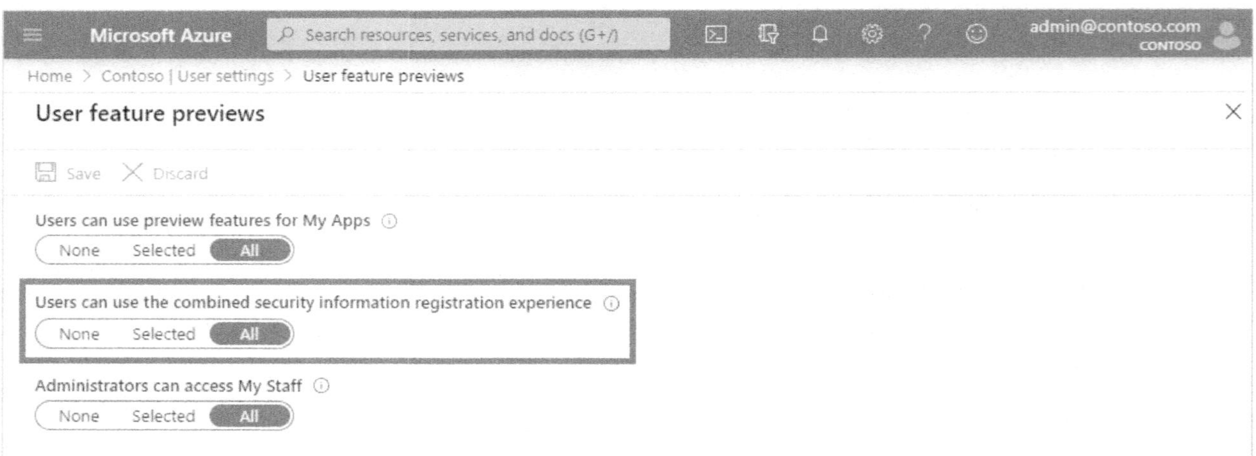

[43] https://docs.microsoft.com/en-us/azure/active-directory/authentication/howto-registration-mfa-sspr-combined

Migrate ADFS to Azure AD

1. ADFS has a greater surface attack area than Azure AD
Examples include NTLM Brute-Force, MFA bypass (see CVE-2019-1126, CVE-2019-0975, CVE-2018-8340, CVE-2009-2508)[44]
2. ADFS can leak relying party trust relationships

Daniel Streefkerk (@dstreefkerk) wrote a PowerShell script that can determine the external ADFS namespace that is being used to control authentication to Office 365.[45] Armed with the name of the ADFS server, you can enumerate all the IDP Apps being used by changing the URL below to match the namespace found: *https://adfs.tailspintoys.ca/adfs/ls/idpinitiatedsignon.htm*
This works on all ADFS 2012 R2 or earlier farms, since this enumeration is disabled by default in 2016 (unless an administrator re-enables it).

2. ADFS can have multiple single points of failure unless designed properly

3. ADFS requires certificate maintenance – resulting in planned downtime

4. ADFS requires more IT overhead than Azure (Backups, Monitoring, Upgrades, Patches)

5. Azure AD Conditional Access offers better security controls than ADFS Claims

6. Azure AD is lightweight and less complex to administer (No Claims Rules)

7. Azure AD (P2) aligns to NIST 800-63b (Scan dark web for breached passwords)

8. Azure AD has a better feature roadmap

9. Moving the Identity Provider (IdP) to Azure AD will contain the blast radius of an on-premises breach.

In the wake of the SolarWinds supply-chain hack of December 2020, the US National Security Agency wrote a rare public Cybersecurity Advisory[46] recommending Azure AD as the Authoritative Identity Provider.

> *"Ensure core privileged cloud administrative users, groups, and roles are not impacted by data synchronized from on-premises environments, and that cloud administrative roles do not authenticate with SAML SSO, but instead rely on cloud-only authentication… **Consider using Azure Active Directory as the Authoritative Identity Provider.** By consolidating identity and access natively in the cloud, tenants relieve themselves from the burden of managing the federation of authentication and the on-premises service and gain more of the protections that the cloud provider has in place, including system hardening, configuration, and monitoring."*

[44] https://cve.mitre.org/find/
[45] https://github.com/dstreefkerk/PowerShell/blob/master/Infosec-Related/Invoke-EmailRecon.ps1
[46] https://media.defense.gov/2020/Dec/17/2002554125/-1/-1/0/AUTHENTICATION_MECHANISMS_CSA_U_OO_198854_20.PDF

Chapter Two – Securing Email in M365

Reports suggest that 91% of data breaches start with a spear-phishing attack.[47]

Next to attacks on identity, the 2nd largest threat to Microsoft 365 is phishing attacks.

A phishing attack is when attackers indiscriminately send emails to a broad range of target mailboxes, hoping to gain initial access to an account or a device. On the other hand, spear-phishing is when the sender targets a specific victim. The attacker will dedicate extra time and creativity to customize the sender address and message body to increase attack effectiveness.

For both forms of phishing, the hacker has two targets for *initial* access:

1. **Identity.** Target the user's credentials by tricking them into clicking a hyperlink or opening an attachment to gain the user's credentials.
   Note: If multi-factor authentication (MFA) is configured properly, then the attacker can be prevented from gaining access to the user's identity.
   and/or
2. **Endpoint.** Target the user's endpoint device by clicking on a link or opening a document to run malicious code on the endpoint.

Primary Motivation for Phishing

Financial gain is the most common motivation behind phishing. The hackers often hope to con someone into wiring money into their bank account or to purchase gift cards and send a picture of the back of the gift card to them. Educating users about these motivations can help them be more cautious and safer.

Unconventional Defense to Phishing

Knowing the enemy's motivation is key to defense. Assume all emails requesting a change of bank account are fraudulent until proven otherwise. I recommend that accounting departments establish a multi-level authentication system when onboarding new customers or vendors.

Level 1 (Transactions < $100,000) Authenticate the sender with out-of-band verification such as a phone call to verify the request.

Level 2 (Transactions > $100,000). Require a verbal passphrase known only to both parties (stored in something like LastPass). The passphrase should be established via a different channel than email (assume a hacker has already gained access to email). The idea behind this verbal passphrase is to thwart deep fake voice attacks, which have already been used in these sophisticated spear-phishing schemes. Expect social engineering attacks; train employees and test them with regular attempts to bypass this system, such as ("Hi, I'm new and just joined, and my boss is out. She didn't give me the passphrase before she left on vacation, and I will get in trouble if we don't get this transaction processed. Can you just help me out this one time?").

To quote the late US President Ronald Reagan, "trust, but verify." In cybersecurity, this quote translates into the security mantra "assume breach," which means that we should always assume that the attacker

[47] https://www2.deloitte.com/my/en/pages/risk/articles/91-percent-of-all-cyber-attacks-begin-with-a-phishing-email-to-an-unexpected-victim.html

has already taken over the email account on either side of the transaction. When the hackers realize that out-of-band authentication is required, it's safe to assume that they will resort to social engineering.

Multi-Layered Defense

I have investigated dozens of breaches involving large financial transfers originating from phishing emails, which could have been prevented with basic email hygiene. This chapter will cover the basic technical fundamentals of email security and Microsoft's advanced countermeasures.

Microsoft Exchange Online Protection (EOP) includes multiple layers of defense against spam and malware. For more advanced attacks such as zero-day malware and spear phishing, Microsoft provides add-ons such as Microsoft Defender for Office 365 (MDO) (Plan 1 or Plan 2). MDO Plan 2 is cumulative in that it contains all the features from EOP and MDO Plan 1. The image below shows the complete set of multi-layered protection provided when MDO Plan 2 is applied to a mailbox.

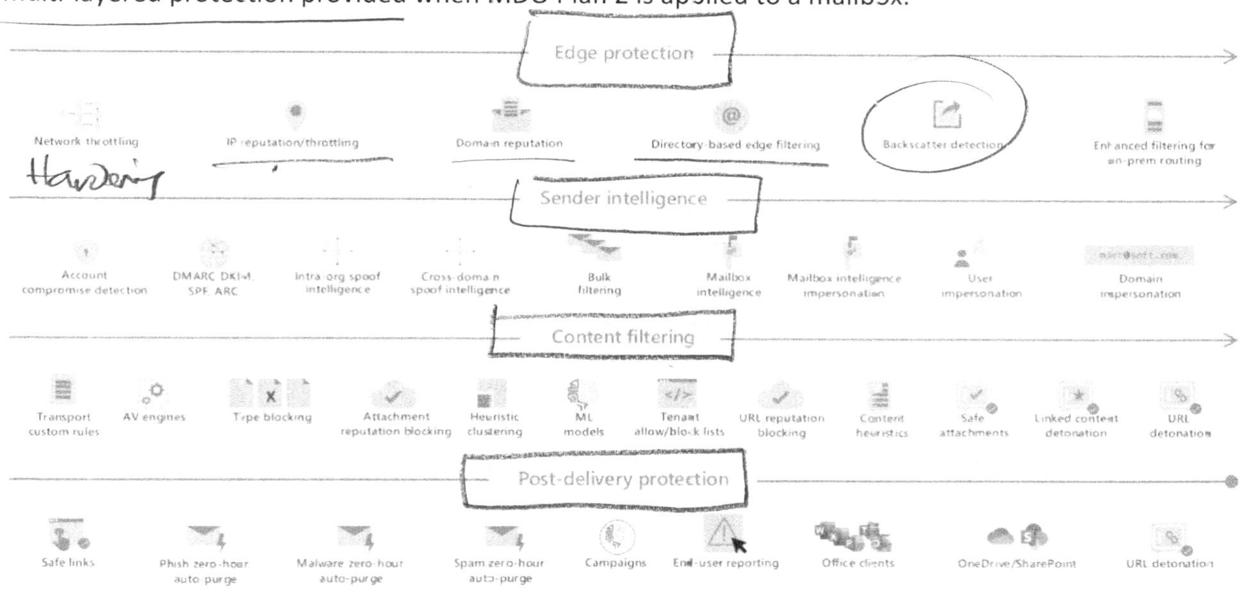

Email Security Fundamental #1 Block Dangerous Attachments by File Extension

By default, EOP scans all emails and attachments with three different antivirus engines. One AV engine is from Microsoft, and the other two are from separate email security vendors that Microsoft licenses.[43] This multi-layered anti-malware protection comes with all licenses inside EOP, and it cannot be disabled even if you prefer a 3rd party email security solution. The only configurable decision for malware is whether to block file extensions commonly used to distribute malware.

[48] https://docs.microsoft.com/en-us/microsoft-365/security/office-365-security/anti-malware-protection-faq-eop?view=o365-worldwide#how-often-are-the-malware-definitions-updated-

Side Note: Which Antivirus Engines does Microsoft use to scan emails for threats?

According to the Microsoft 365 Service Description, Microsoft uses multiple engines to scan for threats. Microsoft reserves the right to change these to improve the service. You can find out which engines are used by downloading a message with Threat Explorer and then examining the message header "X-MS-Exchange-Organization-AVScannedB

```
X-MS-Exchange-Organization-Antispam-PreContentFilter-ScanContext:
 CategorizerOnSubmitted;CategorizerOnResolved;
X-MS-Exchange-Organization-AVScannedByV2: Symantec;Command;Microsoft
X-MS-Exchange-Organization-AVScanComplete: true
X-MS-Exchange-Organization-SenderIntelligence-P2SenderOrgDomainTenantId:
```

yV2." (Threat Explorer is an MDO Plan 2 feature).

Figure 10 After downloading a message from Threat Explorer, you can examine the message headers to see which AV engines scanned the message

By default, Microsoft's EOP "common attachments filter" is disabled, which means that it does not block executables, scripts, or other file types associated with malware campaigns. This filter should be enabled, and additiona file types should be added to the default list.

Navigate to https://security.microsoft.com/securitypoliciesandrules > Threat Policies > Anti-malware and enable the common attachments filter.

When you enable the policy, it will block the following 10 file types:

.ace,.ani,.app,.docm,.exe,.jar,.reg.,.scr,.vbe,.vbs.

The graphical interface allows you to select from close to 100 additional file types to block. You can also add your own custom file types using the set-malwareFilterPolicy Exchange Online PowerShell cmdlet.

The other two available malware configuration options are email notification and ZAP. By default, no alerts are sent to administrators or end-users when malware is blocked (probably because it happens so frequently, and there is nothing actionable that an administrator or user would do in response to the alert). One key security principle is to only alert when actions are required; otherwise, the alerts will be ignored, which is dangerous. The benefit of using this feature instead of an Exchange Transport Rule is that you can strip the attachment and send a message along to the end-user. I tend to block the entire message since if the attachment was dirty, perhaps the message body may contain something dangerous as well.

Malware zero-hour auto-purge (ZAP) quarantines messages that are found to contain malware *after* they've been delivered to Exchange Online mailboxes. By default, malware ZAP is on, and it should be left enabled.

Email Security Fundamental #2 Email Authentication Records[49]

Emails are transmitted across the internet using the SMTP Protocol[50] (Simple Mail Transfer Protocol). When this protocol was first developed in 1981, it was designed to be simple and could not prevent the sender from an impersonation attack (aka *spoofing*). Discussions began in the early 2000s to address this issue, and then a technical paper proposing a solution was published in 2006 called "Sender Policy Framework" (SPF)."[51] The receiving email server uses SPF to verify the sender's IP address against a list of authorized IP addresses maintained by the domain name owner. The domain name owner can publish a DNS TXT record matching the specifications in RFC 4408, like the example below:

"v=spf1 include:spf.protection.outlook.com -all"

The email recipient's mail server will perform a DNS TXT lookup of the envelope "From:" address and then compare the list of IPs from "spf.protection.outlook com" to see if that matches against the IP address of the server that sent the email.

It sounds pretty ironclad, so why are emails still getting spoofed?

Shortly after 2008, modern email clients such as Outlook changed from showing the "From" address on the envelope to inside the content of the email message itself.[52] Since SPF was designed to protect the impersonation of the envelope[53], this change gave rise to Business Email Compromise spear-phishing attacks. We had almost no effective defenses against such attacks until DMARC

RFC 5322.From Protected by DMARC

From: "Jack Johnson" <jack.johnson@contoso.com>
Sent: Monday, October 21, 2021 9:53 AM
To: (Unsuspecting End-User – Probably in Accounting Department) <AccountingClerk@contoso.com>
Subject: RE: Invoice Payment

Figure 11 The RFC5322.From address is used by modern email clients (since 2008), not the RFC5321.From Envelope address

DMARC to the rescue

Domain-based Message Authentication, Reporting & Conformance (DMARC) was published in 2015[54] to prevent impersonation of the newer RFC 5322 from the field that Outlook and other modern mail clients

---

[49] See also Department of Homeland Security Operational Directive 18-01
[50] https://en.wikipedia.org/wiki/Simple_Mail_Transfer_Protocol
[51] Request for Comment (RFC) 4408 https://en.wikipedia.org/wiki/Sender_Policy_Framework
[52] RFC 5322.From
[53] RFC 5321.MailFrom
[54] RFC 7489 (3/18/2015) https://en.wikipedia.org/wiki/DMARC

use. Think of it as the next version of SPF. When properly implemented, it can block attacks such as "CEO Fraud" or "Business Email Compromise" (BEC).

This is what a simple DMARC record looks like when created as a DNS TXT record:

"v=DMARC1; p=reject"

The "p=" stands for the policy, followed by one of three permitted values: Reject, Quarantine, or None.

Did you notice the DMARC record does not contain a list of IP addresses? The authors of DMARC decided to leverage the existing SPF record as the source of authority for authorized sending IP addresses. So, SPF should be seen as a dependency upon DMARC. Therefore, SPF is a prerequisite for DMARC.

At the time of this writing, just 16%[55] of the Fortune 500 have implemented a DMARC record in Quarantine or Reject mode. Consider the Fortune 500 as the most successful businesses in the world (with the most to lose), yet only a fraction of them protect their domain names from being impersonated. I imagine that most small and medium-sized organizations have never even heard of DMARC.

Most of the IT Administrators I have spoken to fail to understand the relevance of DMARC to email security. For example, they may feel DMARC is unnecessary because they have implemented a transport rule to block all external email addresses, where the sender address matches the company's email domain. While this does protect that company's employees from receiving impersonated senders, it does not protect the rest of the world from receiving forged emails. A hacker who sends an email directly from their machine to a supplier's email address will not route through the company's email security infrastructure. Many of the security breach events that I have investigated, involving wire transfer fraud, happened when a customer receives an email with a forged sender email address.

Spoof Intelligence

Defender for Office 365 and Exchange Online Protection (EOP) uses an industry-first technology called Spoof Intelligence. It leverages advanced algorithms to learn about a domain's email sending patterns and can flag anomalies. Most importantly, through this approach of using Spoof Intelligence, Defender for Office 365 and EOP also extends spoofing protection to domains that might not have implemented DMARC yet. Both spoof protection capabilities are enabled by default and are being constantly updated to learn from the latest attacks.[56]

DKIM

DomainKeys Identified Mail (DKIM) is a digital signature that is added to the message header of outgoing emails. DMARC can use DKIM along with SPF to distinguish authorized senders from the impersonated ones. DKIM should be seen as a prerequisite to DMARC. I wouldn't recommend enabling DMARC in Quarantine or Reject mode until both SPF and DKIM DNS records are in place. It's always a good idea to

---

[55] To learn how to query the public DNS records of the Fortune 500 see my blog article https://www.thecloudtechnologist.com/analysis-of-dns-recon-of-the-fortune-500-part-1-of-3/

[56] https://techcommunity.microsoft.com/t5/microsoft-defender-for-office/business-email-uncompromised-part-one/ba-p/2159900

enable DKIM because it will reduce the chance of legitimate business emails being marked as spam. There is one scenario, however, where it can be implemented incorrectly: The last email server that you control must be the one that adds DKIM. For example, in complex networks, you may be routing email from an on-premises Exchange Hybrid Server to Office 365 and then to a 3rd party before it is finally sent to the designated recipient. In this case, you should disable DKIM in O365 and enable DKIM signing by the last hop 3rd party email provider. Otherwise, if Office 365 is your last hop, then you can safely enable DKIM by creating two DNS CNAME records.

DKIM is not enabled by default in Office 365, so after creating two DNS CNAME records[57], you must go into Microsoft 365 to enable it. Microsoft will then check to see that the two DNS CNAME records have been created, and if they exist, MSFT will begin digitally signing outbound emails with DKIM.

SPF TIPS

SPF will fail to work properly if the specifications are not followed precisely. Some of the common mistakes I see are having an SPF record that is too long (maximum 255 characters) or containing too many DNS name lookups (maximum 10).

A service I often use is the Dmarcian SPF Survey (https://dmarcian.com/spf-survey/) because if an SPF record has too many DNS lookups, it will flatten DNS names to IP addresses and deduplicate all IP ranges. If the result exceeds the 255-character limit, it will create the minimum number of SPF records necessary.

DMARC Deployment Strategy

I recommend publishing SPF and DKIM records and then enabling DMARC in "monitor" mode (where the p=none). After reviewing reports (from one of the providers mentioned above like Postmark, Valimail, or Agari), then take actions such as adding authorized sender IPs to SPF or adding additional DKIM records from authorized sending gateways (such as Sendgrid or Mailchimp). Then proceed to quarantine mode (where p=quarantine) by adding a parameter (pct=10) every week, starting at ten percent, and increasing ten percent weekly until you get to 100, and then you can simply remove the PCT parameter. The reason for this cautious rollout method is because DMARC can block legitimately authorized traffic from service providers such as ServiceNow and Salesforce if those senders are not in the SPF record or have not created DKIM records with them.

DMARC Gotchas

There are a few issues with DMARC to be aware of. The first is that it is limited to only the email portion of the RFC5322 from the field, as shown below. This means that the friendly display name can be impersonated. We'll describe later how Microsoft Defender for Office 365 tackles this limitation by adding its anti-impersonation feature that specifically blocks impersonated display names.

[57] To learn how to enable DKIM see the Microsoft Documentation here: https://docs.microsoft.com/en-us/microsoft-365/security/office-365-security/use-dkim-to-validate-outbound-email

The second issue with DMARC happens when the recipient forwards a calendar invite to another person. This will appear as an impersonated forward since the original sender organization is still the meeting organizer, so DMARC will often block those forwarded invites.

Microsoft has decided to adopt the experimental Authenticated Received Chain (ARC)[58] to help establish an authorized chain of custody for an email message. When widely adopted by other email providers, this should solve the primary limitation of DMARC.

DMARC Monitoring

DMARC includes the ability to monitor when domains are being used to send fraudulent emails. For example, you can add the "RUA" parameter to the DMARC record to receive aggregate reports from receiving email servers: "We saw this IP address sending email as you." If only it were that human readable! The actual reports are sent in XML and so frequently that you need an automated solution for parsing them.

Postmark[59] and Valimail[60] offer 'freemium' services providing basic reporting at no cost and extra services for an additional fee. Agari[61] is another vendor offering DMARC setup and brand protection.

Email Recon Script

Daniel Streefkerk (@dstreefkerk) from Sydney, Australia, wrote a handy PowerShell script to check SPF, DKIM, and DMARC for any domain name. I use Daniel's script regularly to quickly advise a client what an attacker would see if they wanted to impersonate the organization.

```
Domain                          : microsoft.com
MX Records Exist?               : True
MX Provider                     : Microsoft Exchange Online
MX (Lowest Preference)          : microsoft-com.mail.protection.outlook.com
SPF Record Exists?              : True
SPF Record                      : v=spf1 include:_spf-a.microsoft.com
                                  include:_spf-b.microsoft.com
                                  include:_spf-c.microsoft.com
                                  include:_spf-ssg-a.microsoft.com
                                  include:spf-a.hotmail.com
                                  include:_spf1-meo.microsoft.com -all
SPF Mechanism (Mode)            : FAIL
Wildcard SPF Record Exists?     : False
Wildcard SPF Record             :
DMARC Record Exists?            : True
DMARC Record                    : v=DMARC1; p=reject; pct=100; rua=mailto:d@rua.agari.com;
                                  ruf=mailto:d@ruf.agari.com; fo=1
DMARC Domain Policy (Mode)      : REJECT
DMARC Subdomain Policy (Mode)   :
O365 Exchange Online?           : Yes
O365 Tenant Name                : microsoft-com
O365 DKIM Enabled?              : True
```

Figure 12 In this example, the Microsoft.com domain name is protected with SPF, DMARC, and DKIM

---

[58] RFC 8617 ARC https://datatracker.ietf.org/doc/html/rfc8617

[59] https://dmarc.postmarkapp.com/

[60] https://go.valimail.com/microsoft.html

[61] https://agari.com/

You can obtain Daniel's script here:
https://github.com/dstreefkerk/PowerShell/blob/master/Infosec-Related/Invoke-EmailRecon.ps1

Email Security Fundamental #3 Exchange Transport Rules

Exchange Transport Rules (ETR)[62] allow you to filter incoming or outgoing email messages. You can create ETR in the Exchange Online Administration Center.[63]

There are several rules that I recommend you create to block various threats.

Rule 1 Block Executable Attachments

This rule blocks any attachment that has executable content. Since threat actors spread malware via executables, this limits business emails to documents (non-executable content).

Rule 2 Block Auto Forwarded Emails

This rule prevents a mailbox from auto-forwarding its email to an external email address.

Note: In Q4 2020, Microsoft created an outbound spam policy to block auto-forwarded messages. Some organizations will choose to keep the transport rule as a safety net in case an administrator modifies the

---

62 https://docs.microsoft.com/en-us/exchange/security-and-compliance/mail-flow-rules/mail-flow-rules
63 https://admin.exchange.microsoft.com/#/transportrules

outbound spam policy to permit auto-forwards. If "Automatic – System-controlled" is selected, then Microsoft will block auto-forwarded emails.

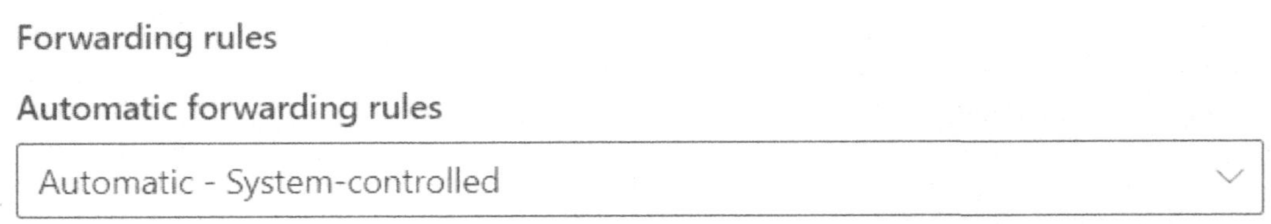

Figure 13 EOP Outbound Spam Policy changed to "System Controlled" in Q4 2020, which blocks forwarded emails.

Rule 3 Block Password Protected attachments

By default, EOP's anti-malware and MDO Safe Attachments cannot scan password-protected attachments unless the password is found in the body of the same email. If the password is found in the body of the email, then Microsoft will use that to decrypt the attachment and scan it for threats. To be safe, it is best to block password-protected attachments since they cannot be scanned for threats.

Rule 4 Block Encrypted Emails

By default, EOP's anti-malware and MDO Safe Attachments cannot scan encrypted attachments. Since Google introduced its own email encryption offering, this rule will block encrypted emails from Google's email service (Gmail).

Rule 5 Block Hyperlinks with IP Addresses

By default, MDO SafeLinks does not scan hyperlinks with IP addresses. Therefore, it's important to prevent links from being sent that contain IP addresses. ETR can use a regular expression to search for this pattern: *(?i)http(s?):\/\/(?:[0-9]{1,3}\.){3}[0-9]{1,3}*

Rule 6 Quarantine DMARC Failures

*Apply this rule if...

The sender is located...	Outside the organization
and	
A message header includes...	'Authentication-Results' header includes 'dmarc=fail'

add condition

*Do the following...

Reject the message with the explanation...	'Sender DMARC policy is to reject this message'

By default, EOP will treat a DMARC failure as a quarantine instead of a reject. This transport rule is designed to conform to the sender's intentions: if DMARC fails, then reject the message.

Rule 7 Set Disclaimers to Reject

*Do the following...

Prepend the disclaimer...	'WARNING EXTERNAL EMAIL'; and fall back to action Reject if the disclaimer can't be inserted.

In 2020, Patriot observed that a few .MSG attachments contained malware but were not getting blocked. The issue was when ETR disclaimers had a failback action to "Wrap," then the subsequent anti-phishing policies failed to block threats. The fix was to change the failback action to Reject or Ignore (where Reject is the recommended option for security). Basically, if a disclaimer cannot be added, then fail close by rejecting the message. Microsoft has since fixed the issue, but the best practice remains in case of any future code regressions, and there seems to be little harm from rejecting messages where disclaimers cannot be added. Since we are on the topic of disclaimers, my disclaimer is that you should always test your rules rather than taking my advice – this book is for educational purposes only, and I'm not responsible for problems that occur due to the advice I give in this book. See what I did there?

Rule 8 Block Open Redirect

*Apply this rule if...

The subject or body matches... '(\/r\/\?)'

add condition

*Do the following...

Prepend the disclaimer... '[POSSIBLE PHISHING OPEN REDIRECT DETECTED - BE CAREFUL ABOUT THE HYPERLINKS IN THIS EMAIL]'; and fall back to action **Reject** if the disclaimer can't be inserted.

One of the top 25 most dangerous software weaknesses is an open redirect.[64] An open redirect is a website that allows anyone to specify a link to an external site. For example:

http://t.emails.acme.com/r/?id=www.acme.com?e=(base 64 string containing the victim email address)

If the domain name's reputation is good, and if the hyperlink has not been used in prior phishing incidents (zero reputation), then the hyperlink may not get blocked. So, this ETR uses a regular expression (\/r\/\?) to find patterns of Open Redirects like "/r/?" in the body or attachment.

Rather than blocking the email or sending it to quarantine, this example shows how to prepend the email with a disclaimer since it is possible for redirects to be used for legitimate purposes.

Email Security Fundamental #4 Blocking Redirects

Once a hacker finds out that you have blocked the auto-forwarding of emails, they may try to enable an Outlook Rule to redirect mail to an external address. The only method I have found to block redirects is to modify the Default Remote Domain[65] to disable forwarding.

[64] https://cwe.mitre.org/data/definitions/601.html

[65] https://admin.exchange.microsoft.com/#/remotedomains

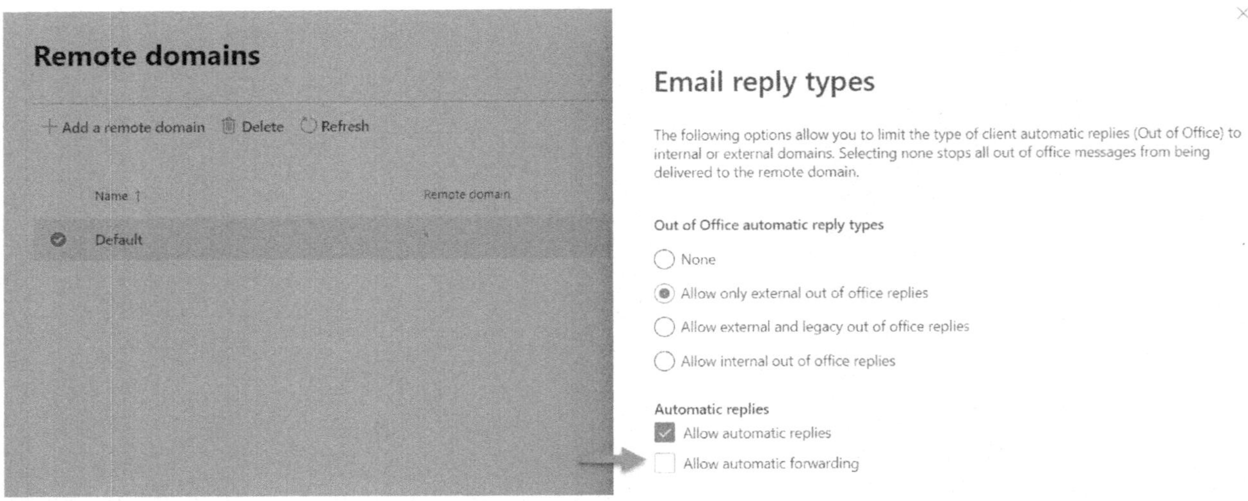

Best Practice Analyzer Tools for Email Security

ORCA

The Office 365 Advanced Threat Protection Recommended Configuration Analyzer (ORCA)[66] is a PowerShell script that was first published in October 2019 and has been continuously updated through at least March 2021.

Installing it is as simple as launching an elevated PowerShell session and then running:

Install-Module -Name ORCA; Get-ORCAReport

It then produces an HTML report containing recommendations for EOP and MDO configurations.

Prerequisites. Exchange Online PowerShell V2 module, which can be installed with: Install-Module -Name ExchangeOnlineManagement

Permissions. To Run ORCA, you need to have the necessary permissions. The "View-Only Configuration" Exchange Online role is needed, which is included in either the Azure AD "Global Reader" or the Exchange Online Role "View-Only Organization Management."

Configuration Analyzer

Microsoft has taken much of the ORCA tool and placed it into the graphical web interface here:

https://security.microsoft.com/configurationAnalyzer

The main benefit of the Configuration Analyzer over ORCA is the one-click fix or the adopt feature that immediately adopts the recommendation or the modify action that takes you right to the policy page to make the changes. It also features a configuration drift analysis and a history tab. The main benefit of the ORCA tool is the portability of the HTML report for sharing with colleagues or change control boards.

---

[66] https://github.com/cammurray/orca

Strict Security Policies

If you don't have time to go through each setting and you just want strong email security in a few mouse clicks, enable the strict policies. Don't be mad when it blocks too much; that is why it is 'strict.' It doesn't advertise itself as 'perfect.'

You might consider the Strict policy as something you would apply to email accounts where you cannot accept much risk of phishing or malware getting through, whereas the 'Standard' policies are the baseline for the rest of the organization.

Beyond the Basics

Microsoft offers advanced email security controls, including attachment detonation, hyperlink inspection, and anti-impersonation. These are included in Microsoft Defender for Office Plan 1. We'll cover Plan 2 features later when we discuss response automation and phishing simulation.

Safe Attachments

MDO Safe Attachments[67] is designed to block malicious attachments based on behavior observed in a sandbox. After EOP scans attachments for known malware, they are opened in parallel against a series of *Windows* sandboxes running in Microsoft's cloud data centers operating with a mix of Windows operating systems and Office versions.

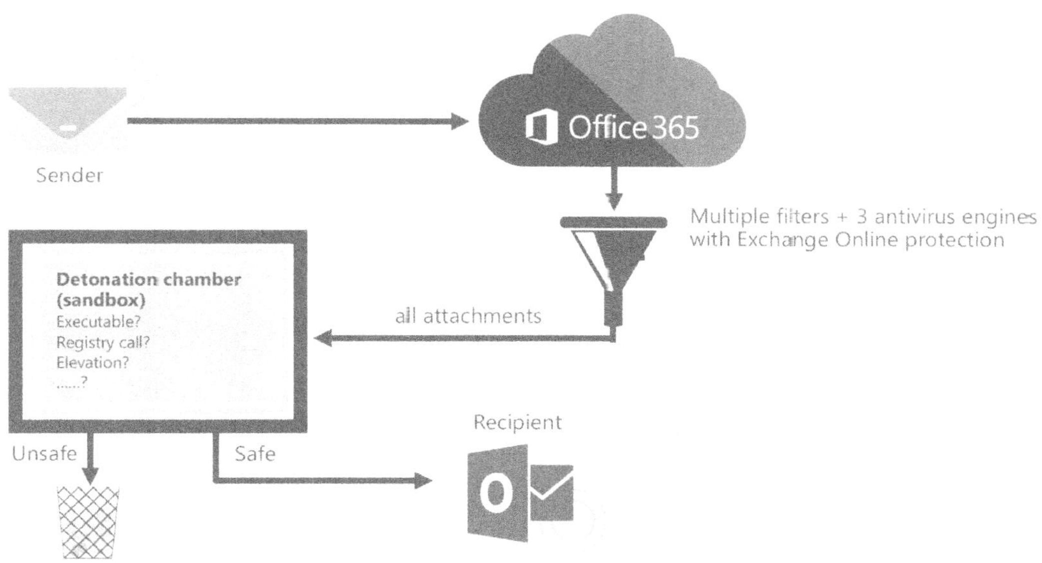

The sandbox is quite sophisticated. For example, if malware attempts to check if it is running in a sandbox, it is seen as suspicious because why would a Microsoft Office or PDF attachment care what the recent file count registry value is? By default, 50% of the detonations take less than one minute, and you can view the exact mail delay latency with the new Mail Latency Report here:

---

67 https://docs.microsoft.com/en-us/microsoft-365/security/office-365-security/safe-attachments?view=o365-worldwide

https://security.microsoft.com/mailLatencyReport

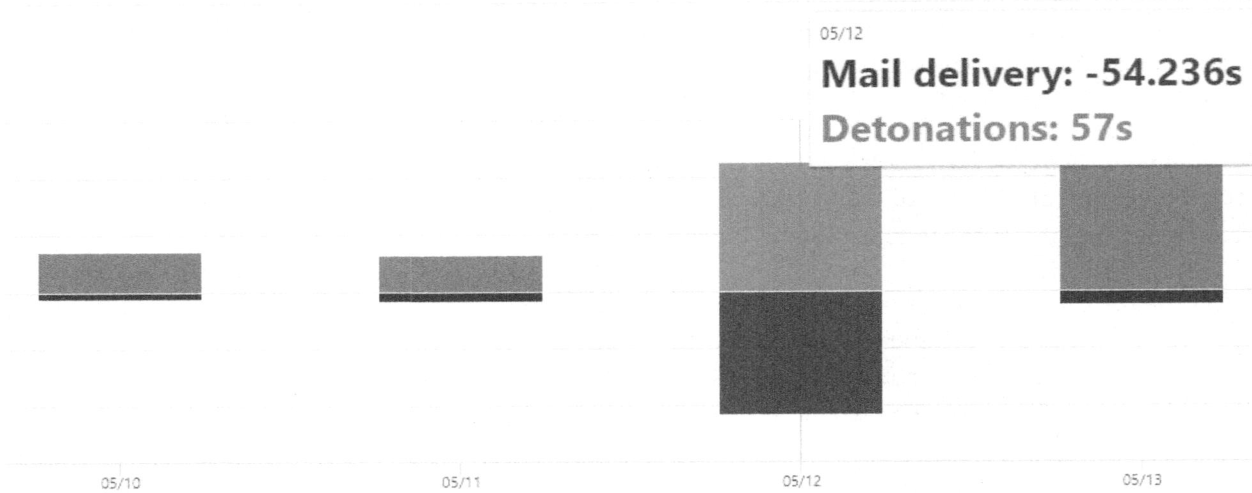

Limitations

It's important to understand that Safe Attachments only detonates files in Windows, and therefore it won't detect exploit behavior in non-Windows computers such as macOS, Linux, Android, or iOS.

Reporting

MDO Safe Attachments includes several reports

- Safe Attachment file types
- Safe Attachments message disposition
- Threat protection status

These reports, along with others, are found here:
https://security.microsoft.com/emailandcollabreport

Recommendations

I recommend configuring MDO Safe Attachments for **Block.** The "Dynamic Delivery" option was originally created when delays in scanning resulted in customer complaints, and its purpose was to allow the message to be received while the scanning was performed on the back-end. This can create a problem in which if the email is forwarded to another recipient who is not protected by the MDO policy, the email is sent without the attachment, which results in confusion. Now that Microsoft has improved the detonation average, I guide my clients to go with Block mode, which sends the message to the server-side quarantine where only administrators can release the message.

I recommend checking the "Apply the above selection if malware scanning for attachments times out or error occurs." By default, the timeout is set to 30 minutes, which means that if the inspection takes longer than 30 minutes, it will take the "Block" action if that is what was selected above. In other words, select this box to fail closed and quarantine attachments that take longer than 30 minutes to scan. Don't be alarmed; the average length of scan attachments is under a minute.

Now that blocked files are sent to the quarantine, it is no longer necessary to enable the "Redirect attachment on detection." This option was required back when the service first launched; at that time, the blocked messages did not go to quarantine and were lost if the redirect option was not selected. As of this writing, the product will warn you that message loss will occur if the redirect option is not selected, which is not the case now since malicious files are sent to the quarantine. So, the warning that appears can be safely ignored.

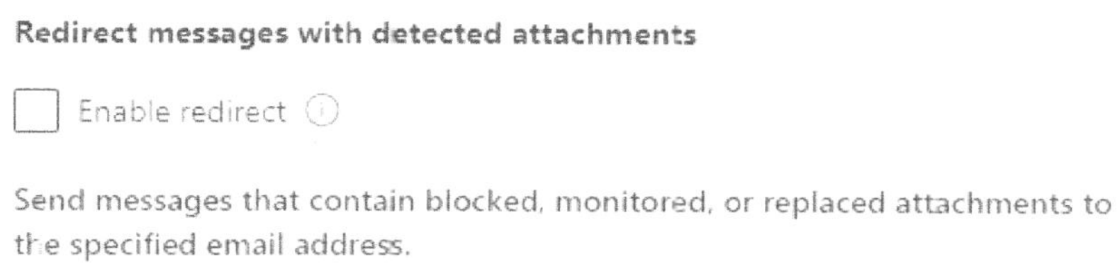

Figure 14 This box is no longer necessary since malicious files are now sent to the server-side quarantine

Advanced Options

When configuring the Safe Attachment policy, you will notice *Global settings* in the top navigation.

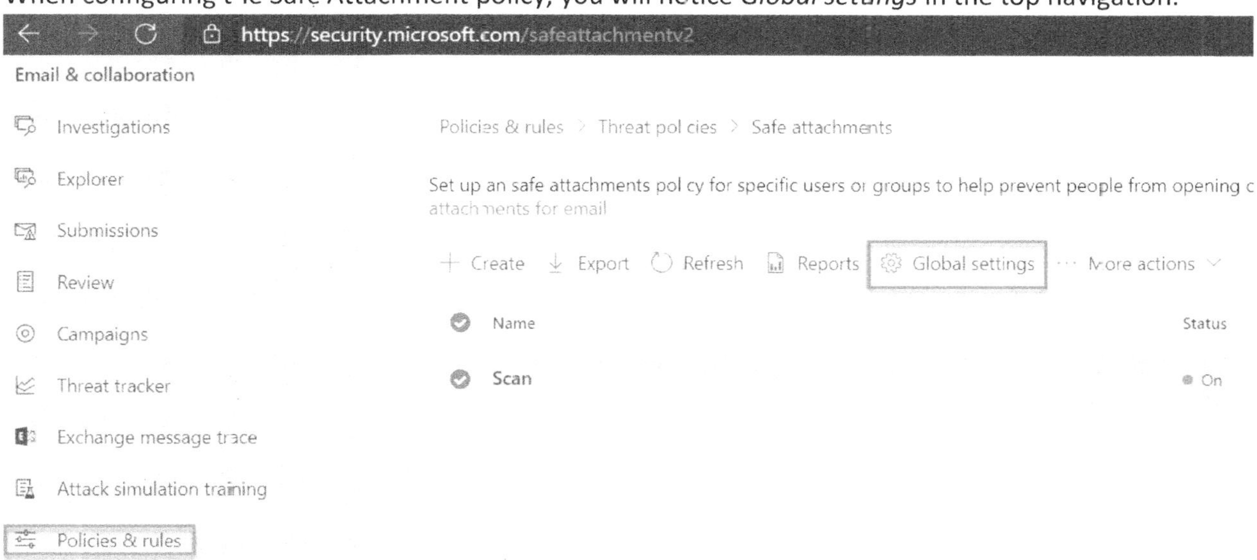

I recommend enabling the radio button to turn on scanning for SharePoint, OneDrive, and Microsoft Teams. Based on my testing, after a malicious file is uploaded, it can take a couple of minutes for a malicious file to be detected (it's not real-time).

The second option to enable Safe Documents requires either the M365 E5 or M365 E5 Security license. This feature will detonate Office documents that originate from outside your organization. This is for scenarios where the attachments are obtained via other channels outside email such as website, USB, etc.

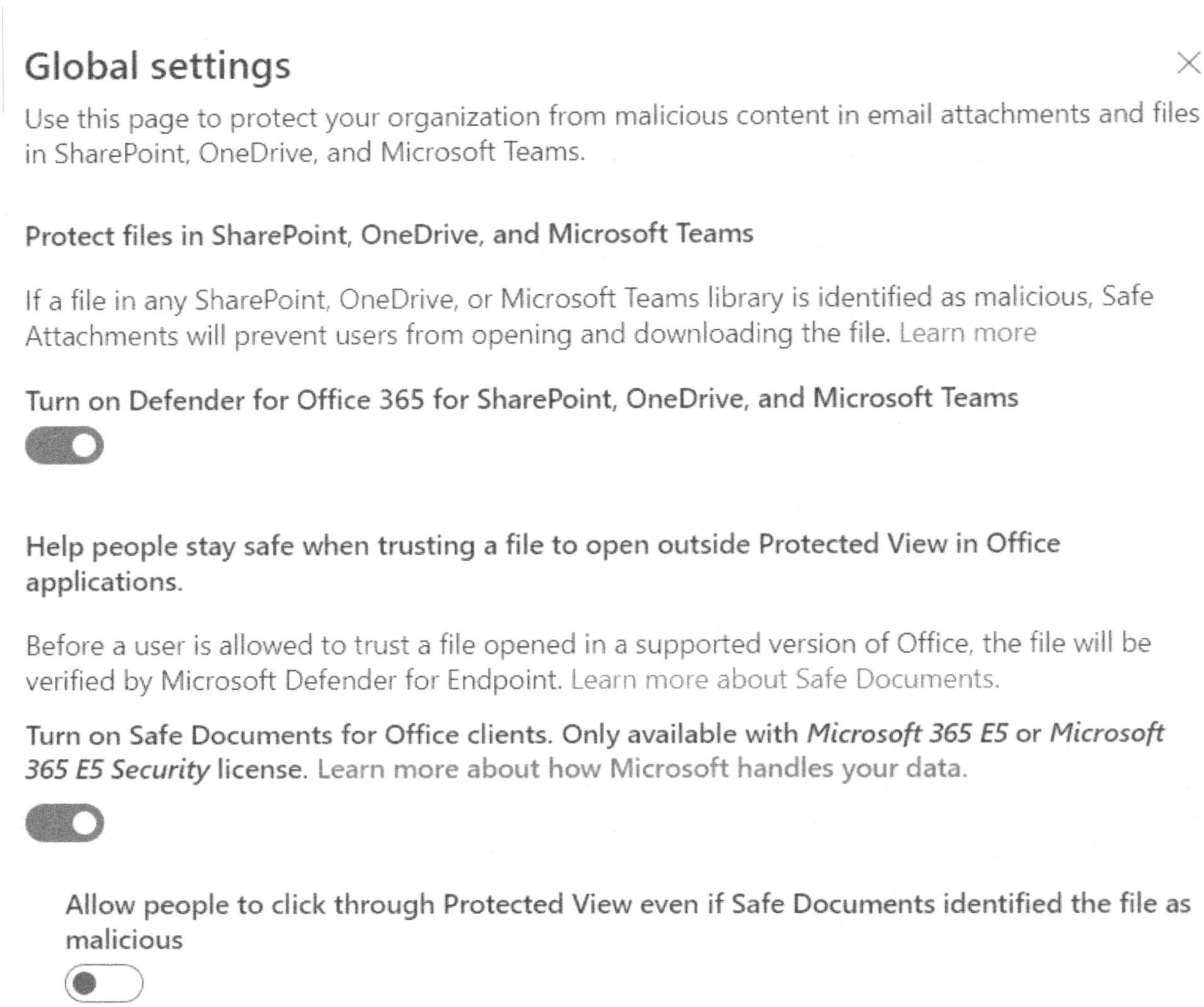

Safe Links

MDO Safe Links are designed to block malicious hyperlinks, either at the time of click or at the time of delivery (this is newer).

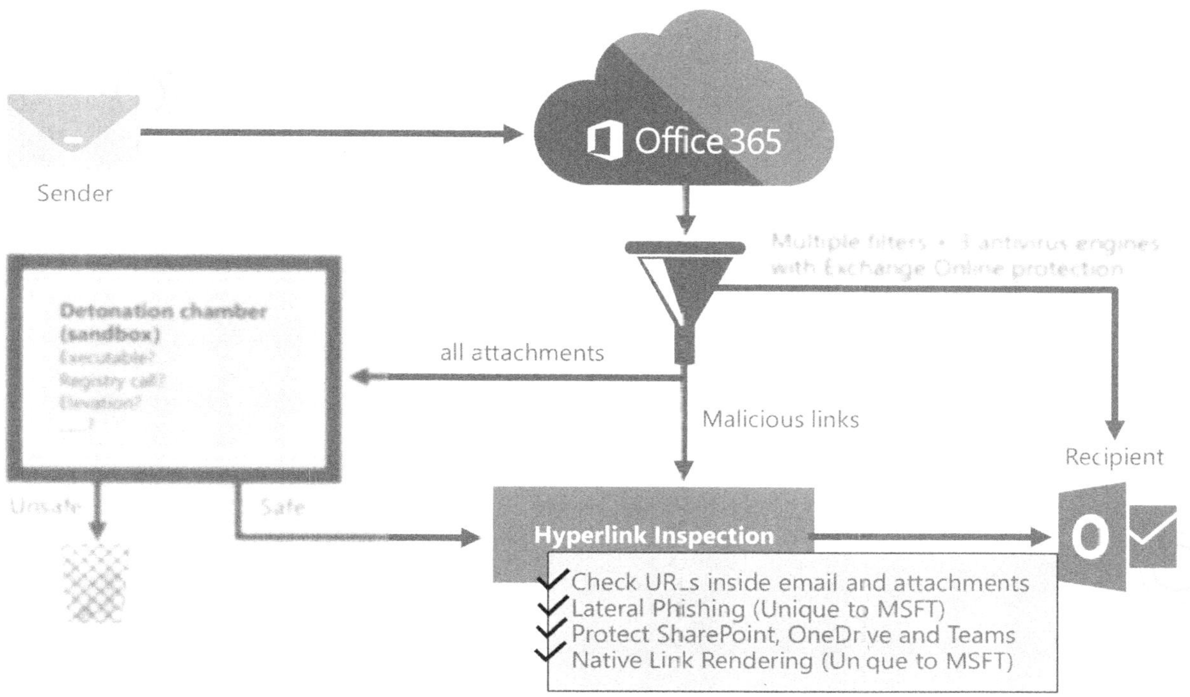

- MDO Safe Links work by rewriting hyperlinks to point to Microsoft to check the reputation and even detonate links inside the same MDO Safe Attachment sandbox. This is used, for example, when a hyperlink points to a file on a website.
- The link can be detonated at the time of delivery before the user clicks on the link, or it can be performed at the time the user clicks on the link. This 'time of click' protection is still the best option, in my opinion, because otherwise, the attacker could swap out the code on the website after it passes through the email security gateways.
- MDO Safe Links offer "Native Link Rendering," where the recipient can hover over the hyperlink and see the original URL rather than the redirected URL. This is helpful when users attend security awareness training and are told to "be careful what you click on." Microsoft is currently the only email security vendor that can show the user the original hyperlink while still performing a redirection to check the link.
- MDO Safe Links protect not only Exchange Online but also hyperlinks found in the other Office 365 productivity solutions such as SharePoint Online, OneDrive for Business, and Teams.
- MDO Safe Links can scan links sent between two internal users (aka lateral phishing). This is important because after an attacker gains a foothold with initial access to a single mailbox, they often will attempt to move laterally inside an organization by sending phishing links to other employees. Because these links originate from trusted senders, it increases the likelihood they will be clicked on.

Limitations

1. Safe links do not function if the website blocks the MDO range of IP addresses. For example, if the hacker hosts malicious content on a website, and then that website blocks outbound (egress) traffic to Microsoft's IP ranges, then Safe links will fail open (unless the link had a prior bad reputation). Hackers know this too; since 2018, the average lifespan of a phishing site has been under 50 minutes.[68]
2. Safe links currently do not check the age of an email domain. For example, if a hacker purchases a domain name today, there is a reasonable chance (based on my testing) that a hyperlink that uses that domain will not be blocked by MDO Safe Links. Other email security vendors block domains if they are newer than 45 days. Hackers know this too (they can read manuals), so they'll often wait the 45 days, or they'll purchase an 'aged' domain from the dark web marketplaces.

3. Safe links do not perform Optical Character Recognition (OCR) of images in attachments or emails that contain instructions for users to browse to malicious links. So, for example, an image that states, "go to website http://mybadsite.com/mybadfile.zip" will not be blocked.
4. Safe links do not work with numeric links such as http://1.1.1.1/threat.zip.

The savvy administrator may say at this point, "wait, I have seen a setting in EOP Spam Policy where I can block Numeric IP addresses found in the URL."

[68] https://zvelo.com/single-use-phishing-urls-need-zero-second-detection

Wouldn't it be cool if that worked so we wouldn't have to create the transport rule? Based on my testing, this doesn't do anything. To block Numeric IP addresses in URLs, you need to create a transport rule (see *Email Security Fundamental #3, Transport Rule #5*).

Recommendations

I recommend configuring MDO Safe Links as shown below:

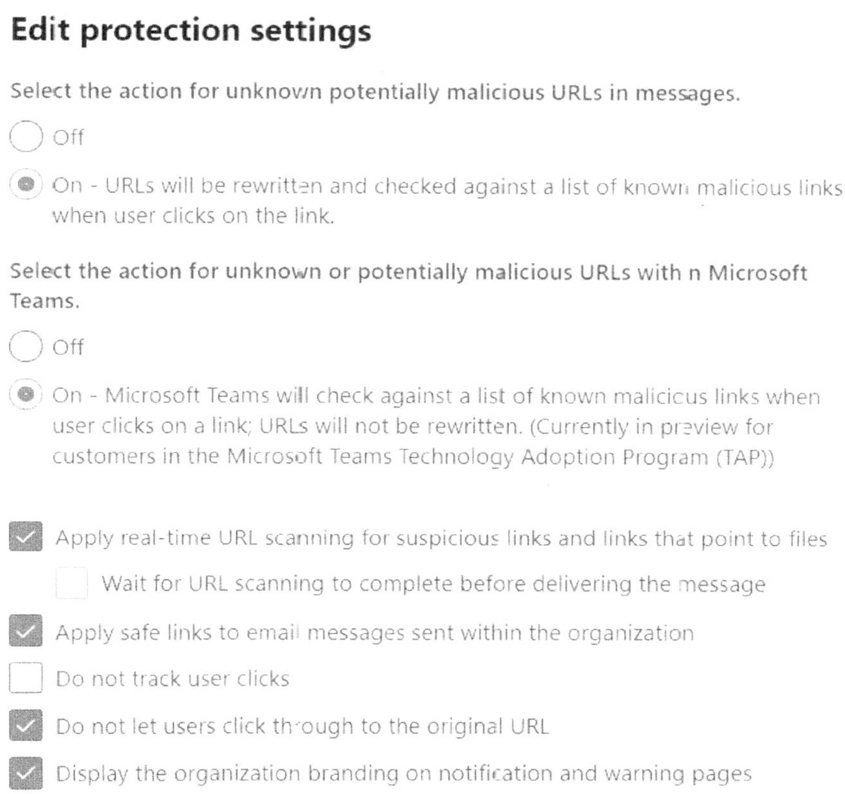

The policy also includes a section to allow-list hyperlinks that should not be re-written. Ironically, you may find it necessary to add Microsoft URLs to the exclusion list.

Reporting

The URL threat protection report provides trend views and detailed views when users click on malicious hyperlinks.

https://security.microsoft.com/reports/URLProtectionActionReport

Advanced Options

Just like how MDO Safe Attachments has ***Global settings***, you'll find that MDO Safe Links also has Global settings. Enable these to define a customer global-block list of malicious URLs and to scan for malicious hyperlinks in other Office 365 products.

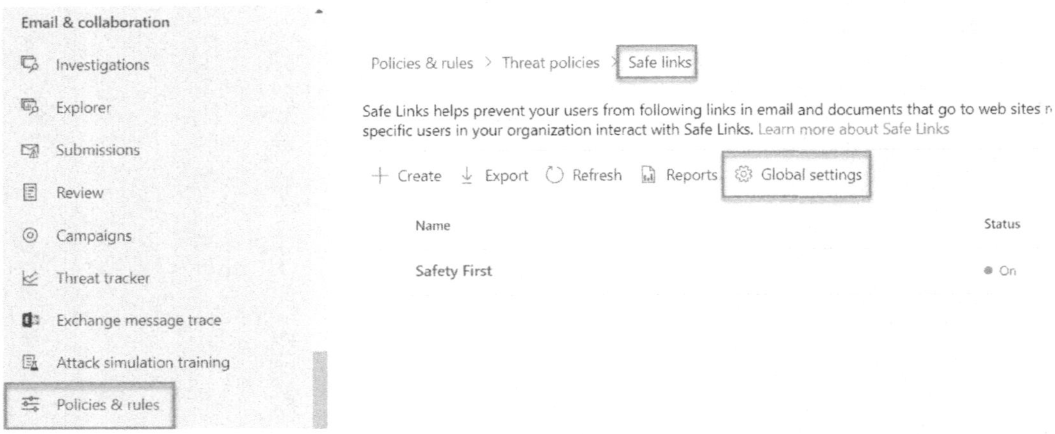

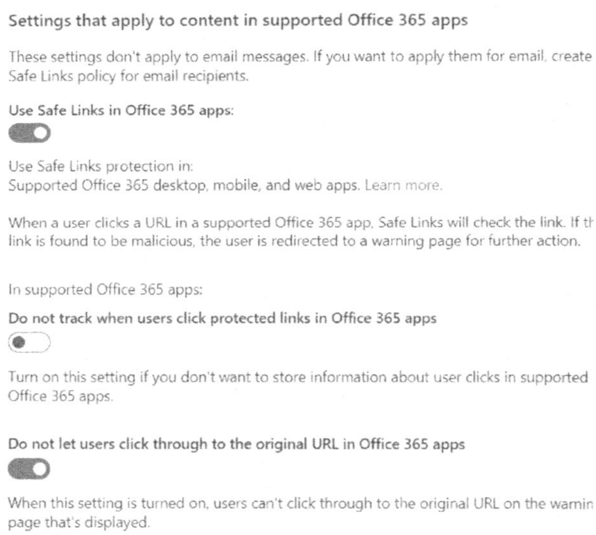

I recommend enabling the "Use Safe Links in Office 365 apps" and selecting "Do not let users click through to the original URL in Office 365 apps." I also recommend leaving "Do not track when users click protected links in Office 365 apps" unselected. This allows you to run forensic reports to determine which users may have clicked on a malicious link. Check with your legal team if General Data Protection

Regulation (GDPR) or other privacy laws require you to enable the "Do not track" option. In general, if you tell the users what you track, then it conforms to the spirit of GDPR.

Anti-Impersonation

Since DMARC was not designed to protect against the impersonation of the display name or cases where the attacker purchases a similar-looking domain name, Microsoft's anti-impersonation feature[69] fills these gaps by blocking impersonated display names and impersonated domain names. The product was designed to protect a company from "Business Email Compromise" (aka "CEO Fraud") and is therefore limited to 350 senders per policy (recently increased from 60). It is most effective when the display name is unique, and we wouldn't recommend it for generic names like "James Smith" or "Robert Brown" as that would result in false positives.

Anti-impersonation can also detect misspelled domain names, which is another tactic that hackers use to increase the effectiveness of their spear-phishing campaigns.

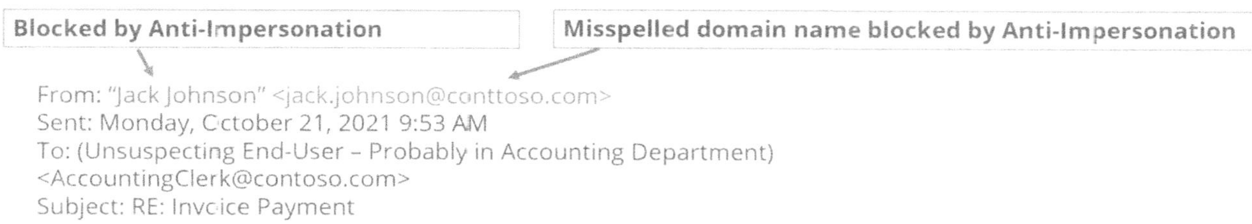

Figure 15 DMARC does not protect against impersonated display names or misspelled domain names. Microsoft anti-impersonation helps solve these two threats.

The display name impersonation protection does not check for nickname substitutions like:

- Douglas for Doug
- Joseph for Joe
- Zachary for Zach
- Etc.

The challenge is the interface only permits one Display Name to be entered per Email Address.

The work-around is to create an SMTP alias for each nickname, and then it lets you add the additional Display Name. If you don't want to create a new SMTP alias for each nickname, then you can add the nicknames directly to the policy using PowerShell, and it achieves the same result without having to create additional SMTP aliases.

The following Exchange Online PowerShell adds a new email address to an existing policy. For example, the pre-existing policy already had a "Ron Smith" pointing to an email address of Ron.Smith@contoso.com, and the following command will add "Smith, Ronald" as a new display name to the same existing email alias.

---

[69] Anti-impersonation requires an extra license which is included in Defender for Office 365 Plan 2 or M365 E5 Security, or full M365 E5.

Set-AntiPhishPolicy -identity (name) -TargetedUsersToProtect @{Add="Smith, Ronald;Ron.smith@contoso.com"}

Microsoft's anti-impersonation feature also permits adding 3rd party domain names (like your customer or supplier domain names). This option can help block emails where the hacker purchased a domain name like your supplier, and they ask for the payment of an invoice, but they change the account details to their own. This doesn't scale well for organizations with dozens of new customers per day since that would require entering every new customer's domain into the policy. If Microsoft added domain name age to the EOP or MDO algorithms (a WHOIS lookup), then they would be more effective at blocking malicious domain names.

Mailbox Intelligence

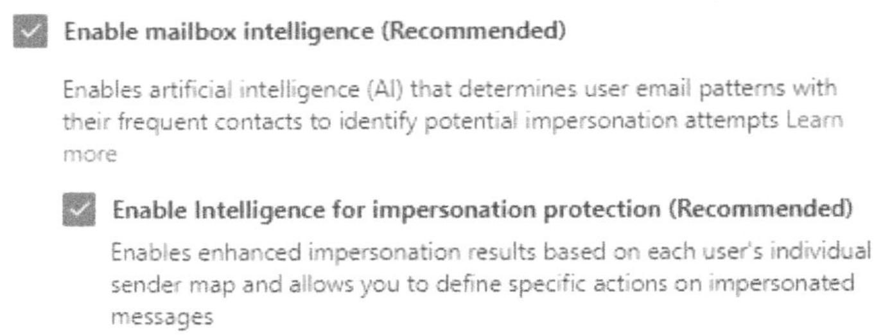

The **Mailbox intelligence**[70] setting is a feature inside the anti-phishing policy. When you enable mailbox intelligence, it starts recording all your sent items so that an Artificial Intelligence engine can prevent the mailbox security from blocking the people you correspond with (avoid false negatives).

Once it has been enabled (for 7 days), you should then proceed to enable the second checkbox: **Mailbox intelligence-based impersonation protection**. This option allows you to specify an action for the impersonation attempts caught by the AI engine (or rather, the lack of sent items to an external contact when the sender matches a user or domain protected by the anti-phishing policy).

As you can see in the admin center, **Mailbox intelligence** must be turned on to see/turn on/turn off **Mailbox intelligence-based impersonation protection** and (optionally) set an action.

Mailbox intelligence = ON while **Mailbox intelligence-based impersonation protection** = OFF means mailbox intelligence is still happening, but no action is taken on messages if mailbox intelligence says "this is an impersonation attempt." Even so, **Mailbox intelligence** = ON while **Mailbox intelligence-based impersonation protection** = OFF can still help reduce false positives. For example, if a frequent contact resembles a protected user in the policy (same name, similar email addresses, etc.), mailbox intelligence can say, "Even though this looks like an impersonation attempt of a protected user, I say that it isn't because these guys have been communicating regularly via email over the last several months."

Another issue that's confusing: the admin center allows you to turn off **Mailbox intelligence-based impersonation protection** but still lets you configure an action, which makes no sense. That action

---

[70] https://docs.microsoft.com/en-us/microsoft-365/security/office-365-security/set-up-anti-phishing-policies?view=o365-worldwide#impersonation-settings-in-atp-anti-phishing-policies

dropdown box and surrounding text should be hidden or grayed out if **Mailbox intelligence-based impersonation protection** = OFF. I understand this is being looked at.

For reference, **Mailbox intelligence** = ON + **Mailbox intelligence-based impersonation protection** = OFF is functionally equivalent to **Mailbox intelligence** = ON + **Mailbox intelligence-based impersonation protection** = ON + Action = No action, if that's of any interest.

FIDO2 U2F Origin Binding

We first looked at FIDO2 U2F in chapter one as a Passwordless authentication solution, and now, we will highlight how it can be used to block phishing attacks with URL Binding. URL Binding is where the website's domain is used as a key component in negotiating the authentication handshake. For example, if a user clicks on a malicious hyperlink inside a phishing email, the authentication will be rejected because the domain in the URL does not match the domain used for registering the security key. Some have gone so far as to call this "totally unphishable authentication."

Google has not had any of its 85,000+ employees successfully phished on their work-related accounts since early 2017, after they began requiring all employees to use physical security keys in place of passwords and one-time codes.[71]

Why Microsoft Defender for Office 365?

There are several reasons why organizations are migrating their email security solution to Microsoft, the main reason being cost savings[72] and security integration with the Microsoft Intelligent Security Graph, which shares signals with other Microsoft solutions[73]. On May 6th, 2021, Forrester named Microsoft, a leader in email security[74]. The other leaders include ProofPoint, Trend Micro, Mimecast, and Barracuda.

The main reason I advise my clients to select Microsoft is that it has a 400% lower miss rate than competitor solutions[75]; It is simply catching more spam and malware than the others. Since Exchange Online sits behind other email security solutions, it can predict the spam and malicious emails that it would have caught. Considering that there are over 200 million users in Office 365, and 81% of all their emails are filtered by Microsoft, it means that Microsoft's machine learning engines have significantly larger models than the competition (470 billion emails per month).

---

[71] https://krebsonsecurity.com/2018/07/google-security-keys-neutralized-employee-phishing/

[72] EOP is free with any purchased Exchange Online plan, and MDO Plan 1 starts at $2.75 per user per month, or even lower for larger organizations often negotiate lower volume discounts or get it as part of a security bundle such as M365 E5 Security.

[73] The Microsoft Security graph allows signal sharing between multiple Microsoft solutions such as Microsoft 365 Defender (Defender for Endpoint, Defender for Office, Defender for Identity), Microsoft Cloud App Security, Azure Identity Protection, and Azure Security Center. The Graph processes over 8 trillion signals per day.

[74] https://www.microsoft.com/security/blog/2021/05/06/forrester-names-microsoft-a-leader-in-the-2021-enterprise-email-security-wave/

[75] Microsoft Ignite 2019 Session BRK2105 23:00 https://www.youtube.com/watch?v=i999KbrBX7c

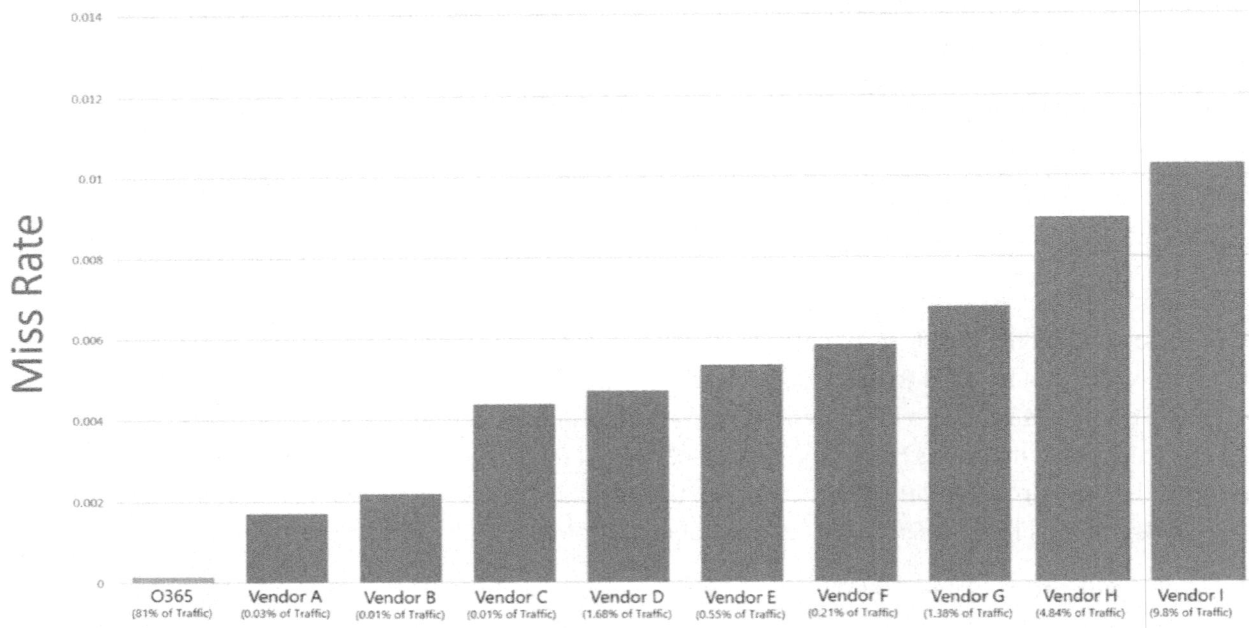

Figure 16 Ignite 2019 Session BRK2105

Evaluating Microsoft Defender for Office 365

I have experienced a high degree of anxiety from organizations that are nervous about making the switch to Microsoft from third-party solutions. The most common concern is whether Microsoft will suddenly allow a ton of spam or phishing emails through or block too many legitimate emails. If you are also considering a switch, then I can empathize with the pressure that the IT department feels, as I was an IT Director for six years. Fortunately, Microsoft provides a way for IT to evaluate the effectiveness of the Microsoft solution before they make the big switch of changing DNS MX records to point to Microsoft.

The first step is to obtain a trial license of Microsoft Defender for Office 365, or Microsoft 365 E5, and then enable a feature called Evaluation Mode (first announced at the Ignite 2019 conference). The Microsoft Defender for Office 365 evaluation set-up card can be found in the Office 365 Security & Compliance Center (https://protection.office.com/homepage) from three access points:

1. Threat management > Dashboard
2. Threat management > Policy
3. Reports > Dashboard

Figure 17 The Microsoft Defender for Office 365 evaluation set-up card first requires an active E5 Trial License

Another way you can evaluate EOP/MDO is to use a test domain, such as a .NET top-level domain (TLD). Many companies have a TLD that they don't use; they purchase it to prevent attackers from using it in phishing campaigns. You could add that domain to Microsoft 365, set up the MX record, and assign the alias to a few users to test EOP/MDO side-by-side with your existing email security solution.

Even if you are happy with your current 3rd party email security solution, there are several benefits for licensing and deploying Microsoft Defender for Office 365.

- MDO uniquely protects malicious content in SharePoint, OneDrive, and Microsoft Teams.
- The Safe Documents feature will sandbox documents that originate from outside of the company email. For example, if a user can access their personal webmail account (Yahoo, Hotmail, Gmail, etc.), then Safe Documents can detonate and inspect attachments for these specific file types: Microsoft Word, Excel, and PowerPoint on Windows.
- Automated incident response (AIR) capabilities (available MDO Plan 2), which we'll review in Chapter Ten, "Responding to a Security Event."

Message Header Forensics

An important skill for email administrators or security administrators is knowing how to read a message header. Like in a deep way, like you were performing a crime scene investigation. The best resource available for understanding message header forensics is an online post by Microsoft MVP Ammar Hasayen. It's almost book-length and too much to cite here but go check it out when you have a chance.

https://blog.ahasayen.com/eop-exchange-online-protection-architecture/

Phishing Simulation

Phishing simulation can dramatically improve the awareness of end-users to spot phishing messages. I have seen studies where click rates were reduced from 38% to less than 5% after 12 months of periodic training.[76] Some phishing solutions have reduced click rates to 2.7%.[77]

In chapter one, we discussed the prior version of Attack Simulator that was hosted in Protection.office.com. The updated version is now hosted in Security.Microsoft.com here: https://security.microsoft.com/attacksimulator

The old phishing simulator was limited to three built-in campaigns. The new simulator starts off with a modular design with five high-level starting points that can be customized with dozens of payloads or your own payloads.

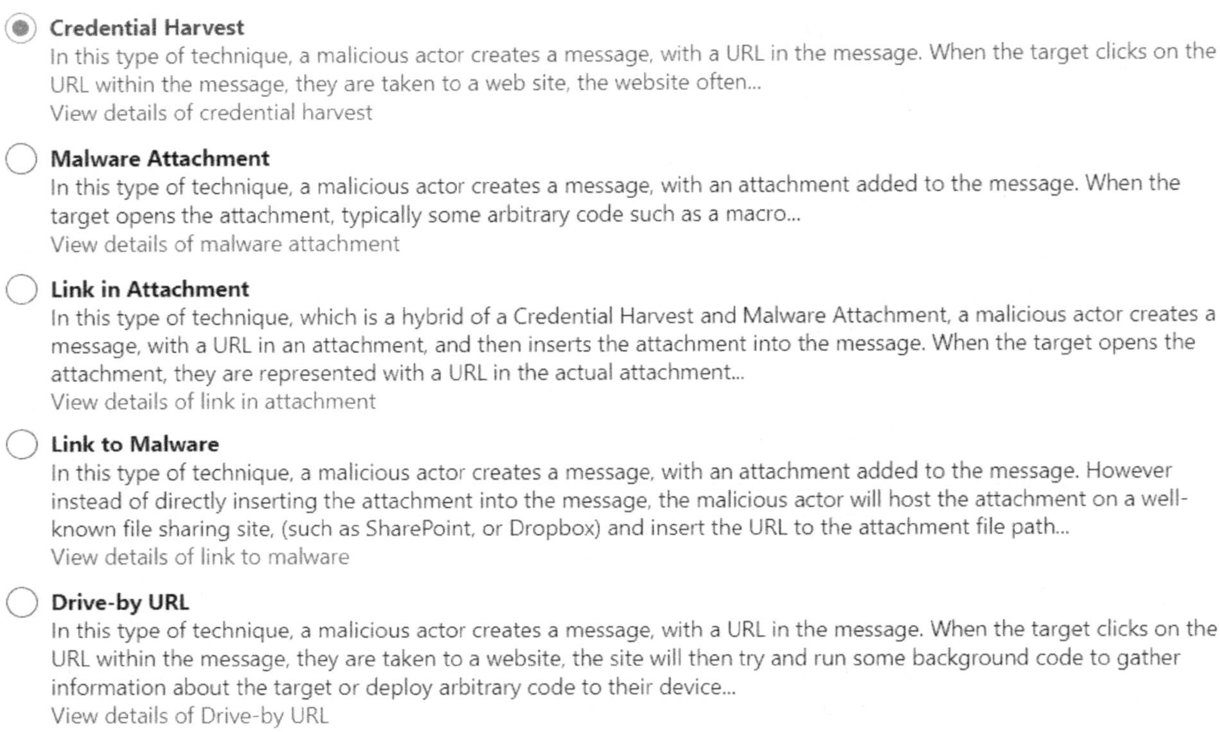

After selecting a category, you can then select from dozens of existing payloads, or you can create your own payload.

[76] https://www.knowbe4.com/resources/point-of-failure-phishing-training-does-not-work/
[77] https://insights.sei.cmu.edu/blog/anti-phishing-training-is-it-working-is-it-worth-it/

Select Payload

Select payload for this simulation technique. You can create or collect your own payloads to add this list. create a new payload, you will be redirected to a payload creation wizard.

+ Create a payload

56 items

Applied filters:

Payload name	Click rate	Predicted Compro...	Simulations launcl
2 Failed Messages	0	39	0
Accounts payable document review	0	20	0
American express password reset	0	45	0
American Express phone number confir...	0	37	0
Black Friday Offer	0	20	0
Capital One bank account locked	0	36	0

Security Awareness Training

Users who fail the phishing simulation are automatically sent to training, which helps measure the effectiveness of the training.

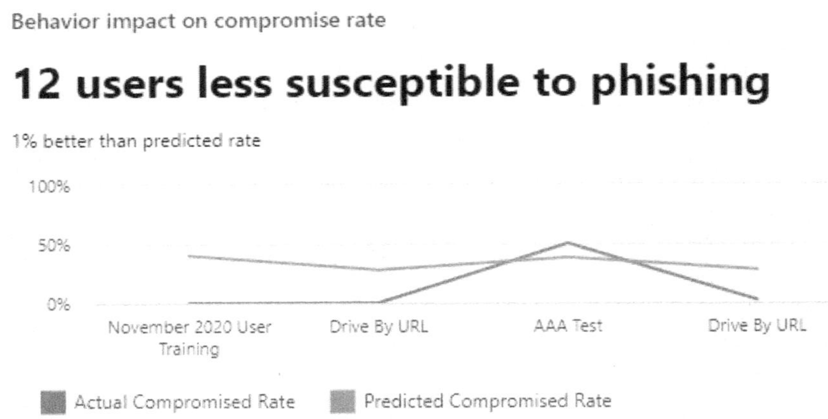

Office Message Encryption (Standard vs. Advanced Features)

Any discussion on email security would be incomplete without encryption. Microsoft 365 supports all the major encryption standards, including Transport Layer Security (TLS)

Office 365 Message Encryption (OME) is a service built on Azure Rights Management (Azure RMS) that lets you send encrypted email to people inside or outside your organization, regardless of the destination email address (Gmail, Yahoo! Mail, Outlook.com, etc.).

To view encrypted messages, recipients can either get a one-time passcode, sign in with a Microsoft account, or sign in with a work or school account associated with Office 365. Recipients can also send encrypted replies. They don't need a subscription to view encrypted messages or send encrypted messages.

How do users benefit from the service?

Message senders benefit from the added control over sensitive emails provided by Office 365 Message Encryption.

Which licenses provide the rights for a user to benefit from the service?

Microsoft 365 E3/A3/G3, Office 365 E3/A3/G3, and Azure Information Protection Plan 1 provide the rights for a user to benefit from Office 365 Message Encryption.

How is the service provisioned/deployed?

Admins create and manage Office 365 Message Encryption policies in the Exchange admin center under **Mail flow** > **Rules**. By default, these rules apply to all users in the tenant. For more information about setting up new Office 365 Message Encryption capabilities, see Set up new Message Encryption capabilities.

How can the service be applied only to users in the tenant who are licensed for the service?

Admins should apply mail flow rules for Office 365 Message Encryption only to licensed users. For more information about defining mail flow rules, see Define mail flow rules to encrypt email messages.

Office 365 Advanced Message Encryption

Office 365 Advanced Message Encryption helps customers meet compliance obligations that require more flexible controls over external recipients and their access to encrypted emails. With Advanced Message Encryption, admins can control sensitive emails shared outside the organization by using automatic policies that can detect sensitive information types (for example, personally identifying information, or financial or health IDs), or they can use keywords to enhance protection by applying custom email templates and expiring access to encrypted emails through a secure web portal Additionally, admins can further control encrypted emails accessed externally through a secure web portal by revoking access at any time.

How do users benefit from the service?

Message senders benefit from the added control over sensitive emails provided by Advanced Message Encryption.

Which licenses provide the rights for a user to benefit from the service?

Office 365 E5/A5/G5, Microsoft 365 E5/A5/G5, Microsoft 365 E5/A5/G5 Compliance, and Microsoft 365 E5/A5/G5 Information Protection and Governance provide the rights for a user to benefit from Advanced Message Encryption.

How is the service provisioned/deployed?

Admins create and manage Advanced Message Encryption policies in the Exchange admin center under **Mail flow** > **Rules**. By default, these rules apply to all users in the tenant. For more information about setting up new Message Encryption capabilities, see Set up new Office 365 Message Encryption capabilities.

How can the service be applied only to users in the tenant who are licensed for the service?

Admins should apply mail flow rules for Advanced Message Encryption only to licensed users For more information about defining mail flow rules, see Define mail flow rules to encrypt email messages in Office 365.

Business Standard or Business Premium?

You'll notice that OME Standard is included in "Azure Information Protection Plan 1" and that is listed as a feature included in the Business Premium. You'll also notice that the Advanced OME is ***not*** included in either Standard or Premium. Microsoft no longer sells the Azure Information Protection Plan 2 SKU, which means customers need to acquire a package to obtain features such as automatic classification.

Message policy and compliance	Microsoft 365 Business Standard	Microsoft 365 Business Premium
Long-term archiving of Exchange Online-based mailboxes	No	Yes[3]
Azure Information Protection Plan 1	No	Yes[2]

Microsoft 365 Business Premium service description - Service Descriptions | Microsoft Docs

Chapter Three – Securing the Corporate Endpoint in M365

We learned from Chapter Two that even with the best security awareness training and phishing simulations, at least 5% of people will still open phishing emails! Therefore, after identity and email, the next battleground is the endpoint (Windows, macOS, Linux, iOS, or Android).

The hacks that are successful against identity and email often rely upon a human mistake. Endpoint security is therefore extremely important because it is often the last layer of defense that stands between a human mistake and a hacker's goals.

Here are just a small handful of techniques that target human mistakes that hackers exploit to gain initial access to an endpoint:

- Browsing a website that contains malware (also known as a drive-by attack)
- Clicking on a malicious advertisement (also known as malvertising)
- Opening a malicious attachment
- Opening a malicious hyperlink from an email or inside an email attachment
- Plugging in a USB drive that contains malware
- Receiving a phone call from "Microsoft Support" that asks to install remote access software

In this chapter, we will explore how Microsoft Defender for Endpoint can be used to secure the corporate endpoint from the attacks listed above.

Why Enable Tamper Protection[78]

To understand the value of Tamper Protection, we first need to understand that malware has evolved to split itself into multiple attack stages. The first stage of the attack is to disable the antivirus client so that more dangerous attack sequences such as Ransomware can execute. This first stage attack is called a "loader," which attempts to disable Antivirus or other security settings via the registry, PowerShell, group policy, WMI, Scheduled Task, or Group Policy Object (GPO).

A dropper is often a script or executable that contains more advanced malware or ransomware inside of itself. For example, it will make a new executable appear on the disk or execute an in-memory (aka file-less) attack such as process hollowing.

Tamper Protection is designed to prevent loaders from disabling real-time antivirus protection. For example, it will prevent the following PowerShell command from working:

Set-MpPreference -DisableRealtimeMonitoring $true

---

[78] https://docs.microsoft.com/en-us/windows/security/threat-protection/windows-defender-antivirus/prevent-changes-to-security-settings-with-tamper-protection

On July 2nd, 2021, the REvil ransomware gang successfully pulled off one of the largest ever ransomware attacks against customers of Kaseya VSA. The gang claimed to ransom 1 million computers (if true, this attack was 5 times larger than the Wannacry ransomware attack of 2017). This attack would likely have been disrupted if customers had enabled the Tamper Protection feature.

The following screenshot shows the loader attempting to disable antivirus before loading the dropper, which is self-contained inside a base64 encoded agent.crt file.

```
"C:\Windows\system32\cmd.exe" /c ping 127.0.0.1 -n 5693 > nul & C:\Windows\System32\WindowsPowerShell\v1.
0\powershell.exe Set-MpPreference -DisableRealtimeMonitoring $true -DisableIntrusionPreventionSystem $true
-DisableIOAVProtection $true -DisableScriptScanning $true -EnableControlledFolderAccess Disabled
-EnableNetworkProtection AuditMode -Force -MAPSReporting Disabled -SubmitSamplesConsent NeverSend & copy /Y
C:\Windows\System32\certutil.exe C:\Windows\cert.exe & echo %RANDOM% >> C:\Windows\cert.exe & C:\Windows\cert.
exe -decode c:\kworking\agent.crt c:\kworking\agent.exe & del /q /f c:\kworking\agent.crt C:\Windows\cert.exe &
c:\kworking\agent.exe
```

The portion of the command above that attempted to disable real-time monitoring would have failed if Tamper Protection was enabled. This means that the later stages of the attack performed by the dropper or ransomware would likely have been prevented since, according to VirusTotal, Microsoft Defender detected the REvil ransomware.

- Tamper Protection does not require Windows 10 E5, but if you have E5, then it can only be disabled via Intune or the Microsoft Defender security console. Therefore, the benefit of the enhanced license is that even a local administrator cannot disable the real-time AV engine. Tamper Protection requires Windows 1903, or the equivalent Windows Server version or higher.
- Tamper Protection prevents more than just real-time protection from being disabled. It also blocks attempts to change: DisableAntiVirus, DisableAntiSpyware, DisableRealtimeMonitoring, DisableOnAccessProtection, DisableBehaviorMonitoring, DisableIOAVProtection registry keys (and more).
- Tamper Protection can now be enabled globally inside the MDE advanced feature settings. So, when should you use Intune to control Tamper Protection, and when should you use the global setting? If you need more granular control on a per device/group basis, then Intune is required.

Using Intune Device Profiles – a step-by-step guide

Create a profile that includes the following settings:

- Platform: Windows 10 and later
- Profile Type: Endpoint protection
- **Settings > Windows Defender Security Center > Tamper Protection**

Steps to Block Manual Intune Unenrollment

If you depend upon Intune to deploy Tamper Protection, you want to prevent a malicious actor from uninstalling Intune; otherwise, the Tamper protection feature can be turned off.

- In Intune, navigate to **Device configuration – Profiles >** ***Profile name*** **> Device Restrictions > General > Manual unenrollment > Block**
- In Intune, navigate to **Device configuration – Profiles >** ***Profile name*** **> Device Restrictions > General > Direct Memory Access > Enabled**

Enable Attack Surface Reduction Rules (ASR)[79]

- ASR Rules are a feature of Windows 10 E3 and Windows 10 E5. The E5 version adds unique rules that are not available in the E3 version, such as the ability to prevent Adobe from spawning a child process like PowerShell, CMD.exe, VBscript, WSH, etc.
- ASR rules can be enabled without MDE, but the benefit of using MDE is centralized reporting. Otherwise, the audits would be decentralized in the local event viewer.
- ASR Rules are branded as part of "Microsoft Defender Exploit Guard," which is a series of Windows 10 security features including Controlled Folder Access, Exploit Protection, and Network Protection.
- Some of the ASR rules require cloud-delivered protection[80] to be enabled. Read the ASR documentation page[81] to identify important caveats before enabling ASR.
- The ASR Rule "Executables that don't meet a prevalence, age, or trusted list criteria" examines .exe, .dll, .scr to determine if they are in an allowed list that MSFT maintains, and since there is no way to add exclusions, so we recommend setting this rule to Audit mode.
- You can enable ASR rules using any of these methods:
    - Microsoft Intune
    - Mobile Device Management (MDM)
    - Microsoft Endpoint Configuration Manager
    - Group Policy
    - PowerShell
- In Intune, navigate to **Device configuration – Profiles >** ***Profile name*** **> Endpoint Protection > Microsoft Defender Exploit Guard > Attack Surface Reduction**.

---

79 https://docs.microsoft.com/en-us/microsoft-365/security/defender-endpoint/attack-surface-reduction?view=o365-worldwide

80 https://docs.microsoft.com/en-us/windows/security/threat-protection/windows-defender-antivirus/enable-cloud-protection-windows-defender-antivirus

81 https://docs.microsoft.com/en-us/windows/security/threat-protection/microsoft-defender-atp/attack-surface-reduction

- I recommend enabling them all to Audit mode for approximately 30 days, then setting them to block after addressing any necessary exclusions that are found after analyzing the audit results.
- For a deep dive on ASR rules, I recommend the four-part blog series available on Techcommunity.microsoft.com[82]

Enable "Block at First Site"

This is a series of configuration items that submit a new executable or script to the cloud. Block at first sight only uses the cloud protection backend for executable files and non-portable executable files that are downloaded from the Internet or that originate from the Internet zone. You can configure this using Intune, SCCM, or Group Policy.

In Intune, navigate to **Device configuration – Profiles >** ***Profile name*** **> Device restrictions > Windows Defender Antivirus**. The settings should be the following:

- Cloud-delivered protection: Enable
- File Blocking Level: High
- Time extension for file scanning by the cloud: 50
- Prompt users before sample submission: Send all data without prompting
- Submit samples consent: Send all samples automatically

Enable MDE Sample sharing for all files

Cloud protection requires that you allow your endpoint to upload the samples to the cloud.

- In Intune, navigate to **Device configuration – Profiles >** ***Profile name*** **> Microsoft Defender ATP (Windows 10) > Sample sharing for all files > Enable**
- In Intune, navigate to **Device configuration – Profiles >** ***Profile name*** **> Microsoft Defender ATP (Windows 10) > Expedite telemetry reporting frequency > Enable**

Enable MDE Automatic Investigation and Remediation

This feature is now enabled by default for new tenants[83]. However, existing tenants that have already configured a policy are not overridden by the change.

How to enable AutoIR

- Create a Role Group in MDE Settings > Permissions > Roles (select a group)
- Create an MDE machine group, set it to all machines, and assign it to Full – Remediate threats automatically
- Enable Automated Investigation in MDE Settings > Advanced Features

---

[82] https://techcommunity.microsoft.com/t5/microsoft-defender-for-endpoint/bg-p/MicrosoftDefenderATPBlog/label-name/Demystifying%20ASR%20rules

[83] https://techcommunity.microsoft.com/t5/microsoft-defender-for-endpoint/microsoft-defender-for-endpoint-automation-defaults-are-changing/ba-p/2068744

- Enable *all* of the MDE Settings > Advanced Features (or as many as you are licensed for, ex: Azure ATP, Intune, MCAS, etc.).

Note: If you have older versions of Windows 10, such as 1803[84] or 1709[85], you will need to deploy an update. Although, instead of spending the time pushing updates, you instead invest that time in upgrading to a supported version of Windows. The enterprise support policy for Windows 10 enterprise is 30 months, and the Profession edition is 18 months. This means that you are no longer receiving security updates if you have these old editions of Windows.

Enable EDR Block Mode

Originally, it was assumed this feature was only applicable when Defender was in passive mode behind another AV client. While that is the primary use case for EDR Block mode,
Microsoft's documentation[86] recommends enabling this feature even when Defender is in Active mode. "We recommend keeping EDR in block mode on, whether Microsoft Defender Antivirus is running in passive mode or inactive mode. EDR in block mode provides another layer of defense with Microsoft Defender for Endpoint. It allows Defender for Endpoint to take actions based on post-breach behavioral EDR detections."

Enable Network Protection[87]

Network protection expands the scope of Windows Defender SmartScreen[88] to block all outbound HTTP(s) traffic that attempts to connect to low-reputation sources (based on the domain or hostname).

Network Protection is branded as part of "Microsoft Defender Exploit Guard" which is a series of Windows 10 security features including Controlled Folder Access, Exploit Protection and ASR rules.

Network Protection can be enabled without MDE, but the benefit of using MDE is centralized reporting. Otherwise, the audits would be decentralized in the local event viewer.

How to enable Network Protection in Intune:

- In Intune, navigate to **Device configuration – Profiles >** ***Profile name*** **> Endpoint Protection > Microsoft Defender Exploit Guard > Network Filtering > Network Protection**

---

[84] https://www.catalog.update.microsoft.com/Search.aspx?q=KB4493464
[85] https://www.catalog.update.microsoft.com/Search.aspx?q=KB4493441
[86] https://www.thecloudtechnologist.com/mdatp-best-practices/_wp_link_placeholder
[87] https://docs.microsoft.com/en-us/windows/security/threat-protection/microsoft-defender-atp/network-protection
[88] https://docs.microsoft.com/en-us/windows/security/threat-protection/windows-defender-smartscreen/windows-defender-smartscreen-overview

Protecting against Drive-By Attacks with SmartScreen[89]

Microsoft Defender SmartScreen protects your system from Drive-by attacks, which are malicious web attacks that tend to start on trusted websites, targeting security vulnerabilities in commonly used software. Drive-by attacks are especially dangerous because they don't require any user interaction – so there's nothing to click, nothing to download – and infection is usually invisible.

Microsoft Defender SmartScreen checks files that you download from the web against a list of reported malicious software sites and programs known to be unsafe. It is an already Built-in feature in Microsoft Edge and Chromium Edge. "Windows Defender Browser Protection" is available as an add-on to Chrome[90]

I highly recommend SmartScreen! You can manage it through Group Policy[91] or Intune.

Web Browser Isolation

SmartScreen is great when it is already aware of a threat. But what about a zero-day drive-by attack when there is no prior reputation for SmartScreen to rely upon? Microsoft Defender Application Guard is the next step in protection by applying virtualization-based security to the web browser so that the underlying operating system is shielded when a user browses to a malicious site. This feature is natively available in Microsoft Edge Chromium or via web browser extension in Google Chrome or Firefox[92].

Application Guard can be enabled in stand-alone or enterprise mode. Application Guard Enterprise Mode works by sending all untrusted web traffic to a virtual container on the same computer (like how Kubernetes works, where the container is a mirror of the host). So as an enterprise administrator, you must first define your trusted websites such as SharePoint Online, OneDrive for Business, then shield all other websites in the VM. The end-user experience is relatively unaffected at first appearance until they attempt to copy content from the website into the actual computer. As an enterprise administrator, you define how much interaction you want to permit between the shielded web browser and the actual computer.

The virtual container that the web browser runs inside can either be completely non-persistent or partially non-persistent so that the cookies and favorites persist. If the virtual machine gets pwned, not to worry, it will be wiped when the user restarts the computer or logs off the machine.

Application Guard is available for Windows 10 Professional or Enterprise Editions version 1809 or higher. The CPU must support extended page tables (aka SLAT) and virtualization-based security extensions such as VT-X (Intel) or AMD-V.

---

[89] https://docs.microsoft.com/en-us/windows/security/threat-protection/microsoft-defender-smartscreen/microsoft-defender-smartscreen-overview
[90] https://chrome.google.com/webstore/detail/windows-defender-browser/bkbeeeffjjeopflfhgeknacdieedcoml?hl=en-US
[91] https://docs.microsoft.com/en-us/windows/security/threat-protection/microsoft-defender-smartscreen/microsoft-defender-smartscreen-available-settings
[92] https://docs.microsoft.com/en-us/windows/security/threat-protection/microsoft-defender-application-guard/md-app-guard-browser-extension

You can manage Application Guard with Intune, Configuration Manager, Group Policy, or 3rd party MDM.[93] For example, in Intune, you can configure Endpoint Security > Attack Surface Reduction Policy > Application Guard for Edge

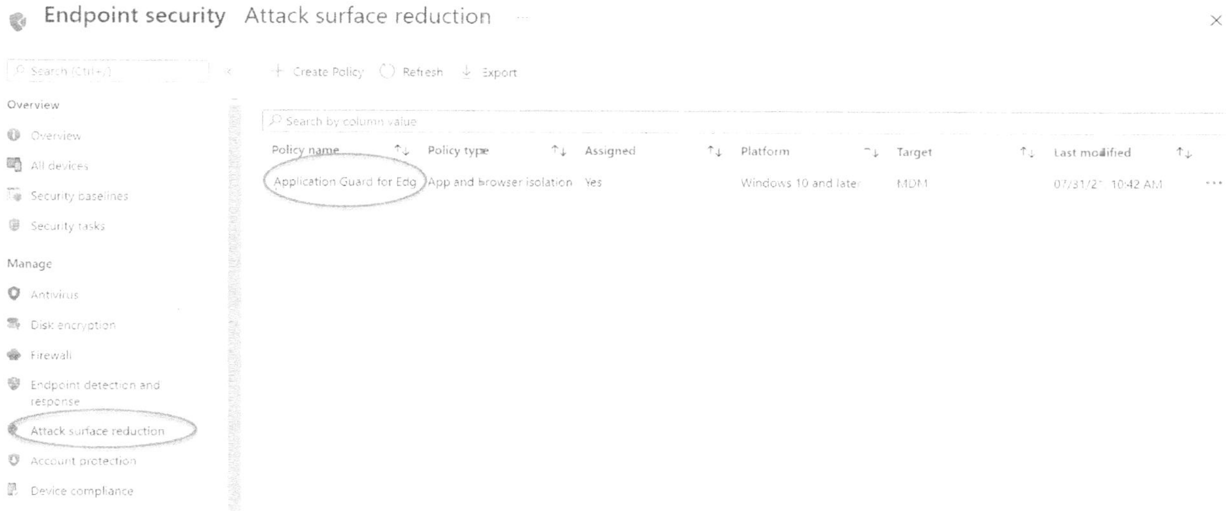

Tip: At least one mandatory network isolation policy must be set. For example, you must configure Cloud Resources or (EnterpriseIpRange and EnterpriseNetworkDomainNames).

Here are some examples of what could be listed in Cloud Resources:

..sharepoint.com|..office.com|..office365.com|..powerbi.com|..windowsazure.com|..bing.com|..azure.com|..microsoft.com|..windows.net|..microsoftonline.com|..microsoftstream.com|..yammer.com

Note: Application Guard is not officially supported in a VM or VDI since you would have to enable nested virtualization on the host[94].

Troubleshooting Tips

In my testing, I found that sometimes web pages would time out. I had to run this command to reset the container: c:\windows\system32\wdagtool cleanup

Otherwise, the container is reset upon reboot or logoff. Which, by the way, is the length of time a compromised container would be allowed to persist.

Check the local event logs:

- Microsoft-Windows-DeviceManagement-Enterprise-Diagnostics-Provide/Admin event log for information about the AllowAppHVSI policy

---

[93] https://docs.microsoft.com/en-us/windows/security/threat-protection/microsoft-defender-application-guard/reqs-md-app-guard

[94] https://docs.microsoft.com/en-us/windows/security/threat-protection/microsoft-defender-application-guard/reqs-md-app-guard

- Microsoft-Windows-WDAG-PolicyEvaluator-CSP/Operational event log for information about any policy changes.

To learn more about deploying the Application Guard, check out the Microsoft documentation[95].

Malicious Office Macros

There are a variety of techniques for preventing malicious macros from running. For example, you could use Endpoint Manager Configuration Manager or Group Policy. But did you know that you can block Macros from running in Microsoft Apps for Enterprise by configuring a cloud-based policy at Config.office.com? Every time Microsoft Office applications launch, they check config.office.com to see if there is a security policy. This is great for those remote endpoints that are not on a VPN to get group policy settings. So, you can effectively manage Office security without MDM enrollment or GPO; the only requirement is that users are signed into their Office with their corporate credentials.

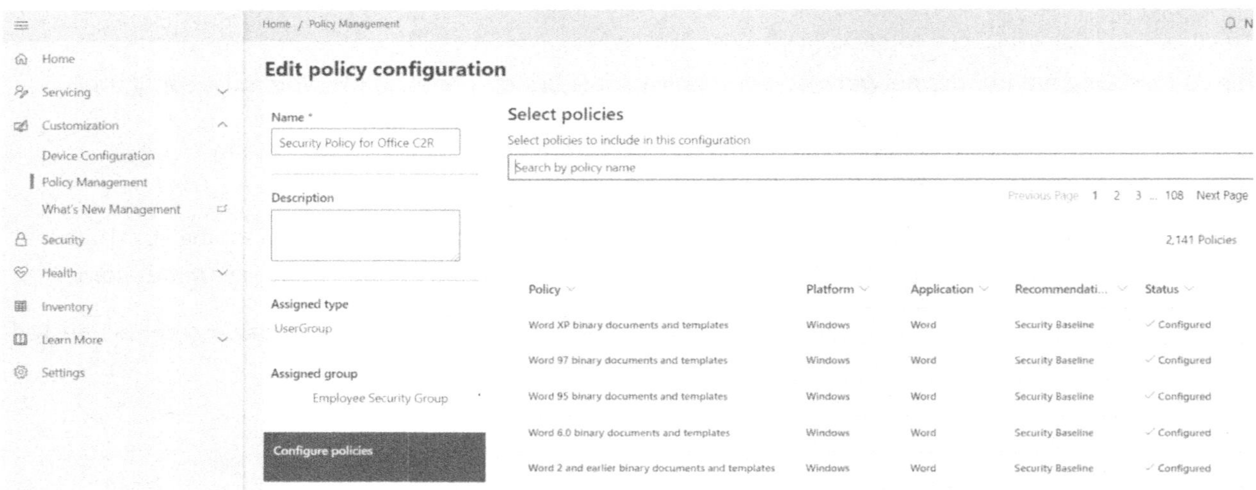

This same configuration can now be managed within Endpoint Manager Intune.[96]

---

[95] https://docs.microsoft.com/en-us/windows/security/threat-protection/microsoft-defender-application-guard/md-app-guard-overview

[96] https://endpoint.microsoft.com/#blade/Microsoft_Intune_DeviceSettings/AppsMenu/officeProPlusPolicies

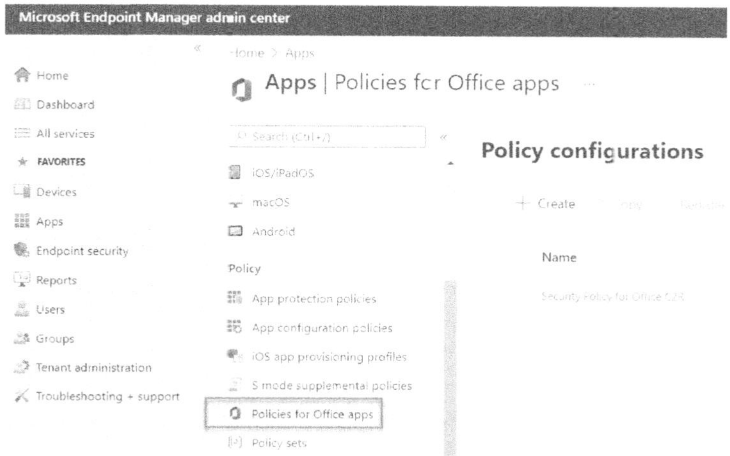

Here are some of the recommended policies to configure:

- Disable Trust Bar Notification for unsigned application add-ins and block them
- Disable all Trust Bar notifications for security issues
- Go to VBA Macro Notification Settings: Enable with "Disable without Notification"
- Disable VBA for Office applications
- Block macros from running in Office files from the Internet

To avoid problems with users who need valid/trusted Macros, you can enable two additional settings:

1. Allow Trusted Locations on the network:

   Lockdown the NTFS and/or Share Permissions to only allow authorized users or admin from adding Macros to this path. Ask each Department to provide Macros for review.

2. Trusted Location #1 (through #20):

   This is where you can specify the network path of where the authorized Macros can run from

There is also an option to use Security Policy Advisor to make recommendations.

It has built-in intelligence to notify you if any of the policies would impact users based on past usage.

	Recommended policy	Feature ↑	Application ↑	Productivity impact ↑	Confidence ↑
Preview	Only trust VBA macros signed using V3 signatures	VBA	Office	0% of users in group	High
New!	Web Pages and Excel 2003 XML Spreadsheets	Fileblock	Excel	0% of users in group	High
	Check ActiveX Objects	ActiveX	Office	0% of users in group	High
	Block macros from running in Office files from the Internet	VBA	Word	0% of users in group	High

It is also periodically updated to include new recommendations, so be sure to check back every so often.

Hardware-based Isolation of Zero-Day Vulnerabilities in Microsoft Office

The above defensive techniques describe defending against currently known threats. However, to protect against zero-day vulnerabilities in Microsoft Office, Application Guard[97] opens untrusted files in an isolated Hyper-V enabled container. If the file turns out to be malicious, the host device is protected. Microsoft 365 E5 or M365 E5 Security licensing is required to use this feature.

Endpoint Manager Endpoint Security

Several of the Intune Configuration Policies listed in this chapter can also be configured in the newer Endpoint Security section of the portal found here. This is where you should build new policies if you do not have an existing Intune deployment.

[97] https://docs.microsoft.com/en-us/windows/security/threat-protection/microsoft-defender-application-guard/md-app-guard-overview#what-is-application-guard-and-how-does-it-work

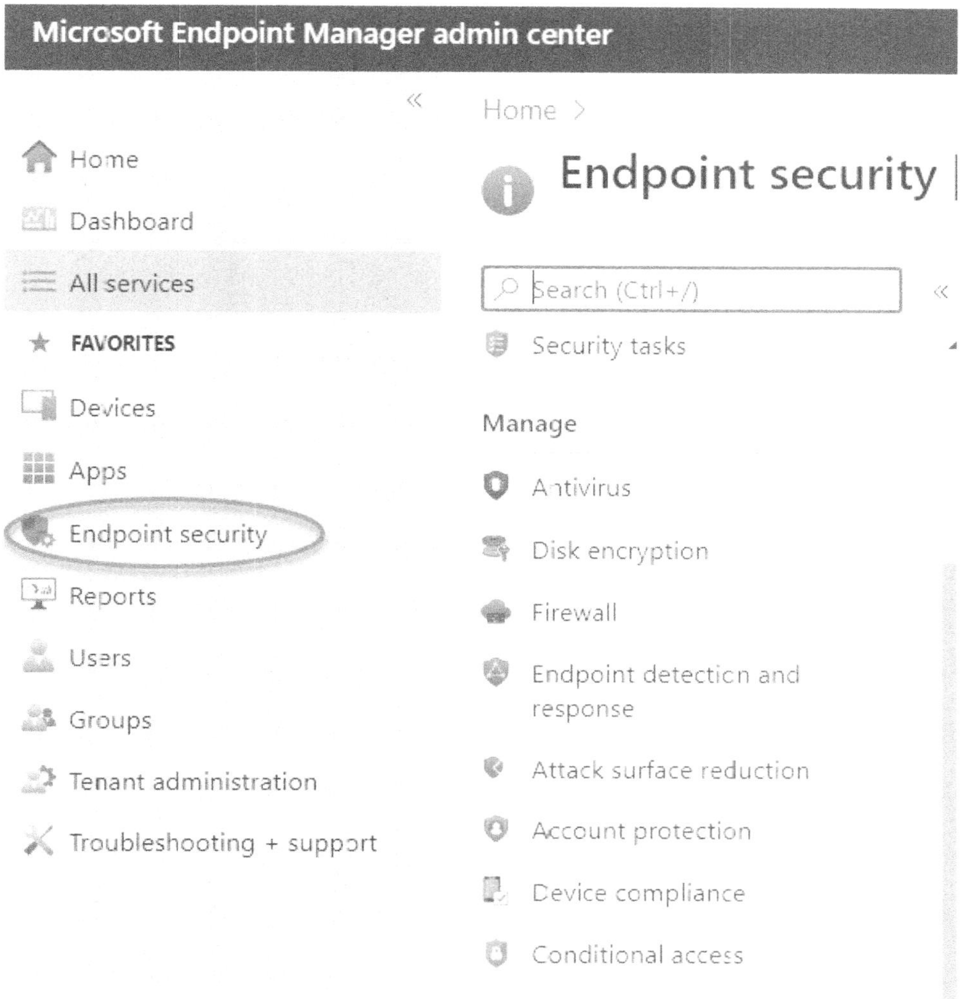

Testing

Once you get your Defender for Endpoint security locked down, it's recommended to test it out in an isolated test lab (for example, in an Azure IaaS VM that has no network connectivity to your business or home network!).

- Download a Ransomware Simulator from GitHub
  https://github.com/bcaseiro/malwaresimulator
- Watch this video to learn about detonating 800 malware samples for testing purposes
  https://www.youtube.com/watch?v=N4Vex7l8jv4&feature=youtu.be

Test Results

For example, on a default Windows 10 system with no additional hardening or customization, the ransomware simulator can encrypt 61% of files, whereas, with the configuration in this chapter, the simulator is blocked completely.

Configuration	% Of files infected by Ransomware Simulator

Windows 10 ("Free") Antivirus	61%
Hardened Configuration	0%

MDE Threat and Vulnerability Management (TVM) includes the Security Recommendations section, which has 74+ recommendations. Check it out inside your MDE Tenant here: https://security.microsoft.com/security-recommendations

Defender for Servers

Microsoft Defender for Endpoint (MDE) supports four versions of Windows Server: 2008 R2, 2012 R2, 2016, and 2019*. Windows Server 2016 was the first version of Windows to feature native antivirus protection (AV).

For those who choose to deploy AV to down-level clients[98], the following table shows the scenarios where AV is already built-in versus where you can deploy System Center Endpoint Protection (SCEP). System Center Endpoint Protection (SCEP) is the AV client used by System Center Configuration Manager (SCCM, however, you do not need SCCM to use SCEP. SCEP is available as a stand-alone distributable that can either be distributed using GPO, System Center Configuration Manager (SCCM), or any software distribution tool of choice.

Server	SCEP or MAA	MMA	MDAV
2008 R2	Yes	Yes	(N/A)
2012 R2	Yes	Yes	(N/A)
2016	No	Yes	Natively Installed
2019	No	No	Natively Installed

TIP: SCEP must be running version 4.10 or greater for AV alerts to appear in the MDE Dashboard

[98] *Some organizations avoid deploying any file-level AV on their server operating systems and decide to only deploy the Endpoint Detection and Response (EDR) monitoring agent (aka MMA hereafter). They do this to avoid application conflicts with AV (which places a 'lock' on a file to scan it), and avoiding the overhead of maintaining exclusion rules. Also, historically (and ironically) it is the 3rd party AV vendors that have had 30% of all vulnerabilities. Attackers like to target the AV vendor because they know it runs with deeper system level privileges. In general, if a server has a host-based firewall enabled, and if administrators are not browsing the internet on risky sites on the server itself, then an argument can be made that using the EDR/MMA agent only for down-level server operating systems may be sufficient. Each organization should weigh the risks and rewards and make their own decision.*

Note: If the Servers are hosted in Azure, then you can deploy the free "Microsoft Antimalware for Azure" (MAA) which is the same antimalware platform that SCEP uses.

SCEP AV client is managed with Group Policy or SCCM[99]. We will cover the details in the document below.

There are three unique deployment scenarios for protecting Windows Server Operating Systems:

Scenario 1) Windows Server 2008 R2 and 2012 R2.

Scenario 2) Windows Server 2016

Scenario 3) Windows Server 2019

Each scenario will be covered in the document below for both Deployment and Configuration Management.

Deployment

Windows Server 2008 R2 and 2012 R2

Step 1) Download the SCEP AV Agent (here) and distribute using your software distribution tool of choice or Group Policy. Or, if you have SCCM, the SCEP install package is in the Client folder of the Configuration Manager installation folder on the site server.

Here is the syntax example to install SCEP silently:

scepinstall.exe /s

Step 2) Download and distribute the MMA agent from the Defender Portal (securitycenter.microsoft.com > settings > onboarding), then use your software distribution tool of choice or Group Policy to push it out.

Obtain the WORKSPACE_ID and WORKSPACE_KEY from the Onboarding instructions in SecurityCenter.microsoft.com > Settings > Onboarding

[99] https://yongrhee.wordpress.com/2020/03/19/managing-system-center-endpoint-protection-scep-epp-aka-antivirus-policies-via-group-policy/

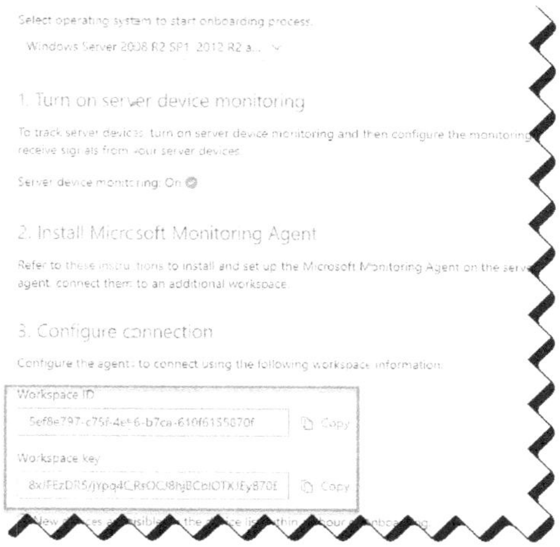

Here is the syntax to use for the installation:

- To extract the agent installation files from an elevated command prompt, run MMASetup-<platform>.exe /c and it will prompt you for the path to extract files to.
    - Alternatively, you can specify the path by passing the arguments MMASetup-<platform>.exe /c /t:<Full Path>.
    - To silently install the agent and configure it to report to a workspace in Azure commercial cloud, from the folder you extracted the setup files to type: setup.exe /qn NOAPM=1 ADD_OPINSIGHTS_WORKSPACE=1 OPINSIGHTS_WORKSPACE_AZURE_CLOUD_TYPE=0 OPINSIGHTS_WORKSPACE_ID="<your workspace ID>" OPINSIGHTS_WORKSPACE_KEY="<your workspace key>" AcceptEndUserLicenseAgreement=1

Important:

The MMA agent has a prerequisite hotfix that should be on your servers if you apply all recommended updates. If you have some older servers that are infrequently patched, be sure to install the prerequisite hotfix (here).

Windows Server 2016

AV is built-in, so you just need to download and distribute the MMA agent from the Defender Portal (securitycenter.microsoft.com > settings > onboarding) then use your software distribution tool of choice or Group Policy to push it out (using the same syntax and method as shown above).

Windows Server 2019

There is no AV or MMA agent to deploy (it is built-in) so just **deploy the license activation script** following the Onboarding instructions in SecurityCenter.microsoft.com > Settings > Onboarding

Note: Azure Defender can also now onboard Server 2019 (this was announced at Ignite 2021 here).

Antivirus Client Configuration Management

Server 2008 R2 and 2012 R2 (SCEP)

You can use Group Policy or SCCM to manage AV configuration settings, however, be aware that there are different Group Policy locations depending on the operating system version.

Click Here for the ADMX templates to manage SCEP settings with Group Policy. (*Note ADMX templates for SCEP settings will be available upon download of the SCEP agent). To learn about distributing the ADMX, make sure you read this article (here)

Computer Configuration –> Administrative Templates –> Windows Components –> Endpoint Protection

This modifies the following registry key: Hkey_Local_Machine > Software > Policies > Microsoft > Microsoft Antimalware

Server 2016 and 2019 (MDAV)

Computer Configuration –> Administrative Templates –> Windows Components –> **Windows Defender Antivirus**

This modifies the following registry key: Hkey_Local_Machine > Software > Policies > Microsoft > Windows Defender

Note: "Server 2019" is also known as Long-Term Service Channel (LTSC). While MDE also supports the Semi-Annual Channel (SAC) versions of Windows Server, it is beyond the scope of this document to discuss the pros and cons of SAC (instead refer to Comparison of Windows Server Servicing Channels).

Managing Exclusions

On Windows Server 2016 and 2019, the built-in AV client automatically excludes paths and files based on the server roles installed like DNS, Active Directory, Hyper-V, File/Print, or Web Server. The exclusions only apply to real-time protection and not scheduled full/quick or on-demand scanning, so it is still important to add exclusions if those scan types are planned. See the first resource link listed below for more information on exclusions.

Unified Installer

As this book was going to print, Microsoft released to public preview a unified installer so that Windows Server 2012 R2 and 2016 now have a single installer for both AV and EDR. The prerequisite is to deploy MS KB5005292[100] first.
Get it here: https://aka.ms/MDE4DLServer

---

[100] https://support.microsoft.com/en-us/topic/microsoft-defender-for-endpoint-update-for-edr-sensor-f8f69773-f17f-420f-91f4-a8e5167284ac

Defender for iOS / Android

Defender for Endpoint for mobile (iOS or Android)[101] can also protect against the following:

- It Automatically blocks malicious web links from SMS, instant messaging apps, browsers, or email.
- It Blocks background connections from malicious apps on the user's device.
- It Allows security admins to create custom indicators (URLs, IP Addresses) for web protection.

My first test using Defender for iOS was successful! I got a smishing attack, and when I wanted to see if Defender would block it, I was pleasantly surprised to see the block page!

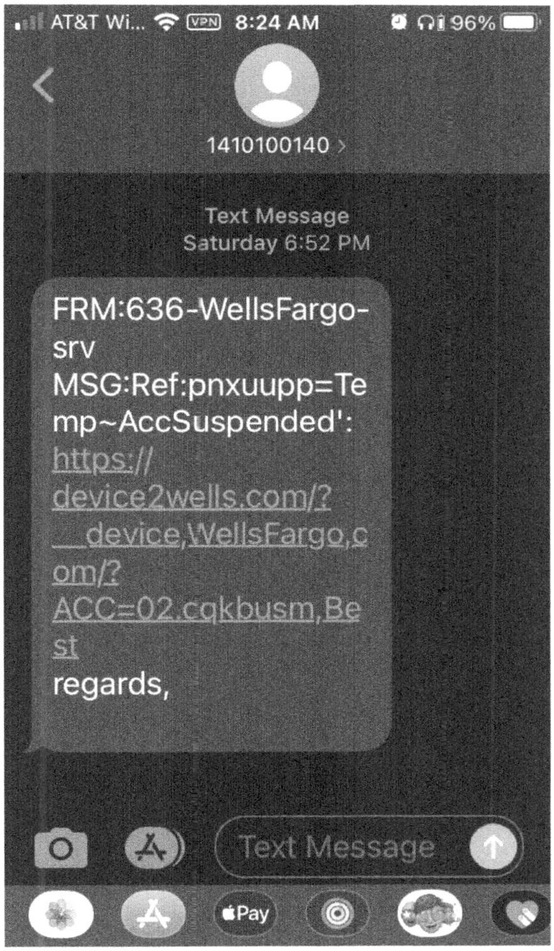

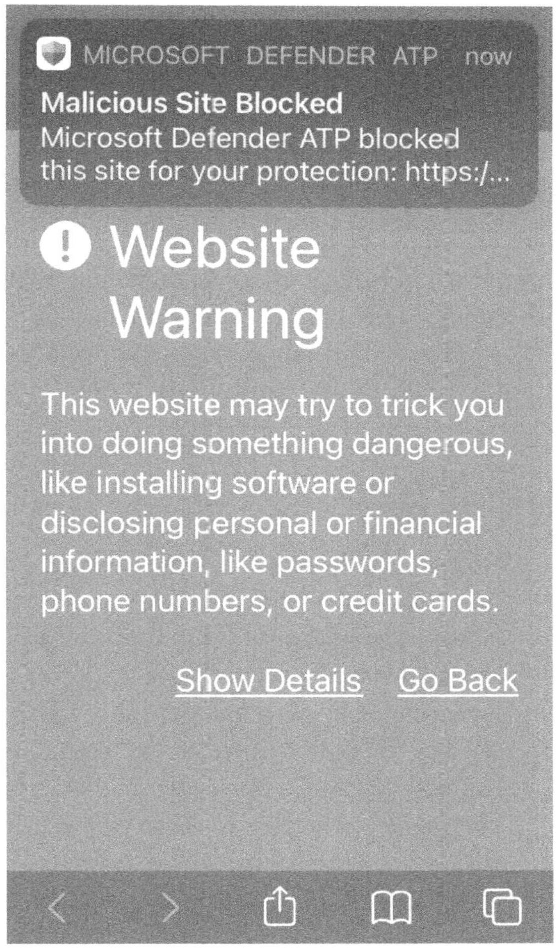

[101] Download from the iOS App Store here: https://apps.apple.com/us/app/microsoft-defender-atp/id1526737990

Chapter Four - Securing BYOD in M365

In the previous chapter, we learned how to protect the corporate endpoint (company-owned devices). In my experience, most organizations permit personal devices to connect to their online services, such as email. When employees connect to corporate resources, it is called "Bring your own device" (BYOD). It's popular because employers gain extra productivity from employees without having to pay for the device or data plan. Employees like the convenience of not having to carry two phones.

There is a security tradeoff with personal devices, so in this chapter, we'll learn about BYOD security controls. For example, by default, Microsoft 365 does not prevent personal devices from connecting to services such as Exchange Online, SharePoint Online, OneDrive for Business, Teams. And by default, nothing prevents an employee from downloading data from these services on a personal device that lacks security controls such as virus protection or encryption. So, the first question is: do you want to entirely block all personal devices from connecting to M365 resources such as Exchange Online? Or is there a way to achieve a balance of security while allowing employees to use personal devices for work?

The answer to this question is not simple. Each organization must decide how much risk is acceptable and compare that to the attractive cost savings from a BYOD policy. Consider the cost of outfitting a workforce of thousands of employees with a $700 smartphone and a $100 per month data plan. Does the cost of a data breach exceed this cost?

Let's weigh the risks of allowing personal devices to connect to Microsoft 365 against the benefits.

BYOD Risks to consider

- How will you remove intellectual property or sensitive information such as customer information when an employee quits or is terminated?
- How will you ensure that sensitive information is encrypted so the data remains safe even if the device is lost or stolen?
- How will you ensure that malware, ransomware, or backdoors do not spread from personal devices to corporate networks? In 2021 there were at least 17 zero-day vulnerabilities found in Apple's iOS mobile operating system[102]. Darkweb marketplaces and some commercial companies sell access to these vulnerabilities to the highest bidder. [103]
- Hackers can modify their User-Agent string to appear to be a mobile phone even though they are connecting from a weaponized Linux distribution such as Kali Linux[104]. Will you modify your policy so that all mobile phones must be managed?

Benefits of a BYOD policy

- Employees don't have to carry two phones around in their pockets.
- Reduced company expenses.

---

[102] https://therecord.media/apple-patches-iphone-zero-day-in-ios-15-0-2/

[103] https://www.wired.com/story/untold-history-americas-zero-day-market/

[104] https://tech.nicolonsky.ch/bypassing-conditional-access-device-platform-policies/

- Flexible business models. In healthcare organizations, it's incredibly common for some of the physicians to be contractors with their own equipment. Often doctors work for themselves or someone else, and they use the hospital as a facility to perform their procedures.

Wait and carefully think before you say, 'that list of risks looks bad!' Yes, but before you march into the CFO's office and ask to purchase company phones for each employee, first, imagine where they are coming from. Today, each employee uses their personal phone for work, which avoids the overhead of the company expense for the phone and cellular plan. Imagine how the CFO would react if you said, "We are thinking that this idea of allowing personal devices to connect to our business systems may increase risk beyond the benefit of the cost savings. We would like you to buy each employee a thousand-dollar smartphone and an additional twelve hundred dollars annual expense per employee for a mobile phone contract."

First, evaluate the Microsoft options for securing remote access to Microsoft 365: Intune App Policies, MCAS access and session policies, Azure Virtual Desktop, Cloud PC (Windows 365), and Azure AD Application Proxy.

For personally-owned mobile phones, I recommend using Intune App Protection Policies to encrypt and protect business applications on personal phones. Then, I recommend using Azure AD Conditional Access policies to block applications that are not managed by Intune App Protection Policies.

Intune App Protection Policies for Personal Devices

Intune App Protection Policies begin when the corporate identity of the user signs in to an 'enlightened' application on iOS or Android. An enlightened application is one that is wrapped with the Intune software development kit (SDK). The enlightened applications are basically 'wrapped' so that they can make an API call to Intune to verify if a policy exists. Each user must first have an Intune license assigned to them and then an Intune App Protection policy assigned to them.

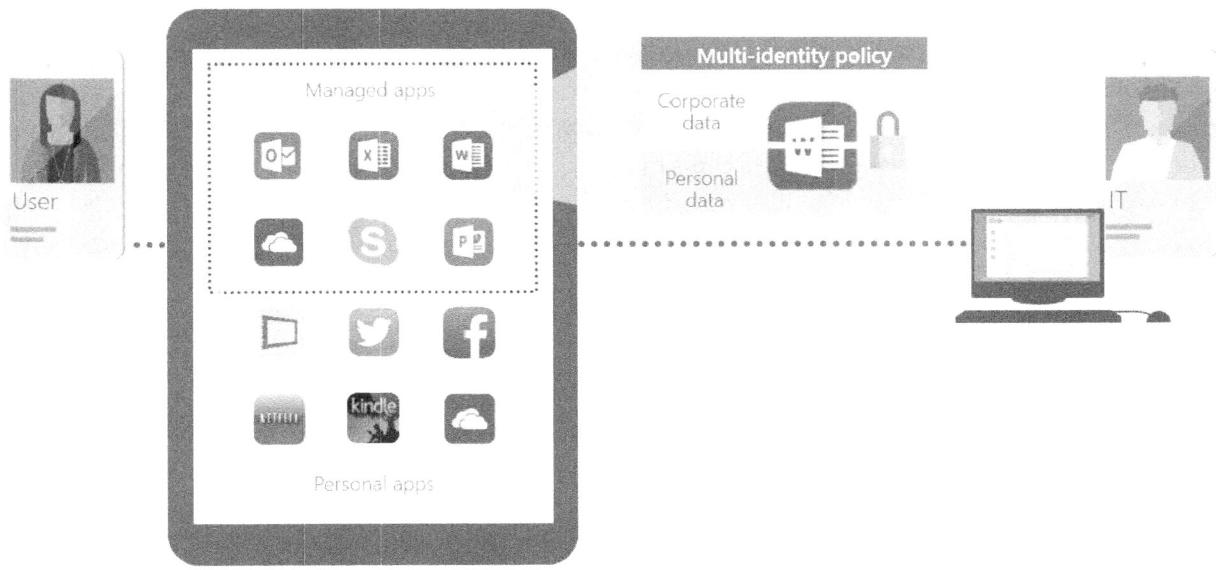

Here are some use cases for app protection:

1. Selectively wipe just corporate data from a personal device when the employee leaves your organization or if their device is lost or stolen
2. Prevent corporate data from being copied or saved into a personal application
3. Prevent corporate data from being backed up into a personal iCloud backup container
4. Force encryption and access control such as a PIN or biometric unlock when the application is launched (helpful if you can't force an overall device PIN)
5. Require that the device must be running a minimum supported version. Microsoft calls this feature "Conditional Launch." The managed application won't launch if the device is running an old version. Why is it so important? Between January to July 2021, there have already been 13 zero-day vulnerabilities in iOS.[105]

Recommendation: Configure MAM policies with a conditional launch to the latest supported version of iOS or Android with the Warning setting, so that devices that are not at that level will receive the warning. For example:

Min OS version	14.7.1	Warn
Min OS version	14.5.1	Block access

Azure AD Conditional Access Policies for Personal Devices

Once you have configured Application Policies, the next step is to configure a conditional access policy to require the use of those managed applications, otherwise, in the case of Exchange Online, a user could simply use any 3rd party ActiveSync client to bypass the Intune Application policies.

Another reason to require managed applications in CA policies is to prevent hackers from manipulating the UserAgent string to make their web browser appear to be a mobile device. This is important to be aware of because many organizations' conditional access policies are only applied to Windows or Mac devices, since they don't own the mobile devices, they are reluctant to apply policy to personally owned devices. This leaves a gap that hackers can exploit. To close the gap, you must create a conditional access policy to require compliant applications to prevent the hacker from masquerading their Windows

[105] https://therecord.media/apple-releases-fix-for-ios-and-macos-zero-day-13th-this-year/

or Linux hacking station as a mobile device as shown in the Chromium web browser setting here:

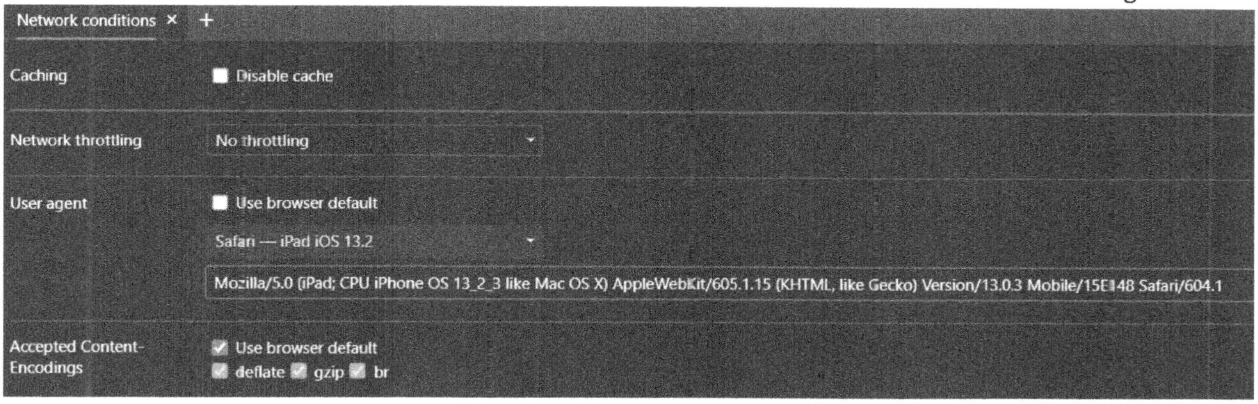

Securing Personal Devices with Microsoft Cloud App Security access and session policies

What about personally owned computers such as Windows, macOS, and Linux? An important information security principle is "Zero Trust."

The Zero Trust model assumes breach and verifies each request as though it originates from an open network. Regardless of where the request originates or what resource it accesses, Zero Trust teaches us to "never trust, always verify." Many home computers may not be running the latest EDR software, and who knows whether they have been patched. Is the firewall or Bitlocker enabled? There is no way to know without installing an agent to validate these things. This is where it gets tricky - most people do not want their home computer enrolled into a company's mobile device management system like Intune for privacy reasons. Therefore, many organizations will opt instead to block personal computers from connecting to corporate resources.

There is a significant increase in risk if personal computers are not blocked. How would you differentiate someone's home computer from a nation-state threat actor who is connecting from a VPN inside your country? Without device-based authentication using Hybrid Azure AD Join or Intune MDM enrollment, then any APT threat groups can connect to your tenant.

For organizations that are not threat modeling against nation-state or cybercrime groups, there are some middle-of-the-road options such as permitting web browsers from personal computers, or Virtual Desktop Infrastructure (VDI). Wait you might say, shouldn't VDI be considered a top-tier remote access solution? The issue is, user-based MFA can be bypassed, so if the VDI is accessible from the Internet and you are only performing user-based MFA, then it can be bypassed. In my opinion, any internet-based connection should authenticate the device – even when accessing a VDI solution.

Microsoft offers a few VDI options such as Azure Virtual Desktop or Cloud PC. VDI is a great fit for thick-client apps. However, for web-based applications, there are two light-weight options that require less cost and overhead such as using Microsoft Cloud App Security (MCAS) Session Policies or Azure AD Proxy.

Here are some of the things you can do with MCAS access and session policies

- **Prevent data exfiltration**: You can block the download, cut, copy, and print of sensitive documents on, for example, unmanaged devices.
- **Require authentication context**: You can reevaluate Azure AD Conditional Access policies when a sensitive action occurs in the session. For example, require multi-factor authentication on the download of a highly confidential file.
- **Protect on download**: Instead of blocking the download of sensitive documents, you can require documents to be labeled and protected with Azure Information Protection.
- **Encrypt uploads**: Before a file is uploaded you may want to scan the contents for sensitive information. If the content includes regulated data such as credit cards, or personally identifiable information, you can block the upload or force it to be encrypted with a particular label.
- **Block malware**: You can protect your environment from malware by blocking the upload of potentially malicious files. Any file that is uploaded or downloaded can be scanned against Microsoft threat intelligence and blocked instantaneously.
- **Monitor user sessions for compliance**: Risky users are monitored when they sign into apps and their actions are logged from within the session. You can investigate and analyze user behavior to understand where, and under what conditions, session policies should be applied in the future.
- **Block custom activities**: Some apps have unique scenarios that carry risk, for example, sending messages with sensitive content in apps like Microsoft Teams or Slack. In these kinds of scenarios, you can scan messages for sensitive content and block them in real-time.
- **Access Control**. Both, Azure AD Conditional Access and MCAS, can block access based on hybrid domain join membership or Intune enrollment. However, at the time of this writing, only MCAS can check for certificates without having to rely upon AD FS. In the future, Microsoft is working on adding native certificate-based authentication directly into Conditional Access policies as well.

Securing Personal Devices with Azure Virtual Desktop or Cloud PC

The primary difference between AVD and Cloud PC (aka Windows 365) is consumption-based billing or fixed billing, respectively. Otherwise, remote access from the internet is the same (Web Browser or Client) and can be controlled by Conditional Access Policy such as requiring Multi-Factor Authentication.

By default, data transfer from a personal computer to the AVD or Cloud PC is unrestricted, but this can be configured via policy in the administrative interface or via PowerShell.[106]

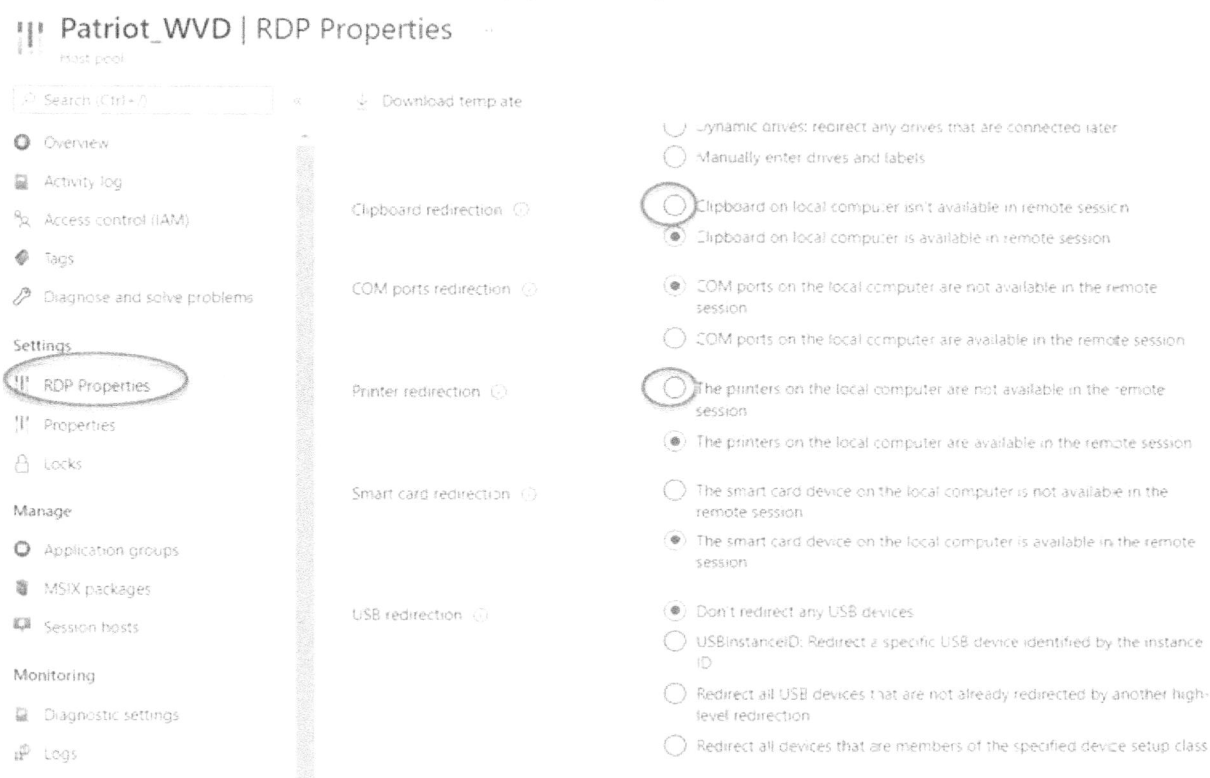

For example, you may want to:

- Disable clipboard redirection.
- Disable USB device redirection.
- Disable redirection of plug and play devices.
- Disable local drive redirection.
- Disable printer redirection.
- Block Screen Capture[107]

The AVD client for Windows 10 has a unique feature that can prevent the host machine from taking screenshots of the applications running inside the WVD. This is done by adding a registry key to the AVD host computer in azure that is hosting the virtual machines. Since only the Windows client supports this,

[106] https://docs.microsoft.com/en-us/azure/virtual-desktop/customize-rdp-properties
[107] https://docs.microsoft.com/en-us/azure/virtual-desktop/security-guide#enable-screen-capture-protection-preview

you could create a conditional access policy that prevents other operating systems from connecting to WVD (block mac, mobile and browser clients).

reg add "HKLM\SOFTWARE\Policies\Microsoft\Windows NT\Terminal Services" /v fEnableScreenCaptureProtection /t REG_DWORD /d 1

There are many other security considerations for hardening AVD that go beyond the scope of this section. See the footnotes for more information.[108]

Securing Personal Devices with Azure AD Proxy

Azure AD Proxy is a virtual machine you deploy on the inside of your network that creates a reverse tunnel so that external users can access internal web-based applications without a VPN connection. It is included in the Azure AD Premium P1 or Enterprise Mobility + Security E3 or M365 E3 license bundles.

You can control access to Azure AD Proxy with Conditional Access Policy (such as requiring an MFA prompt) or requiring Hybrid Domain Join or Intune Compliance machines.

Azure AD Proxy is considered more secure than Virtual Private Networks (VPN) because:

- Microsegmentation. This is a key component of Zero Trust and the principle of least privilege: only publish applications that the employee needs to access. Most VPNs provide access to the entire flat network.
- Integrates with Conditional Access, so you can force MFA and even posture check using Intune compliance policy.
- Integrates with Microsoft Cloud App Security (MCAS), so you can block, encrypt, or scan uploads or downloads for malware

[108] https://docs.microsoft.com/en-us/azure/virtual-desktop/security-guide

Chapter Five – Detecting Anomalies in M365

Microsoft offers several solutions to detect anomalies in user behavior, otherwise known as ***User and Entity Behavior Analytics (UEBA)***. UEBA uses large datasets to model typical and atypical behaviors of humans and machines within a network, and then policies can be created to alert, block, or orchestrate a response.

Microsoft has at least five products that use some form of UEBA. Some of these offer only detection like MDI and Sentinel, whereas others can block such as MCAS or Azure Identity Protection.

1. Microsoft Cloud App Security (MCAS) uses UEBA to detect and block anomalies in the cloud. MCAS can also orchestrate a response using Microsoft Power Automate (formerly known as Flow). For example, it can isolate a machine in Defender for Endpoint, or suspend a user account.
2. Microsoft Defender for Identity (MDI) detects anomalies in the on-premises data center but does not have any blocking technology. MDI is more Intrusion Detection System (IDS) than Intrusion Prevention.
3. Azure Active Directory Premium P2 includes a feature called Azure Identity Protection that also detects and blocks anomalous sign-ins such as impossible travel and unfamiliar sign-in properties like a new user agent
4. Azure Sentinel is a 100% cloud-based *Security information and event management (SIEM)* that includes UEBA over some source types. Azure Sentinel uses Azure Logic Apps to perform automation (aka Security Orchestration, Automation, and Response, or SOAR).[109]
5. Insider Risk Management uses behavioral anomalies to detect risky insider behavior. On the employee's last day, did they mass delete or mass download?

MCAS, MDI, and Azure Identity Protection create an aggregate user risk score. This user risk score can help defenders identify insider risk or compromised accounts. The risk score can be seen in the main Microsoft Cloud App Security Dashboard.

[109] https://docs.microsoft.com/en-us/azure/sentinel/automation-in-azure-sentinel

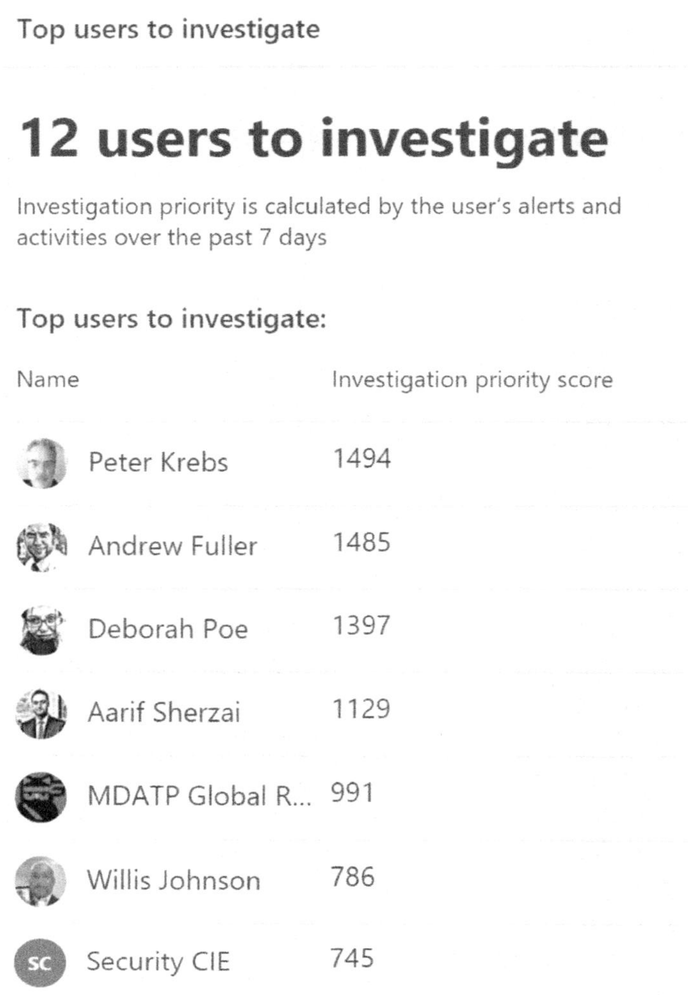

User Risk can be applied to Conditional Access Policies to proactively block sign-ins at the front door. This reduces the number of security incidents that SOC teams must investigate.

Azure Identity Protection

Azure Identity Protection is sometimes called "risk-based MFA" because conditional access can be configured to take actions based upon user risk. For example, the policy shown below is configured to block when User Risk is High.

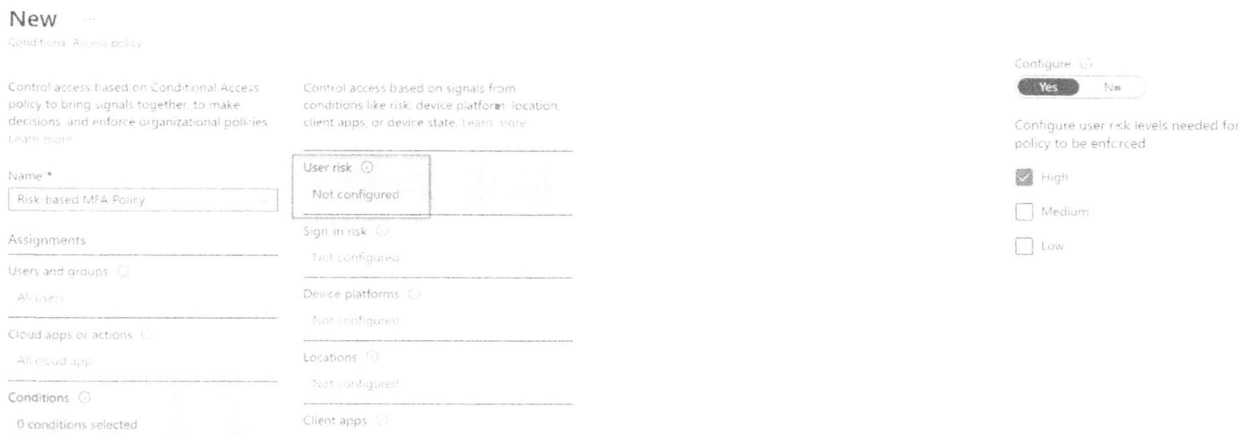

You can then have a separate conditional access policy configured to force MFA when User Risk is Medium. This is the primary advantage of configuring user risk via Conditional Access instead of inside the Azure Identity Protection portal, which only allows a single policy.

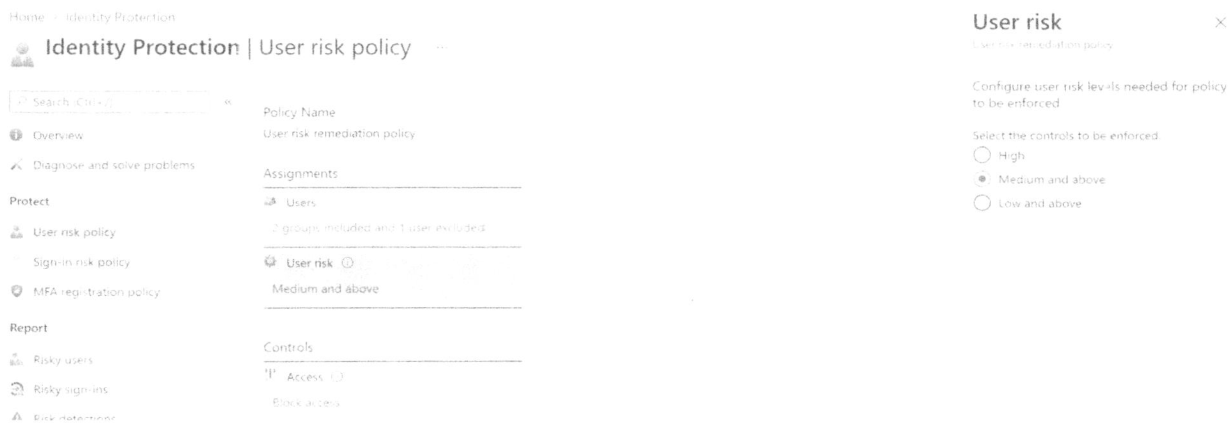

Azure Identity Protection uses both Machine Learning and behavioral-based indicators such as:

- Unfamiliar Sign-in Properties
- Suspicious Browser
- Atypical Travel
- Anomalous Token
- Token Issuer Anomaly

Unfamiliar Sign-In

This risk detection type considers past sign-in history (IP, Latitude / Longitude, and ASN) to look for anomalous sign-ins. The system stores information about previous locations used by a user, and considers these "familiar" locations. Risk detection is triggered when the sign-in occurs from a location that's not already in the list of familiar locations. Newly created users will be in "learning mode" for a while where unfamiliar sign-in properties risk detections will be turned off while our algorithms learn the user's behavior. The learning mode duration is dynamic and depends on how much time it takes the algorithm to gather enough information about the user's sign-in patterns. The minimum duration is five days. A user can go back into learning mode after a long period of inactivity. The system also ignores sign-ins from familiar devices and locations that are geographically close to a familiar location.

We also run this detection for basic authentication (or legacy protocols). Because these protocols don't have modern properties such as client ID, there's limited telemetry to reduce false positives. We recommend our customers move to modern authentication.

Unfamiliar sign-in properties can be detected on both interactive and non-interactive sign-ins. When this detection is detected on non-interactive sign-ins, it deserves increased scrutiny due to the risk of token replay attacks.

Suspicious Browser

Suspicious browser detection indicates anomalous behavior based on suspicious sign-in activity across multiple tenants from different countries in the same browser.

Atypical Travel

This risk detection type identifies two sign-ins originating from geographically distant locations, where at least one of the locations may also be atypical for the user, given past behavior. Among several other factors, this machine learning algorithm considers the time between the two sign-ins and the time it would have taken for the user to travel from the first location to the second, indicating that a different user is using the same credentials.

The algorithm ignores obvious "false positives" contributing to the impossible travel conditions, such as VPNs and locations regularly used by other users in the organization. The system has an initial learning period of the earliest of 14 days or 10 logins, during which it learns a new user's sign-in behavior.

Use the "Named Locations" in Conditional Access Policy to enter the locations used by your organization.

Anomalous Token

This is a new detection that indicates that there are abnormal characteristics in the token such as an unusual token lifetime or a token that is played from an unfamiliar location. This detection covers Session Tokens and Refresh Tokens.

Token Issuer Anomaly (SAML Only)

This risk detection indicates the SAML token issuer for the associated SAML token is potentially compromised. The claims included in the token are unusual or match known attacker patterns. For example, in the wake of the SolarWinds hack, attackers used a hacking technique known as "Golden SAML" where they used the on-premises ADFS token signing certificate to mint authentication requests to Azure AD. This detection was added because of that incident.

Microsoft Cloud App Security

Microsoft Cloud App Security product can be configured to detect or block anomalous activities.

The anomaly detection policies are automatically enabled, but Cloud App Security has an initial learning period of seven days during which not all anomaly detection alerts are raised.

After seven days, each session is compared to the activity, when users were active, IP addresses, devices, and so on, detected over the past month, and the risk score of these activities.

These detections are part of the heuristic anomaly detection engine that profiles the environment and triggers alerts with respect to the learned baseline.

These detections also use machine learning algorithms designed to profile the users and sign-in patterns to reduce false positives.

Anomalies are detected by scanning user activity. The risk is evaluated by looking at over 30 different risk indicators, grouped into risk factors, as follows:

- Risky IP address
- Login failures
- Admin activity
- Inactive accounts
- Location
- Impossible travel
- Device and user agent
- Activity rate

Azure Sentinel

Azure Sentinel also offers UEBA for the following sources[110]:

- Syslog (Linux)
- SecurityEvent (Windows)
- AuditLogs (Azure AD)
- SigninLogs (Azure AD)
- OfficeActivity (Office 365)
- BehaviorAnalytics (Azure Sentinel UEBA)
- Heartbeat (Azure Monitor Agent)
- CommonSecurityLog (Azure Sentinel)
- ThreatIntelligenceIndicators (Azure Sentinel)

[110] https://docs.microsoft.com/en-us/azure/sentinel/identify-threats-with-entity-behavior-analytics?WT.mc_id=Portal-Microsoft_Azure_Security_Insights#entity-insights

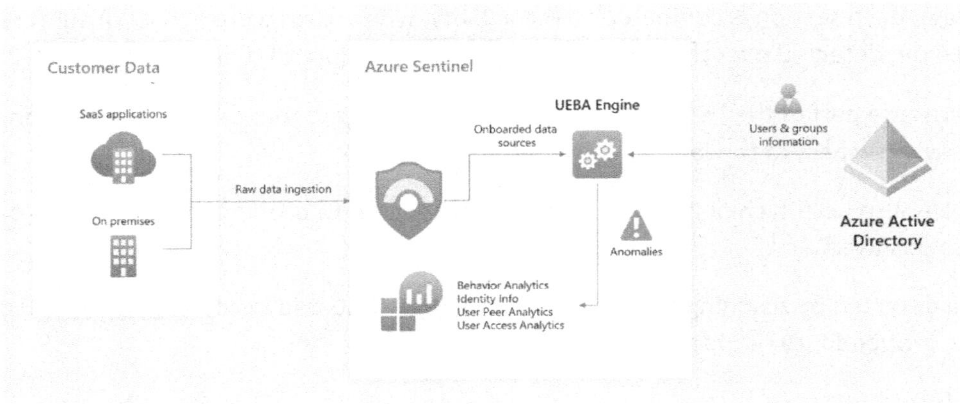

Microsoft Defender for Identity

Microsoft Defender for Identity (MDI) uses User and entity behavioral analytics (UEBA) for Active Directory (on-premises). This is a 'post breach' IDS agent for Domain Controllers to identify attackers who are already inside your network. Always "assume breach" and hunt for adversary TTPs. The average time an attacker goes undetected is 200 days. It has been said, "There are two kinds of companies: those that have been hacked, and those that don't realize they have been hacked."

MDI is very lightweight to deploy – an agent is installed on the domain controllers, and then the DC's will stream activity to Azure where the behavioral data is collected. It's much more efficient than the predecessor technology, Advanced Threat Analytics (ATA) which required on-premises database servers to store this information.

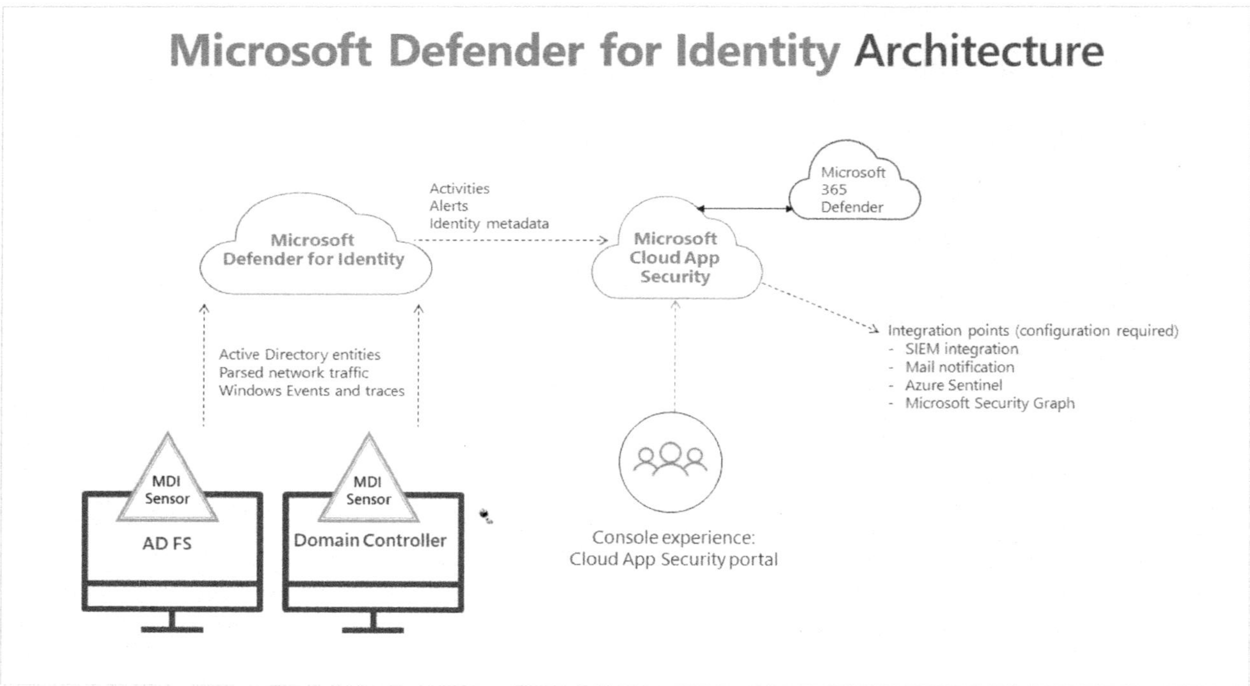

Insider Risk Management

Up to 49% of employees say they have downloaded, saved, or sent work-related documents to their personal accounts before leaving or after being dismissed from a job.[111]

Microsoft's Insider Risk Management alerts on behavioral anomalies so that you can investigate risky behavior. It can be triggered manually, or automatically via integration with Human Resource Information Systems (HRIS) – for example when an employee turns in their resignation.

Some organizations require their employees to sign confidentiality agreements to protect their customers or intellectual property. The information provided by this tool can help organizations enforce these policies.

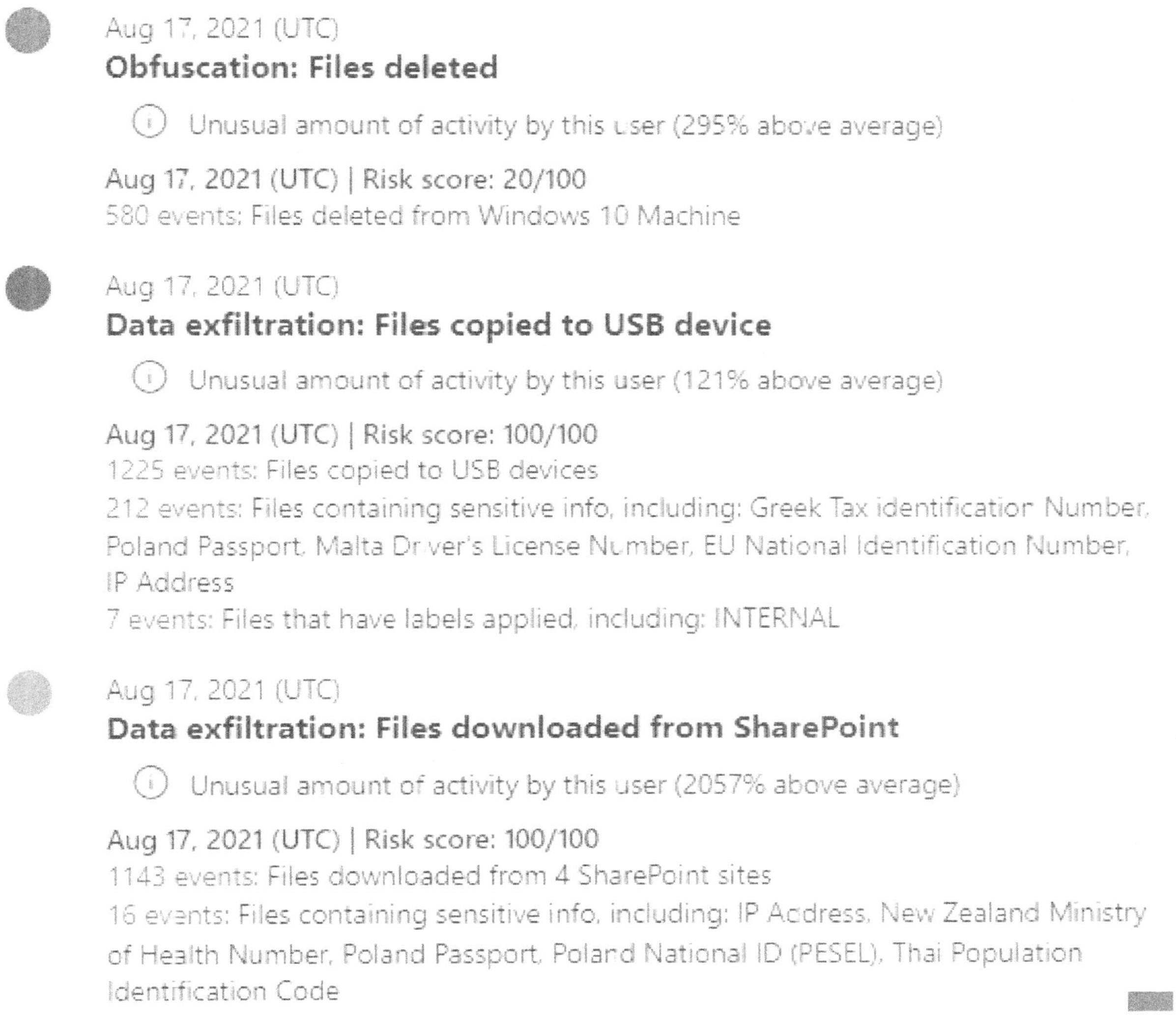

Here are the activities detected by Insider Risk Management:

- Copying files to USB

[111] https://www.tessian.com/blog/insider-threat-statistics/

- Deleting files from a device
- Sharing SharePoint files with people outside the organization
- Sharing SharePoint folders with people outside the organization
- Sharing SharePoint sites with people outside the organization
- Downloading content from SharePoint
- Adding people outside the organization to priority SharePoint sites
- Adding people inside the organization to priority SharePoint sites
- Downgrading sensitivity labels applied to SharePoint files
- Removing sensitivity labels from SharePoint files
- Removing sensitivity labels from SharePoint sites
- Accessing sensitive or priority SharePoint files
- Granting access to sensitive or priority SharePoint resources to people outside the organization
- Requesting access to sensitive or priority SharePoint resources
- Deleting of SharePoint files
- Deleting of SharePoint files from the first stage recycling bin
- Deleting of SharePoint files from the second stage recycling bin
- Unusual mass downloading of content from a connected cloud app
- Unusual mass sharing of content from a connected cloud app
- Anonymous IP address activity in a connected cloud app
- Activity after termination in a connected cloud app
- Multiple failed logins in a connected cloud app
- Activity is above the user's usual activity for that day
- A User had a previous case resolved as a policy violation
- Deleting of SharePoint folders
- Deleting of SharePoint folders from the first stage recycling bin
- Deleting of SharePoint folders from the second stage recycling bin
- Sending email with attachments to recipients outside the organization
- Downloading content from Teams
- Sending Teams messages that contain sensitive info types (preview)

- Adding users outside the organization to a Teams private channel
- Adding users outside the organization to a Team
- Sharing file links with people outside the organization in a Teams private channel (coming soon)
- Sharing folder links with people outside the organization in a Teams private channel (coming soon)
- Sharing file links with people outside the organization in a Teams chat (coming soon)
- Using Microsoft Edge to copy files to personal cloud storage
- Copying sensitive or priority content to the clipboard
- Printing files
- Transferring files to a network share
- Using a browser to download content from a third-party site
- Using a browser to download content from an unallowed domain
- Moving sensitive or priority content to a new location on a device
- Reading sensitive info
- Renaming files on a device
- Creating hidden files
- Mounting USB to a device
- Archiving files on a device
- Defense evasion - Attempt to bypass security controls
- Unwanted software - Unapproved or malicious software
- Physical access after termination or failed access to sensitive asset

Chapter Six – Defending against Human Operated Ransomware in M365

Ransomware attacks are increasing at an alarming rate. Experts estimate there was one ransomware attack every 10 seconds in 2020, compared to every 40 seconds in 2016.[112] Half of all malware attacks in Q3 2020 involved ransomware. Ransomware authors are earning an estimated $102 million per month[113]. It's safe to say that if organizations continue paying ransoms, then ransomware attacks will keep growing. I'll share a few experiences I have had in dealing with ransomware attacks and what I recommend you do to reduce your risks.

I remember getting a phone call to help one of the largest cities in the United States when more than 4,000 computers and 700 servers were encrypted by the ransomware, making it one of the biggest ransomware attacks against a US City Government.

A few months later, I received a similar call from another city. In this case, their email was already in Exchange Online, so their email was not encrypted. This time, I helped them integrate their on-premises VPN to integrate with Azure MFA. By the end of 2020, over 78% of states in the USA reported ransomware attacks in at least one municipality[114].

If your on-premises Exchange Server becomes encrypted by ransomware, I recommend rebuilding it in Exchange Online because any on-premises server can be hit again in a future ransomware attack. I am not aware of any publicly documented attack against Exchange Online. While Kevin Mitnick demonstrated on YouTube how the attack could theoretically occur[115], there are no known instances of this technique happening.

Why is Exchange Online more resilient against ransomware attacks than on-premises Exchange? The first reason is Microsoft applies security patches before they are publicly available. Since Microsoft creates the security patches, we can expect them to be deployed faster than anyone else. Many organizations I know wait days or weeks because they are just as concerned about a patch causing an outage as they are about a cyber-attack.

Another reason why Exchange Online is more resilient against ransomware is how Microsoft has architected its design. The Database availability groups (DAG) provide a lagged copy, so even if their primary servers are hit, there is a lagged copy that will be protected. Exchange Online has multiple database availability groups: 4 active and 1 lagged by 14 days of delayed transaction logs. If a ransomware attack affects the mailbox server that hosts the active copy of a mail transaction, failover to another active DAG takes place, transparent to customers. All three copies of a mail transaction in the active databases would have to be affected by the ransomware attack to fall back on the lagged DAG. Failure isolation mechanisms reduce the blast radius of a ransomware attack.[116]

---

112 https://cybersecurityventures.com/cybersecurity-almanac-2019/
113 https://therecord.media/treasury-said-it-tied-5-2-billion-in-btc-transactions-to-ransomware-payments/
114 https://www.sungardas.com/en-us/blog/ransomware-attacks-on-us-government-entities/
115 https://www.youtube.com/watch?v=VX59Gf-Twwo
116 https://docs.microsoft.com/en-us/compliance/assurance/assurance-malware-and-ransomware-protection

In 2021 we learned that attackers had developed zero-day vulnerabilities for on-premises Exchange Servers that had been exploited in the wild even before a patch could be made available. DearCry ransomware was developed to spread ransomware against unpatched Exchange Servers. Exchange Online was not subject to these same exploits.[117]

Facts

- If you pay the ransom - 30% of the time they will *not* give you the decryption key. Therefore, your backup system is absolutely critical to the mission of the IT Department.
- Sometimes decryption keys are available for free at NoMoreRansome.org (newer ransomware is often not there)
- Sometimes Ransomware is meant to distract from the larger goals of the hacker (Data Exfiltration of Intellectual Property). This happened with Hermes Malware against the Bank of Taiwan and Bank of Bangladesh
- Ransomware operators have at their disposal zero-day exploits (these can be purchased in zero-day marketplaces for 1 to 2 million dollars. Since some large ransomware payments are 4 million, attackers can achieve ROI).
- Ransomware authors can be state-sponsored. According to the United Nations, North Korea uses ransomware to collect money against US-based companies to evade US Sanctions. They have earned 2 billion in ransom thus far.
- Ransomware authors have claimed to bribe corporate insiders at Tesla and Accenture to deploy ransomware in those companies' networks[118]. Therefore, it would be wise to expand the scope of insider risk programs to include threat models of ransomware payments to insiders. Consider adding this to security awareness training or phishing emails: "would you like to earn a million dollars by planting ransomware on your company network" Then have discussions with these employees about life choices.

6 TB of files stolen, $50 million ransom demand

In conversations seen by the Cyble research team, the LockBit ransomware gang claims to have stolen six terabytes of data from Accenture and are demanding a $50 million ransom.

The threat actors claim to have gotten access to Accenture's network via a corporate "insider."

- Check with the Department of Treasury before paying a ransom otherwise you may be in trouble with US Government for aiding terrorists. On October 1st, 2020 the US Treasury Department issued a memo that jail or fines await those who pay terrorists with ransom payments.[119]

---

117 https://redmondmag.com/articles/2021/03/12/exchange-dearcry-ransomware.aspx

118 See https://www.wired.com/story/tesla-ransomware-insider-hack-attempt/ and https://www.cpomagazine.com/cyber-security/accenture-downplays-the-lockbit-ransomware-attack-that-reportedly-encrypted-2500-computers-leaking-6-terabytes-of-data/

119 https://home.treasury.gov/system/files/126/ofac_ransomware_advisory_10012020_1.pdf

Microsoft Solutions for Ransomware:

- Enable Defender for Office 365 to scan email for Ransomware
- Enable Windows 10 Attack Surface Reduction rules to block ransomware
- Use Microsoft Defender for Endpoint's EDR feature to detect ransomware activity
- Enable Microsoft Defender for Endpoint "Block at First Sight"
- Backup all laptop data to OneDrive. OneDrive keeps versions of files, so you can restore them to the previous backup.

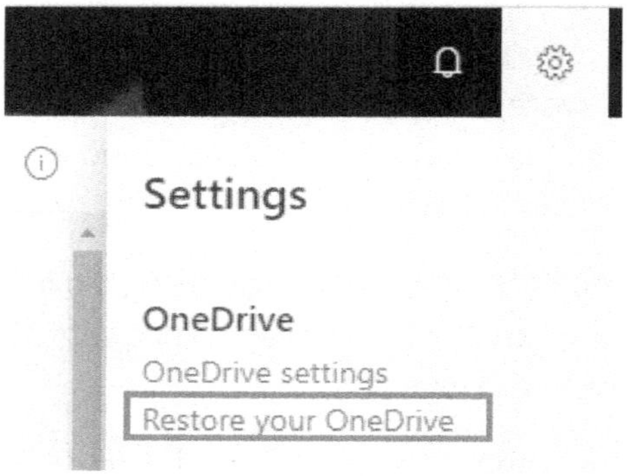

- Backup Server data to an offline or something with versioned restore.
- Controlled Folder Access (Requires Defender AV), and Applocker.[120]

Recommendations

- Plan Ahead: If you backup offsite (to Cloud or a DR site) – then the internet download speed can hinder recovery times. How long does it take to download multiple terabytes on a 100 Megabit Internet connection? Take that into consideration when designing for RPO and RTO compliance.
- Keep all Cloud Administrator logins separate from on-premises privileged users so that if there is a supply-chain attack targeting on-premises, it won't spread to Office 365. Make sure workstations that sign into Cloud Administrator accounts are isolated from the domain and are not used for any other purpose (dedicated workstations for privileged access).
- If you backup to cloud storage such as Azure, check to see if an additional authentication pin can be required for deleting backups. Currently, the following DPM and MABS versions support a security PIN.[121]
    - DPM 2016 UR9 or later
    - DPM 2019 UR1 or later
    - MABS v3 UR1 or later

---

[120] Windows 10 Controlled Folder Access and Applocker require significant IT overhead to setup and maintain because they require a list of authorized executables to function as allow-listing solutions. Some of my colleagues in Cybersecurity recommend them for the most critical workstations. There are bypass techniques, so they are not perfect, but for sure better than not having them if you have the time and resources to maintain them. I recommend CQURE training for application allow-listing https://cqureacademy.com/webinar/whitelisting

[121] https://docs.microsoft.com/en-us/azure/backup/backup-azure-security-feature#authentication-to-perform-critical-operations

- Check to see if your offsite backup provider supports WORM (Write Once, Read Many). For example, Azure Blob storage supports Immutable storage.[122]

- Have an Incident Response Plan ready (NIST 800-184, NIST 1800-11, and http://aka.ms/IRRG) For example, it's important to not perform a restore until after there is sufficient confidence that the attacker's ability to remain persistent in the environment has been eliminated, otherwise, the restore files could become re-infected – wasting valuable time and frustrating end-users.

- Test backups as frequently as you are willing to accept data loss (Assume attackers will tamper/disrupt Backups)

    - Recovery Point Objective (RPO) = The amount of acceptable Data Loss. 1 Day? 1 Week? Test backups that often.

Backups are the next best thing to have after prevention because if the backups are protected from hackers, then you do not have to pay the ransom. At most you'll have a disruptive event while data and operations are unavailable while restoring from backup, but at least you won't be rewarding the hacker's bad behavior with payments.

Questions to ask your backup administrator:

1. Are the most critical systems being backed up? Can you prove it to me?
2. Are backups tested (aka Restored) at least once a year?
3. Is there a process in place that when a new system is brought online that it is added to the backups?
4. When a backup job fails, is their alerting in place and if so, who responds, and is there evidence that failed jobs are remediated?
5. Which Administrators have access to the Backup Systems?
   Note: Assume Ransomware authors will target Administrators
    - Do these administrators use a separate username and password to log in to Backups than their regular Administrator Credentials?
    - Do these administrators use a dedicated workstation to sign into the Backup System with credentials only used for Backups?
    - Is the workstation or Backup server joined to Active Directory? (We want to make sure that if a hacker becomes domain admin in Active Directory that they cannot automatically sign into your backup system)
    - Recommendation: The Backup Servers should not be joined to the Active Directory Domain. You should have three sets of backups: offline, remote (cloud or DR site), and online (for fast restores). Assume the hacker will delete the online and cloud backups, the Offline backups will save you but they are the costliest for IT Overhead to maintain and operate. Think of it as either paying a million dollars per year for backups or paying a million dollars for a ransom payment.

Questions to ask your endpoint or desktop engineering team.

1. Are host-based firewalls enabled? This will prevent ransomware from spreading machine to machine (ex: PsExec, etc.)

---

[122] https://docs.microsoft.com/en-us/azure/storage/blobs/storage-blob-immutable-storage

2. Are host-based intrusion detection systems or EDR (Endpoint Detection and Response) enabled?
3. Verify that 'tamper protection' has been enabled on the host to prevent AV from being disabled by a malware loader.
4. Perform a software audit and make sure that tools like TeamViewer are not installed – we see a lot of attacks where hackers come in via these types of software.
5. Have users been removed from Local Administrator Groups?
6. Are hosts regularly getting security updates deployed for ***both*** Windows and Non-Windows Security Updates?
7. Consider Application White-Listing such as AppLocker. It won't prevent all ransomware but it will slow down advanced hacking groups.

Questions to ask your Server or Network Administrators

1. Are Administrators using separate "privileged access workstations" or are they using the same workstation for privileged tasks that they use for everyday email and web browsing?
2. Is the perimeter network security (Firewall and VPN) limiting ports to the bare minimum?
3. Do all internet-facing hosts have multi-factor authentication enabled (Especially VPN, RDP, VDI, Citrix?) Several of the largest ransomware events happened due to weak VPN credentials.
4. Are all internet-facing hosts patched quickly after the 2nd Tuesday of every month (aka Patch Tuesday?)
5. To reduce the risk of ransomware spreading to servers, prevent IT Administrators from being able to browse web pages while logged onto a server. If servers are in a separate IP subnet, create an ACL to block outbound 80 and 443 requests from the server subnet. The caveat is you could potentially break applications that rely on external connections to the internet. Therefore, you could enable the ACL with logging mode enabled so you could then create a whitelist of allowed sites and then block everything else. The downside is this will increase the administrative burden of the firewall administrator to maintain the ACL. However, the alternative of permitting an IT Administrator to browse websites while logged onto servers is to accept the risk of infecting the entire Server farm with a worm, virus, or Ransomware.

Chapter Seven – Auditing M365

There are four primary audit log locations in Office 365. Depending on the license level, these logs have varying lengths of retention.

1. Office 365 "Unified Access Log"
    1. Enabled by 'opt in' (The first time you visit the log page, it asks if you want to enable it.)
    2. Goes back 90 days
    3. Accessible here: https://compliance.microsoft.com/auditlogsearch?viewid=Test%20Tab
    4. Documentation: Search the audit log in the Microsoft 365 compliance center – Microsoft 365 Compliance | Microsoft Docs
    5. There are four options for extending the logs beyond 90 days
    6. Option 1: purchase M365 E5 (or other licenses) "Advanced Audit" which can extend this log to 1 year
    7. Option 2: purchase '10-Year Audit Log Retention Add On' (This add-on first became available for purchase in March 2021). Note: This policy is *not* retroactive.
    8. Option 3: Extend this into Sentinel to get correlation and default query templates
    9. Option 4: Use a 3rd party SIEM to query the Office 365 Management API.
       TIP: When you purchase the "Advanced Audit" license, it will reduce the throttling that occurs when querying the API (so for example you will see data in Splunk much faster!).
    10. Option 5: PowerShell
2. Azure AD Audit Log
    1. Enabled by Default
    2. Goes back 30 days with an Azure AD P1 license (or 7 days with an Azure AD-Free)
    3. Accessible here: Azure Audit Log
    4. Documentation: Audit logs in Azure Active Directory | Microsoft Docs
    5. Latency. Audit logs have a latency ranging from 15 minutes to an hour
    6. Activities. A complete list of each activity audited is available (here)
    7. Limits. The export limit from the web interface is 5,000 records. You can get around this by exporting the logs through one of the options below, which can also be used to extend retention.
    8. Option 1: Extend this log into Azure Log Analytics (aka Azure Monitor) to go beyond 30 days (learn how here)
    9. Option 2: Extend this log into Sentinel to get correlation and default query templates (learn how here)
    10. Option 3: PowerShell or Graph API.
3. Azure AD Sign-in log
    1. Enabled by Default
    2. Goes back 30 days with an Azure AD P1 license (or 7 days with an Azure AD-Free)
    3. Accessible here: Azure Sign-in Log
    4. Documentation: Sign-in logs in Azure Active Directory | Microsoft Docs
    5. Latency. Sign-in activity logs can take from 15 minutes to up to 2 hours for some records. According to the documentation, 95% of all logs will show up in 2 minutes.
    6. Limits. The export limit from the web interface is 5,000 records. You can get around this by exporting the logs through one of the options below, which can also be used to extend retention.
    7. Option 1: Extend this log into Azure Log Analytics (aka Azure Monitor) to go beyond 30 days (learn how here)

NOTE: Unlike the Azure Audit Log, the Azure AD Sign-in logs require an Azure AD P1 or higher license to export into Log Analytics.

8. Option 2: Extend this log into Sentinel to get correlation and default query templates (learn how here)
9. Option 3: PowerShell or Graph API.

4. Microsoft Cloud App Security
    1. Goes back 6 months
    2. Not enabled by default, requires configuration. You must go to "Connected Apps" then click the three dots to make it include the additional log sources as shown here:

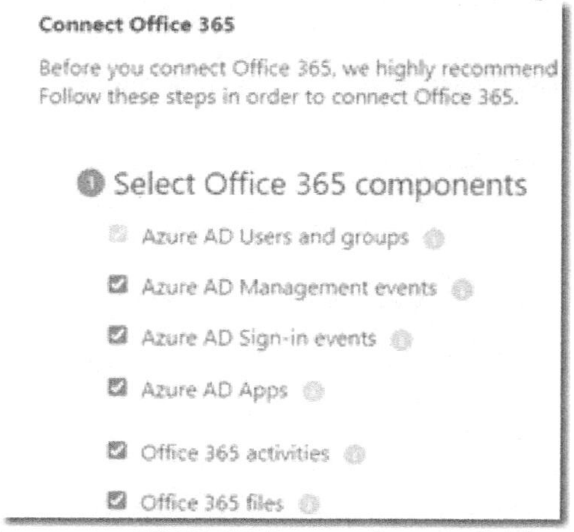

    3. Requires an M365 E5 license or O365 E5 license (or available via Stand Alone)
    4. Accessible here: https://portal.cloudappsecurity.com/#/audits/
    5. Option 1: Extend this log into Sentinel to go beyond 6 months

Reporting

There are a few useful built-in reports that analyze the logs and produce findings.

- Risky sign-ins – A risky sign-in is an indicator for a sign-in attempt that might have been performed by someone who is not the legitimate owner of a user account.

  Latency can range from as little as 5 minutes to a maximum of 2 hours.

- Users flagged for risk – A risky user is an indicator for a user account that might have been compromised
  Latency can range from as little as 5 minutes to a maximum of 2 hours.
    - Risk Detections. Azure AD uses adaptive machine learning algorithms and heuristics to detect suspicious actions that are related to your user accounts. Each detected suspicious action is stored in a record called **risk detection**.

Here are the latencies associated with when the risk detections will appear:

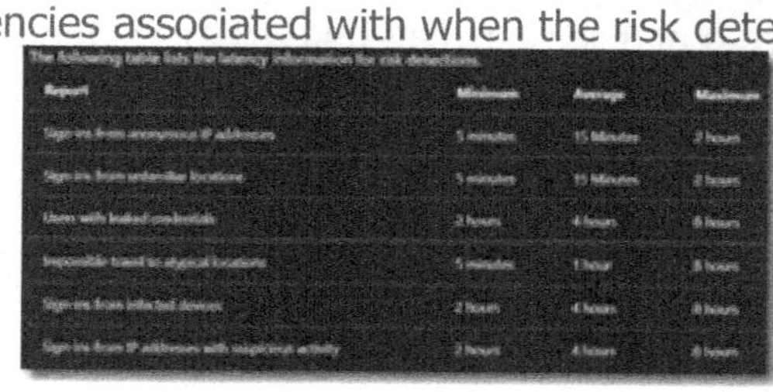

Advanced Audit License

As noted above, the new Advanced Audit License extends the retention of the UAL audit log to 1 year and speeds up 3rd party API throttling. A 3rd useful capability is the additional fields that get audited when this license is applied to mailboxes. The ability to log the 'MailItemsAccessed' (some may know this as MessageBind, that is what it was called in on-premises Exchange). Additional entries including exactly which items were sent from the compromised account are also logged.

The Send event is also a mailbox auditing action and is triggered when a user performs one of the following actions:

- Sends an email message
- Replies to an email message
- Forwards an email message

Investigators can use the Send event to identify emails sent from a compromised account. The audit record for a Send event contains information about the message, such as when the message was sent, the InternetMessage ID, the subject line, and if the message contained attachments. This auditing information can help investigators identify information about email messages sent from a compromised account or sent by an attacker. Additionally, investigators can use a Microsoft 365 eDiscovery tool to search for the message (by using the subject line or message ID) to identify the recipients the message was sent to and the actual contents of the sent message. You can also run the Search-UnifiedAuditLog -Operations Send or Search-MailboxAuditLog -Operations Send commands in Exchange Online PowerShell.

The MailItemsAccessed mailbox auditing action covers all mail protocols: POP, IMAP, MAPI, EWS, Exchange ActiveSync, and REST.

This is useful in a forensic investigation because it logs which emails were accessed. Imagine the relief of a Legal team when a hacker only accessed 10 items instead of a million items, and none of those 10 items contained PII or PHI data.

Note: When a protocol such as POP, IMAP, or MAPI over HTTPS (aka Outlook Anywhere) syncs a folder, then a single audit event is logged that the folder contents were synced rather than an entry for each item in the folder. (Reference).

Note: If an attacker generates more than 1,000 audit records in 24 hours in a mailbox, then this audit log is paused for 24 hours =(So a crafty hacker could overwhelm the log in order to hide activities (the pause occurs for 24 hours). (Reference)

Mailbox Search Events

The SearchQueryInitiatedExchange event is triggered when a person uses Outlook to search for items in a mailbox. Events are triggered when searches are performed in the following Outlook environments:

- Outlook (desktop client)
- Outlook on the web (OWA)
- Outlook for iOS

- Outlook for Android
- Mail app for Windows 10
- Investigators can use the SearchQueryInitiatedExchange event to determine if an attacker who may have compromised an account looked for or tried to access sensitive information in the mailbox. The audit record for a SearchQueryInitiatedExchange event contains information such as the actual text of the search query. The audit record also indicates the Outlook environment the search was performed in. By looking at the search queries that an attacker may have performed, an investigator can better understand the intent of the email data that was searched for.

SharePoint Search Events

Like searching for mailbox items, the SearchQueryInitiatedSharePoint event is triggered when a person searches for items in SharePoint. Events are triggered when searches are performed in the following types of SharePoint sites:

- Home sites
- Communication sites
- Hub sites
- Sites associated with Microsoft Teams

Investigators can use the SearchQueryInitiatedSharePoint event to determine if an attacker tried to find (and possibly accessed) sensitive information in SharePoint. The audit record for a SearchQueryInitiatedSharePoint event contains also contains the actual text of the search query. The audit record also indicates the type of SharePoint site that was searched. By looking at the search queries that an attacker may have performed, an investigator can better understand the intent and scope of the file data being searched for. You can also run the Search-UnifiedAuditLog -Operations SearchQueryInitiatedSharePoint in Exchange Online PowerShell. You must enable SearchQueryInitiatedSharePoint to be logged so you can search for this event in the audit log. For instructions, see Set up Advanced Audit.

In addition to the events listed above, there are also unique audit events that are only audited when the Advanced Audit license is owned:

- Microsoft Forms
- Microsoft Stream
- Microsoft Teams
- Yammer

Alerting

You can configure Alert Policies to notify you when certain things happen. This can be done in M365, Azure Monitor, MCAS, or Sentinel.

Audit Log Bypass

This article describes how it is possible for a user with administrative rights to bypass Mailbox audit logging, so be sure to document the configuration, and any changes to this configuration during a forensic investigation.

Manage mailbox auditing – Microsoft 365 Compliance | Microsoft Docs

PowerShell Modules

There are a variety of PowerShell modules available, designed to automate gathering the logs or searching them for use in forensic investigations. If you find any more, send me a DM on Twitter at @ITGuySocal

1. Hawk

```
Install-module -name hawk

AzureADPreview\Connect-AzureAD

Connect-ExchangeOnline

Start-HawkUserInvestigation -UserPrincipalName <UPN>

Start-HawkTenantInvestigation
```

2. DFIR-O365RC

3. Azure AD Toolkit (This is what Microsoft's DART team uses)

4. CrowdStrike Reporting Tool for Azure (CRT)

5. Sparrow (this is what the US Government's CISA's Cloud Forensics team wrote back in December 2020 to identify activity in a tenant asscciated with the TTPs used by the hackers who compromised SolarWinds).

6. 365BlueTeamKit by Chaim Black

7. Office 365 Extractor by Joey Rentenaar and Korstiaan Stam from PwC Netherlands Incident Response team

8. Mandiant Azure AD Investigator This is similar to Sparrow in that it was built to detect artifacts that may be indicators of Nobelium/UNC2452/Sunburst or other threat actors that use those same techniques.

Chapter Eight - Responding to a Security Event in M365

Microsoft documentation lists the following steps that should be performed when responding to a compromised email account in Office 365[123]:

Step 1 – Reset the Password

Step 2 – Remove suspicious email forwarding addresses

Step 3- Disable any suspicious inbox rules

Step 4 – Unlock the user from sending email

Step 5 – Block the user from signing in (optional)

Step 6 – Remove the user from any administrative roles (optional)

Step 7 – Verify sent items, check other accounts, verify contact Information

In addition to the steps above recommended by Microsoft, here are some additional recommendations:

- Enable Multi-factor authentication
- If forwarding was enabled, check all other accounts that have forwarding enabled and see if there are any other accounts that appear to have suspicious forwarding enabled
- Check to see if there were any oAuth application grants created by the user during the timeframe the attacker had access to the account
- Check the Security Reports: Risky sign-ins, users flagged for risk, and risk detections
- Use the URL Trace report to see who else may have clicked on the same hyperlink
- Check the audit logs and see which emails were 'hard deleted' from the user's mailbox, this is an unusual extra deletion step and is often performed by the hacker when they try to cover their steps. You can prevent the permanent deletion of emails by enabling an email retention policy so that you can preserve forensic evidence.

All this takes time! Fortunately, Microsoft Defender for Office 365 Plan 2 includes Automated investigation and response (AIR)[124]. AIR runs automated investigation processes in response to (1) well-known threats (2) threats that are submitted by end-users via the Report Phishing plug-in or (3) threats manually submitted by administrators.

AIR will automate the types of tasks that email or security administrators have to perform when a phishing email slips by the defenses. For example, it will check to see which mailboxes received the same email, and then automate the removal process to eliminate the manual effort of removing email with PowerShell. Ultimately, this leads to a faster response time and reduces risk. For every minute that

---

[123] https://docs.microsoft.com/en-us/microsoft-365/security/office-365-security/responding-to-a-compromised-email-account?view=o365-worldwide

[124] https://docs.microsoft.com/en-us/microsoft-365/security/office-365-security/office-365-air?view=o365-worldwide

a malicious email is left in an inbox, a user could click a dangerous link or unleash the next ransomware threat.

AIR Playbook

The following steps are performed automatically by AIR during an automated investigation

1. Analyze user activity anomalies in Microsoft Cloud App Security
2. On-demand check of domain reputation from Microsoft's ISG and external threat intelligence sources
3. Detect anomalies based on historical mail flow sending patterns for users in your organization
4. Extract indicators from the header, body, and content of the email for investigation
5. Investigate mail delegation access for user mailboxes related to this investigation
6. Investigate any violations detected by Office 365 Data Loss Prevention (DLP)
7. Detect intra-org and outbound malware or phish originating from users in your organization
8. Investigate any mail forwarding rules for user mailboxes related to this investigation
9. Email cluster analysis based on header, body, content, and URLs
10. On-demand check on URL reputation from Microsoft's ISG and external threat intelligence sources
11. On-demand check of IP reputation from Microsoft's ISG and external threat intelligence sources
12. Email cluster analysis based on outbound mail flow volume patterns
13. On-demand detonation triggered with Office 365 ATP for emails, attachments, and URLs

Recovering from a privileged account takeover

There is additional diligence that must be performed when an administrative account is taken over.

1. Audit Exchange Transport Rules to see if they have been modified.
2. Reset all privileged accounts in Azure AD
3. Invalidate refresh tokens issues for users (Revoke-AzureADUserAllRefreshToken)
4. Audit service principal credentials
5. Audit service principal permissions and reply URLs
6. Audit federation settings and verified domains
7. Rotate the AD FS token-signing and token-decrypting certificates
8. Audit accounts created during the timeframe of when the attacker had admin privs

On-prem:

1. If Seamless SSO is used, remediate the AZUREADSSOACC computer account
2. Remediate on-premises AD DS connector account
3. Remediate Azure AD connector account
4. Remediate on-premises ADSync Service Account
5. Audit/reset accounts on DCs
6. Rotate the AD FS token-signing and token-decrypting certificates
7. Rotate Kerberos ticket-granting ticket account twice
8. Reset all service accounts
9. Rotate secrets associated with remote access MFA token generation

Chapter Nine – Security Operations in M365

Microsoft provides free "Ninja Training" for IT and Security Administrators to gain proficiency with Microsoft security products.

Ninja Training

1. Microsoft Defender for Identity https://aka.ms/mdininja
2. Microsoft 365 https://aka.ms/m365dninja
3. Microsoft Defender for Endpoint https://aka.ms/mdeninja
4. Microsoft Cloud App Security https://aka.ms/mcasninja
5. Microsoft Defender for Office 365 http://aka.ms/MDONinja

Daily, Weekly, and Monthly Security Tasks

I am often asked, "There are so many Microsoft administrative portals! What should our security team be checking?" Here are some recommended tasks for security operations teams.

Daily Tasks

1. Review Microsoft 365 Incidents
   https://Security.microsoft.com > Incidents
2. Check Action Center to see if anything is waiting for an Administrator to Approve
   https://security.microsoft.com/action-center
3. Release items from quarantine upon request and Analyze items using Threat Explorer as needed

Weekly Task List

1. Review General Security Reports
   - Microsoft Security Center Reports
2. User Risk
   - Evaluate User Risk in MCAS
3. Endpoint Risk
   - Device Compliance Reports in Microsoft Endpoint Manager
   - Antivirus Agent Status (Must click 'generate again')
   - Detected Malware (Must click 'generate again')
   - Defender for Endpoint Threat Protection Reports
   - Device Health and Compliance Reports
   - Vulnerable Devices
     - As needed: Work on patching vulnerable software
   - Devices that are falling behind on major operating system updates:
     https://endpoint.microsoft.com/#blade/Microsoft_Intune_Enrollment/ReportingMenu/windowsUpdateReporting
   - Review TVM Reports
     https://security.microsoft.com/tvm_dashboard
   - Review Microsoft's Threat Analytics Reports
     Do you have any devices matching?
     https://security.microsoft.com/threatanalytics3
   - Spend time threat hunting

Monthly Task List

1. Review Microsoft 365 Defender Dashboard (Home Page)
   - Review Device Risk, User Risk, Device Compliance, Active Incidents, Devices with Malware, & Security Score
2. Review Defender for Endpoint Security Recommendations

3. Review SecureScore

4. Review Identity Score

5. Review Compliance Score

6. Perform Attack Simulations

Metrics and KPI

The metrics you measure will have a significant effect on the behaviors and outcomes of security operations. Focusing on the right measurements will help drive continuous improvement in the right areas that meaningfully reduce risk.

To ensure that security operations are effectively containing attackers access, the objectives should focus on

- Reducing time to acknowledge an alert to ensure that detected adversaries are not ignored while defenders are spending time investigating false positives.
- Reducing time to remediate a discovered adversary to reduce their opportunity time to conduct an attack and reach sensitive systems.
- Prioritizing security investments into systems that have high intrinsic value (likely targets / high business impact) and access to many systems or sensitive systems (administrator accounts and sensitive users).
- Increase focus on proactively hunting for adversaries as your program matures and reactive incidents get under control. This is focused on reducing the time that a higher-skilled adversary can operate in the environment (for example, skilled enough to evade reactive alerts).

For more information on how Microsoft's SOC uses these metrics, see https://aka.ms/ITSOC.

O365 SOC Operational References

1. Organizing Security Operations Teams
2. Microsoft Security Best Practices for Security Operations
3. Watch this Ignite video to see how 1000 events were reduced to 10 actionable actions MyIgnite - Microsoft 365 Defender: Stop attacks and reduce security operations workload by 50% with automated cross-domain security
4. Security Roadmap – Top Priorities for the first 30, 90, and beyond
5. Mark Simos maintains a wiki list of helpful resources https://aka.ms/markslist

Chapter Ten – Build a Cyber Defense Lab

The best way I have found to secure M365 is through hands-on labs. The environment changes so frequently that building your own lab is the best way to gain proficiency with security tools.

Step 1 - Create your M365 lab environment

Time to complete: ~30 Minutes

TIP: Complete all steps with your web browser running in 'Incognito' or 'InPrivate Mode' to ensure you are isolated from your production tenant.

In Microsoft Edge or Google Chrome, it is found here:

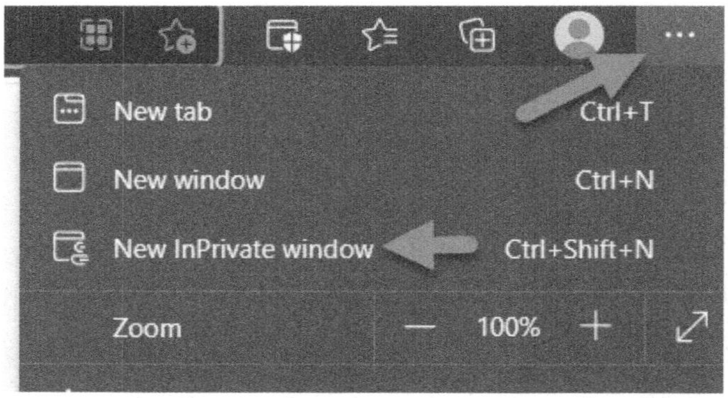

Think up a fictitious company name. For example, you could use a variant of "Contoso"

Optional: Create a new email account that you can use to sign up for an M365 trial tenant.
Note: If you prefer to use your own personal email account for the lab, that's fine, just skip this step:

Browse to https://outlook.live.com/owa/?nlp=1&signup=1 and look for the big blue button to create a new email account.

Sign up for a Microsoft 365 E5 trial subscription

1. In your web browser, open an Incognito (Safe Browsing) Tab and copy and paste this URL into that tab: **https://bit.ly/M365E5Trial**

2. In step 1 of the **You've selected Microsoft 365 E5"** page, enter your new email account address.
3. In step 2 of the trial subscription process, enter the requested information, and then perform the verification.
4. In step 3, You'll probably want a custom domain name for your business at some point. For now, choose a name for your domain using onmicrosoft.com. We recommend something disposable like MyTenant123.onmicrosoft.com.

NOTE: You may have to click Next a few times.

5. For step 4, Create your username and password to sign in to your account.

For this lab, use something you will remember like 'admin' (Or be more creative if you like!)
This value will be referred to as the **global administrator**.

6. Click on "**Manage my subscription**"
7. In Microsoft 365 E5 Setup, select **Continue using *your (YourUserID)@TenantName*.onmicrosoft.com for email and signing in**, and then select **Exit and continue later**.

You should see the Microsoft 365 admin center. If you need to get back to this, go to https://admin.microsoft.com

Ensure all services are enabled

Setting up a new tenant takes a few minutes for things to be provisioned on the backend. To ensure things are ready for the lab exercises, ensure you can access these links using the same InPrivate browser by opening these four sites in new tabs (one per site):

1. https://security.microsoft.com (<- Microsoft Defender Security Console)
2. https://endpoint.microsoft.com (<- Endpoint Manager Console)
3. https://aad.portal.azure.com (<- Azure Active Directory)
4. https://admin.microsoft.com (<- M365 Admin Console)

Create a non-privileged User Account, for example: "Jane Doe"

1. Sign into https://admin.microsoft.com (<- M365 Admin Console)
2. Click Users on the left navigation > Active Users > Add a user

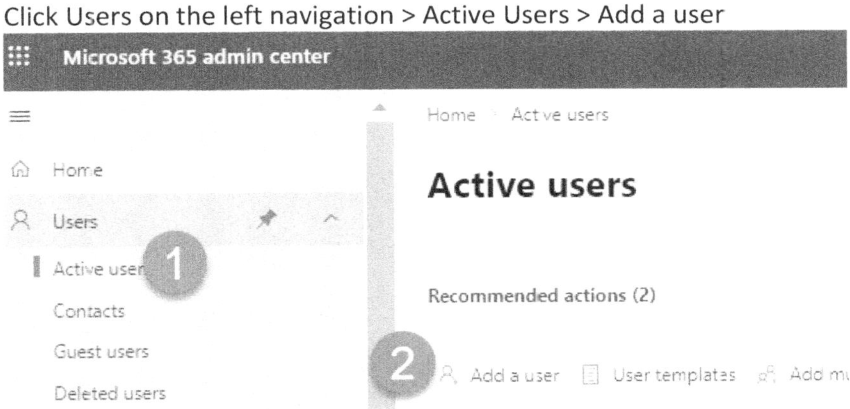

3. Complete the wizard and assign an M365 E5 license

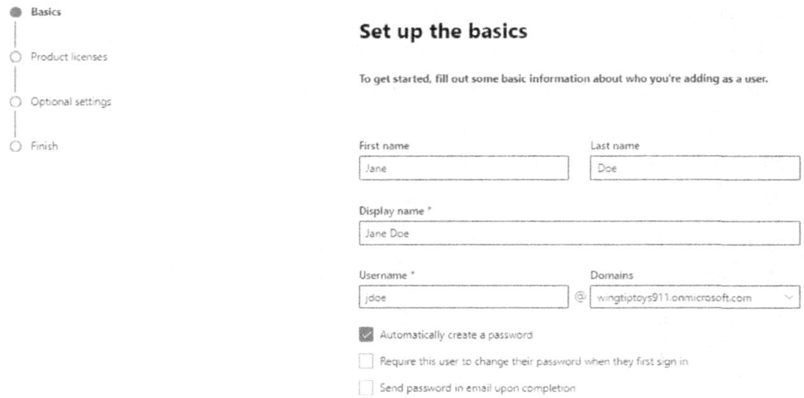

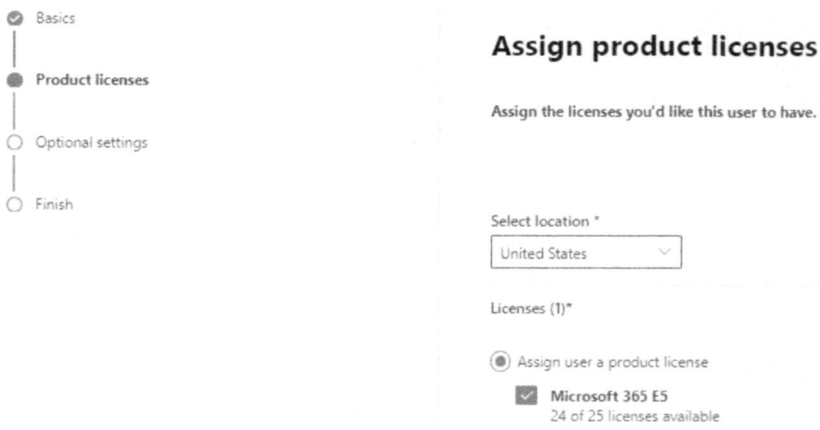

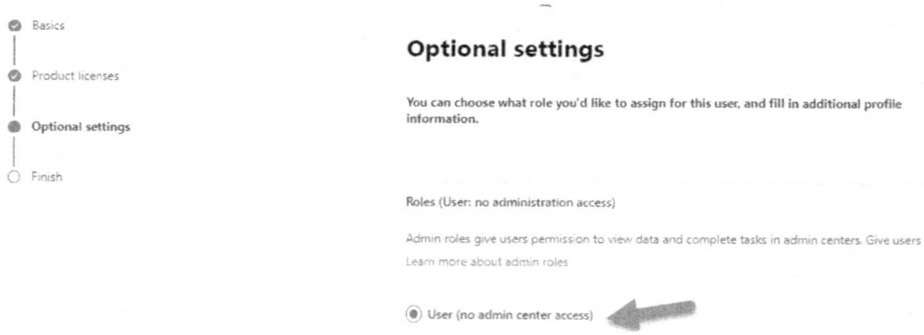

Step 2 –Prepare a Workstation

Estimated Time to Complete = 15 Minutes

You can either use a spare laptop, a virtual machine, or you can create a virtual machine inside the Defender for Endpoint Evaluation lab. We recommend Windows 10 for this lab.

1) Logon to Security.Microsoft.com and on the left Navigation browse to Endpoints > Evaluation & Tutorials > Evaluation Lab (or click here: Microsoft 365 security - Microsoft 365 security)

2) You will see "Hang on! We're preparing new spaces..." (This can take ~10 minutes, time for that coffee refill!)

3) Click Setup Lab

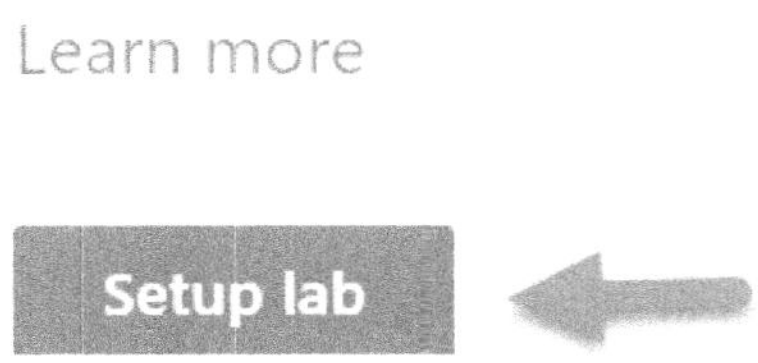

4) Select 3 Devices for 72 hours each

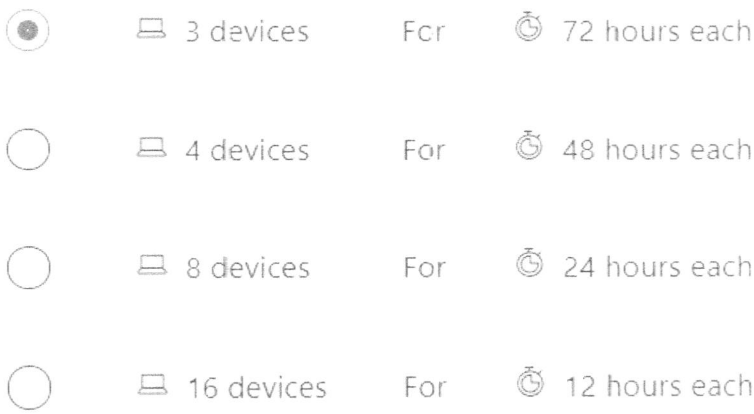

5) Consent to all four EULAs to install the threat simulators, making sure all four checkboxes are "checked" and providing contact information where requested

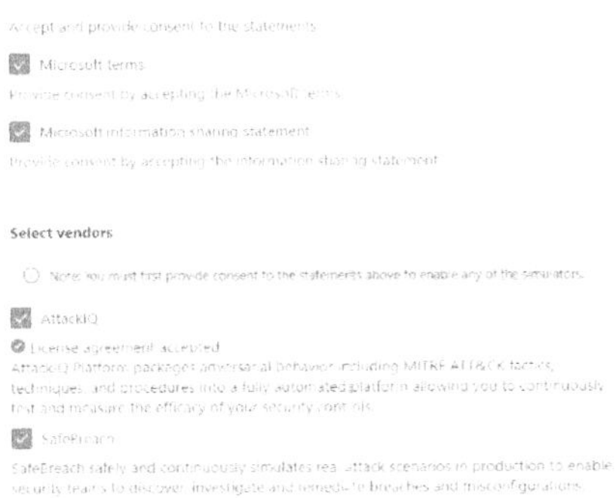

6) Click Setup Lab to complete the wizard
7) Click Add Device
(TIP: Either wait 48 hours before 8/17, otherwise your VM will expire. You can also

repeat this step the morning of the event)

8) Accept the Defaults

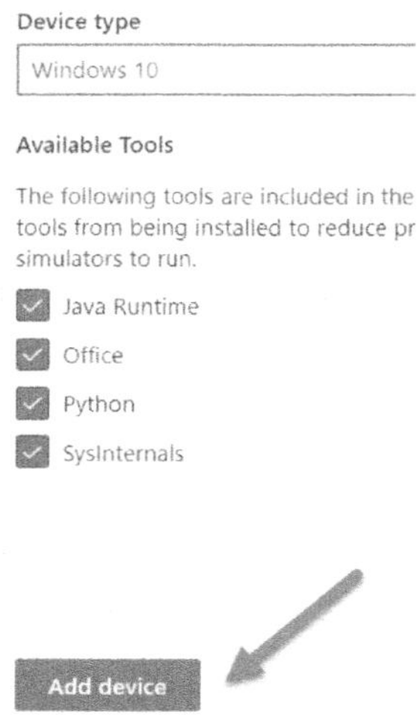

9) Click the Devices Tab and wait until Status changes from 'Setting up' to "Active" (This can take ~10 minutes)

10) When it shows Active, click on the three dots to the right and then click Connect

11) Open the RDP file that is downloaded to connect to your VM

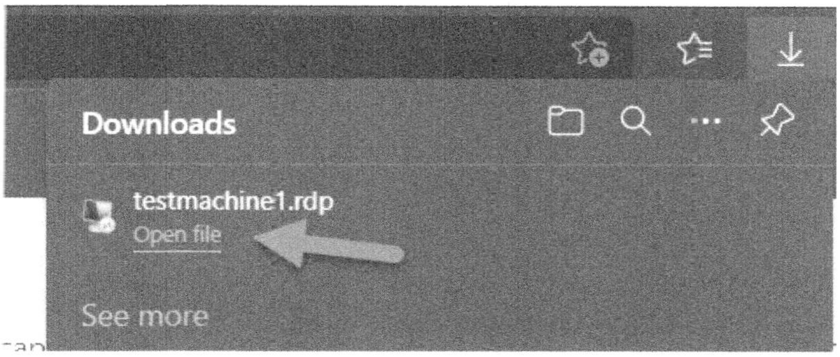

12) Follow the prompts to sign in!

Step 3 – Configure Microsoft Endpoint Manager (Intune)

Estimated Time to Complete = 15 Minutes

In a real-world environment, you might use Group Policy, Microsoft Endpoint Manager Configuration Manager, or MEM Intune to harden Windows 10. In this lab, we are going with MEM Intune[125] because it offers a quick start wizard that enables a nearly complete configuration in a few mouse clicks, so we can hit the ground running.

1) In the same Incognito / InPrivate Web Browser, open a new tab
2) Copy and paste this URL into the new tab: https://Endpoint.Microsoft.com
   (Caution: going forward, anytime you a hyperlink in this document, please assume you should copy and paste the link into your Incognito tab, instead of clicking on the link. If you click on a link, it may open in a standard web browser signed into your production environment, which would not be good!)
3) In the bottom-right, find the "Deploy Windows 10 in cloud configuration" and select the "Start" button to begin the wizard

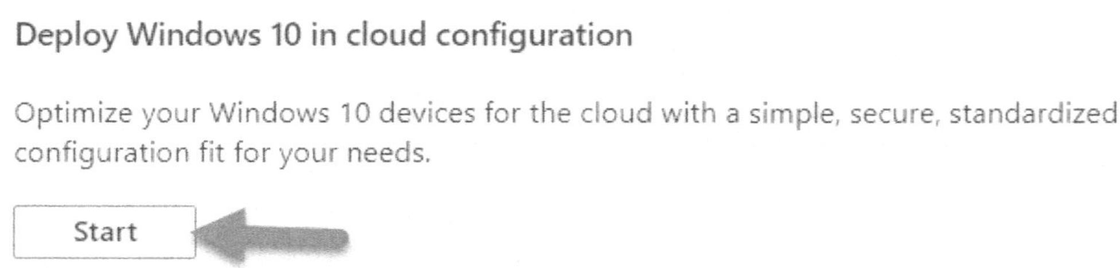

4) Click Next
5) Leave the Default for "Apply device name template"
6) For the resource prefix name, enter something like MyLab then click Next
7) Select any Apps you want to install (optional) then click Next
8) Enter a Group Name like "Lab Users" then click Next
9) On the last step of the wizard click **Deploy**
10) Browse to the MDM Automatic Enrollment Page
    Endpoint.microsoft.com > Devices > Enroll Devices > Automatic Enrollment
    (Or copy and paste the link below)
    https://endpoint.microsoft.com/#blade/Microsoft_Intune_DeviceSettings/DevicesEnrollmentMenu/windowsEnrollment

[125] The steps are following to configure Intune are from the excellent resource "Windows 10 in cloud configuration" by Ravi Ashok (MSFT) and Stan White (MSFT)
Windows 10 in cloud configuration (microsoft.com)

11) Change MDM User Scope to ALL then click Save

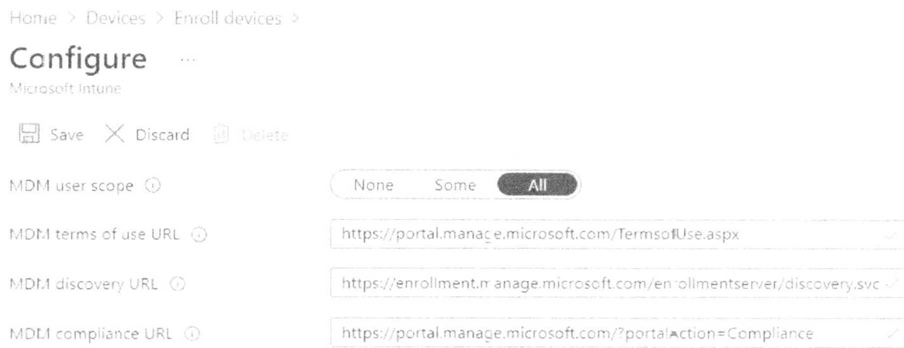

12) We are going to now disable the Security Baseline so that we can selectively configure some of these settings by hand in the workshop. Navigate to Endpoint Security > Security Baselines > Windows 10 Security Baseline

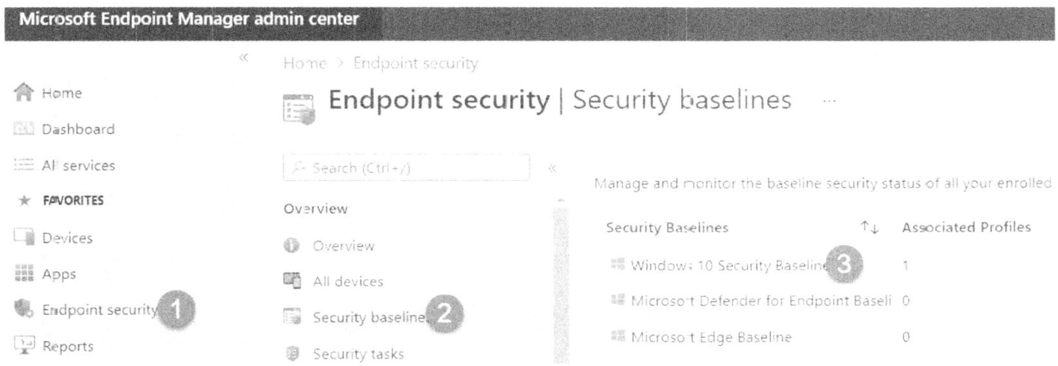

MDM Security Baseline - Microsoft Endpoint Manager admin center

13) Click on the profile > Properties > Assignments (Edit)

14) Click Remove then Review and Save

> The Security Baseline does some great things, like disabling SMB v1, and NTLM but until you test these settings thoroughly against all your legacy applications, it shouldn't be applied to production systems until testing is thoroughly complete. In most cases, you'll end up creating custom policies 'inspired' by the baseline.

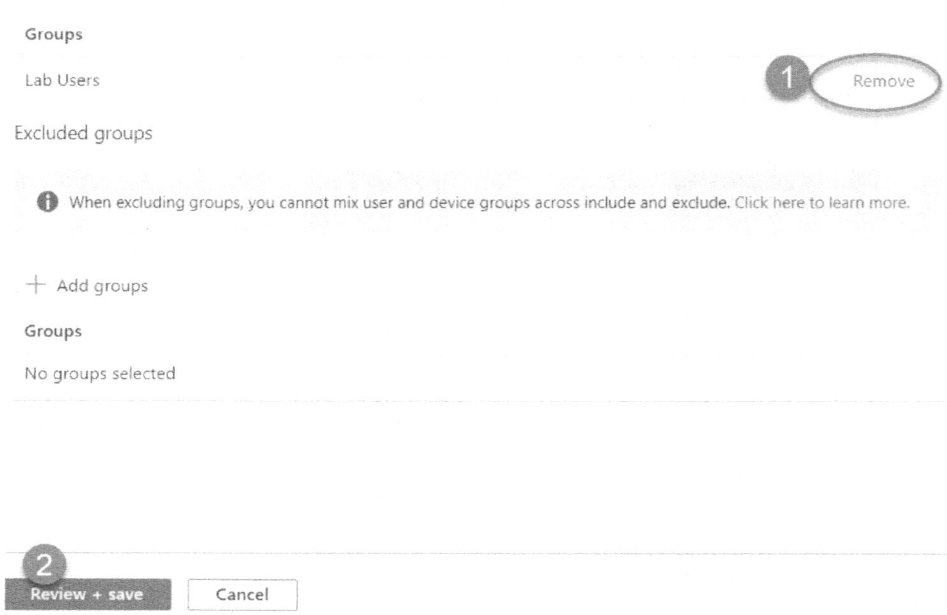

15) Navigate to Groups

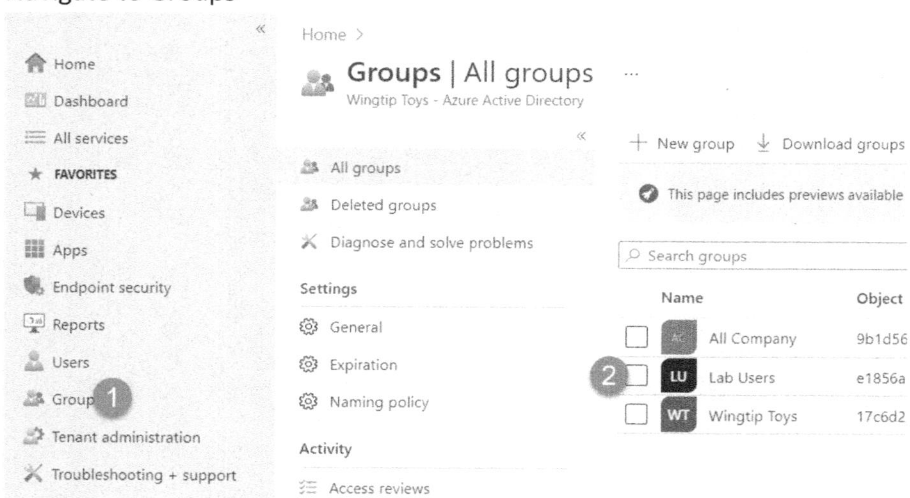

[Groups - Microsoft Endpoint Manager admin center]

16) Select the group you created (eg: Lab Users) and click "members" to then "add members"

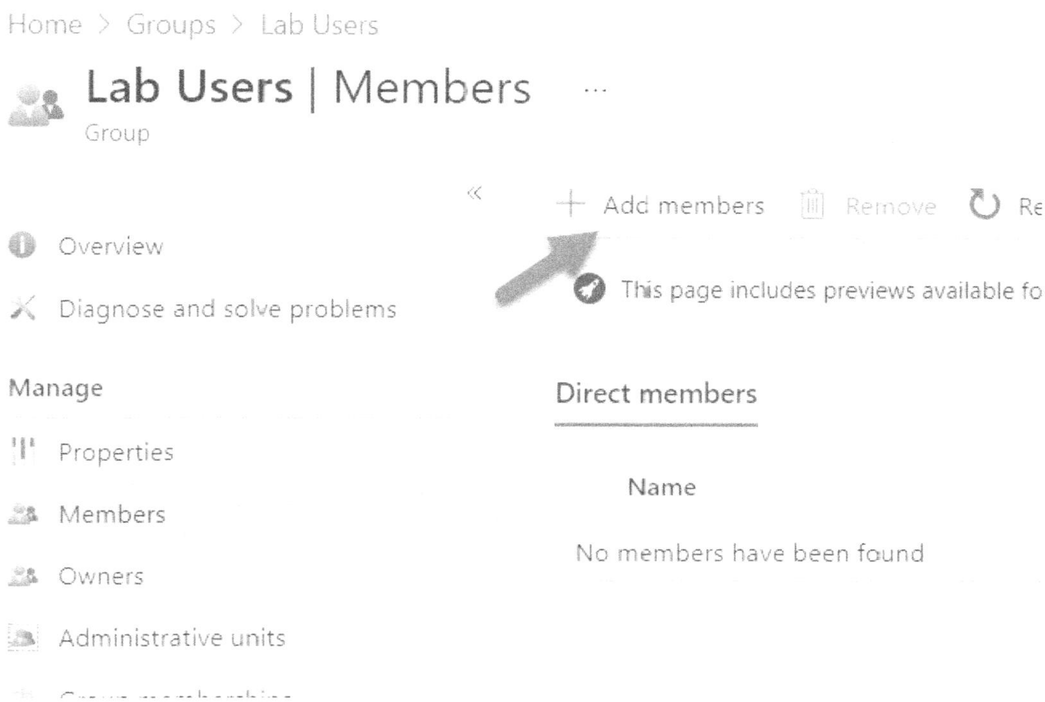

17) **IMPORTANT STEP** Add the non-privileged user account that you created in step 1 (e.g "Jane Doe")

Step 4 – Enroll your VM into Intune

We will now enroll one machine into Intune.

1. On the desktop of the WIN10 computer, select **Start > Settings > Accounts > Access work or school**
   (DO NOT CLICK CONNECT)

2. Click "Enroll only in device management" as shown below:

This will do an Azure AD Registration, not an Azure AD Join (this is a requirement for this Lab).

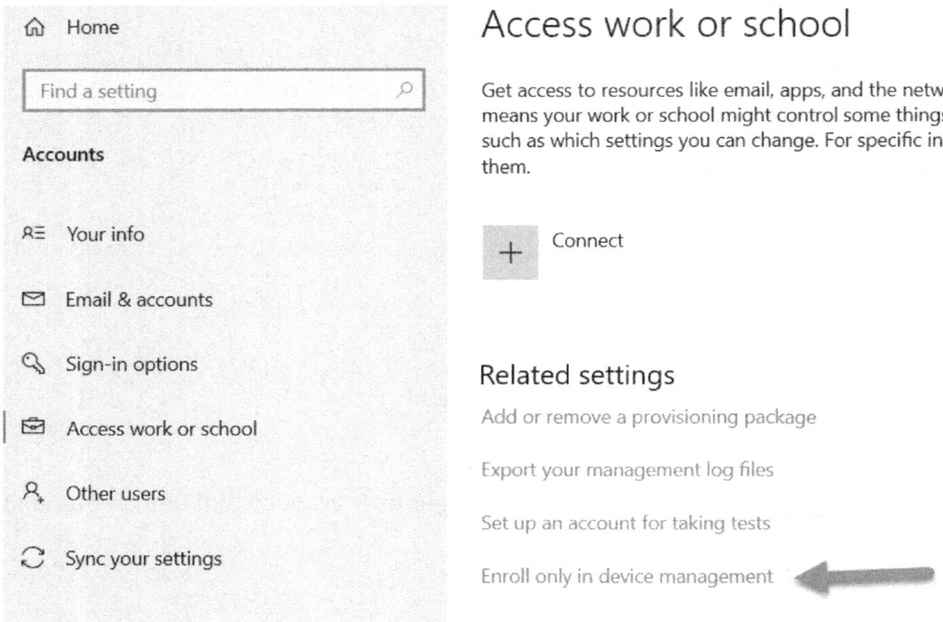

3. **IMPORTANT STEP** enter the NON-Admin account credentials (Example: the Jane Doe Account)
   This is important because it establishes 'user affinity' in Intune as the Primary owner of the device. This allows Intune policies to be applied to this device even though it is not an Azure AD joined device.

4. Then close the settings window. You will see a pop-up message "setting up your device" which you can dismiss by clicking "Got it."

5. After a few minutes, you should be able to see your Device show up in Endpoint.microsoft.com > Devices

TIP: To force Intune to sync changes, follow these steps;

1. *From the Intune Administrative console (endpoint.microsoft.com > devices)*

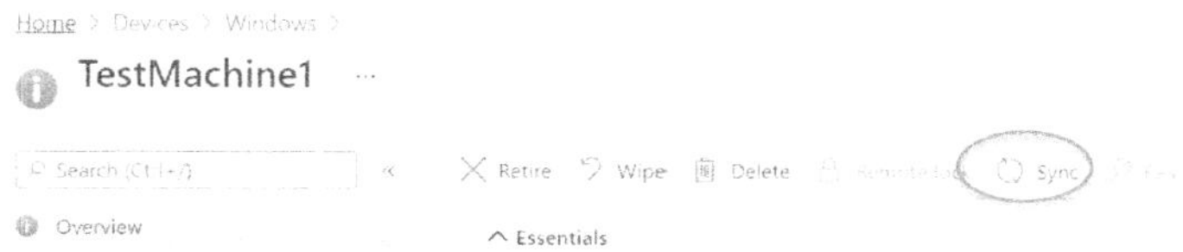

OR

2. *Inside Windows 10 (Settings > Access Work or School > Click Info, then click Sync)*

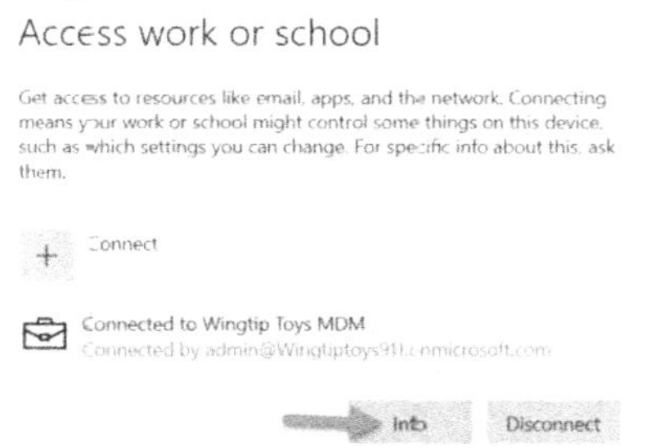

https://endpoint.microsoft.com/#blade/Microsoft_Intune_DeviceSettings/DevicesWindowsMenu/windowsDevices

Getting Started

Now that your lab has been created, it's time to perform these lab exercises:

1. Identity (Zero Trust)
2. Email Security
3. Windows 10 Security

Sign in to your Lab

1) Sign in to your new evaluation tenant (not your production tenant!)
   Tip: remember, open a web browser in "InPrivate Mode" or "Incognito Mode"
2) Sign in to your Virtual Machine

Lab 1 – Microsoft Zero Trust

We start protecting against Ransomware by first securing the Identity, because most data breaches can be traced back to weak credentials that can be easily guessed ("Summer2021!") or stolen (over 8 billion passwords have been leaked or are for sale online), or phished credentials (1 in 3 users will click on a Phishing link).

Using Identities online without multiple factors of authentication is like having a computer plugged directly into the internet without a Firewall. You're allowing any random hacker in the world to take a shot at your identity.

Security Defaults vs Conditional Access Policies

Every new Microsoft 365 Tenant has "Security Defaults" enabled. Security Defaults are great because it forces MFA on all accounts, but **we must disable Security Defaults** so that we can configure Conditional Access Policies to require Device Authentication (A key principle of Zero Trust Security Strategy).

1) In your Lab (InPrivate/Incognito Browser) Sign in to the Azure Active Directory Portal at https://aad.portal.azure.com

2) Click Azure Active Directory > Properties > Manage Security Defaults

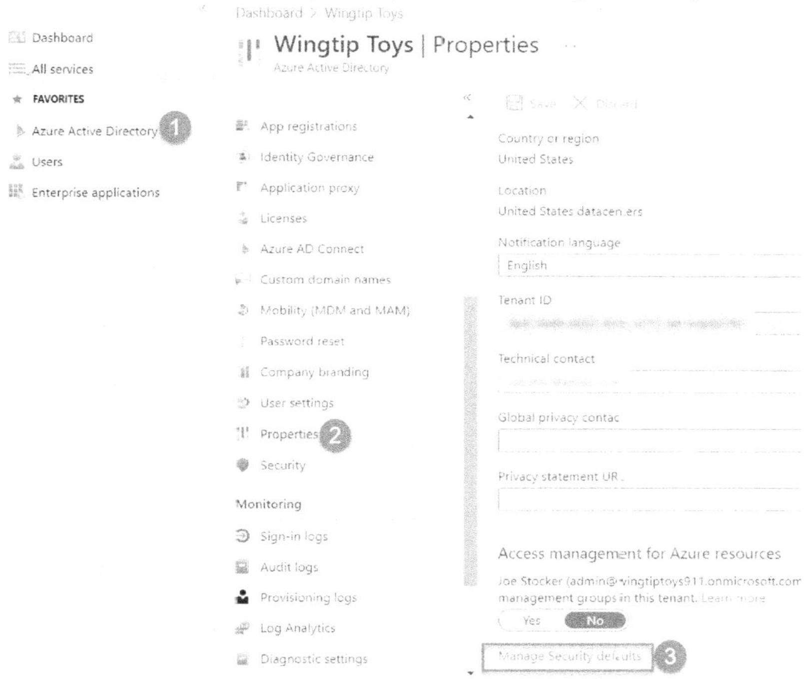

3) Click “No” and “My organization is using Conditional Access” then click Save

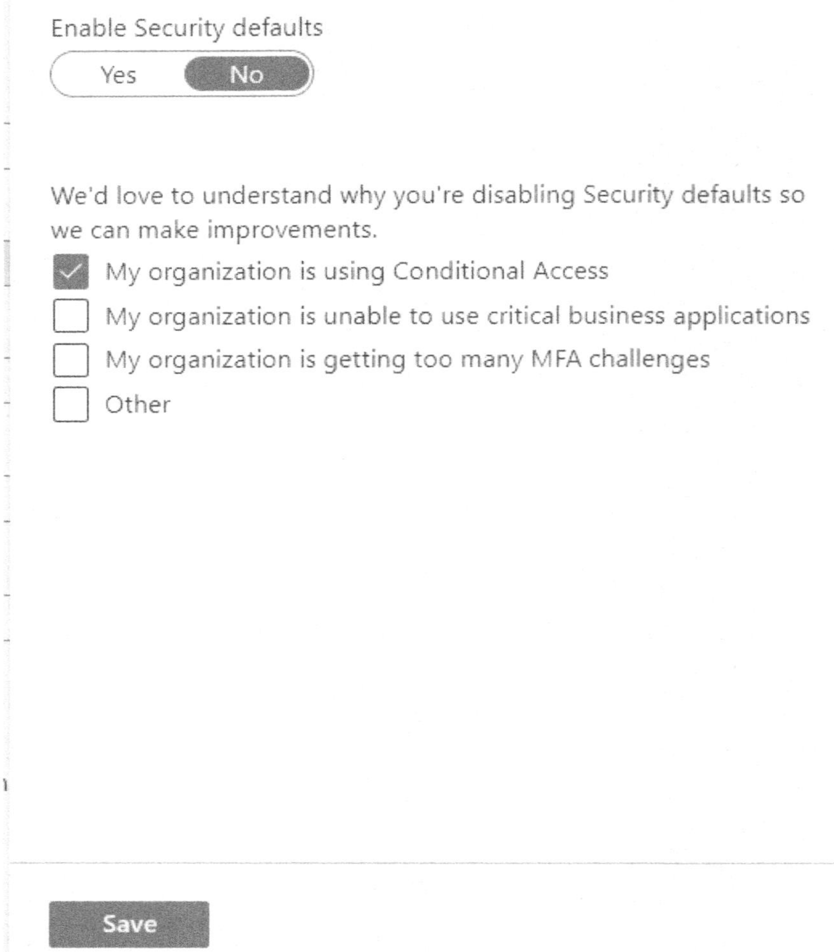

4) Sign into Endpoint.Microsoft.com with your lab credentials

5) Click Endpoint Security > Conditional Access

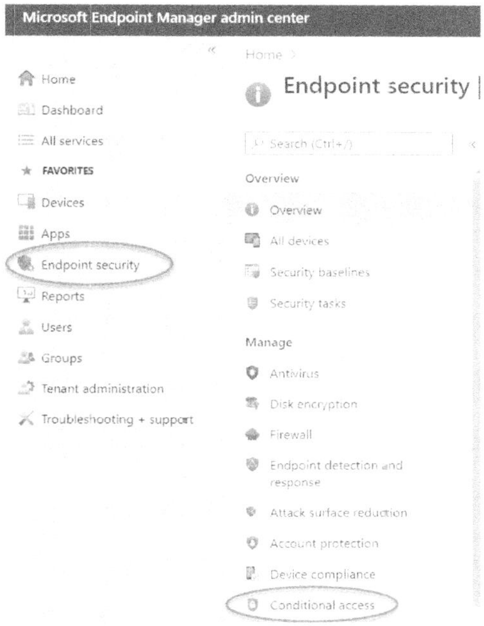

6) Create a new Policy named "CA01 – All Users – PC and Mac - Require Compliant Device"

- Apply to All Users
- Exclude your global administrator account ("This is known as a 'Break Glass' Account") so that if you make a mistake, you don't lock yourself out.
- Apply to All Cloud Applications, and Exclude the "Microsoft Intune Enrollment" App
- Change the Conditions to: Include Any Device and Exclude: Android and iOS TIP: The reason why we are excluding Android and iOS is that in most organizations, employees are allowed to use their personal phones. If you are one of the lucky organizations where your employer provides the smartphone, or they give you a stipend for you to enroll your phone into Intune MDM, awesome, don't select the exclude and then skip the other policy below (CA04).
- Under Access Controls > Grant, select the "Require device to be marked as compliant"

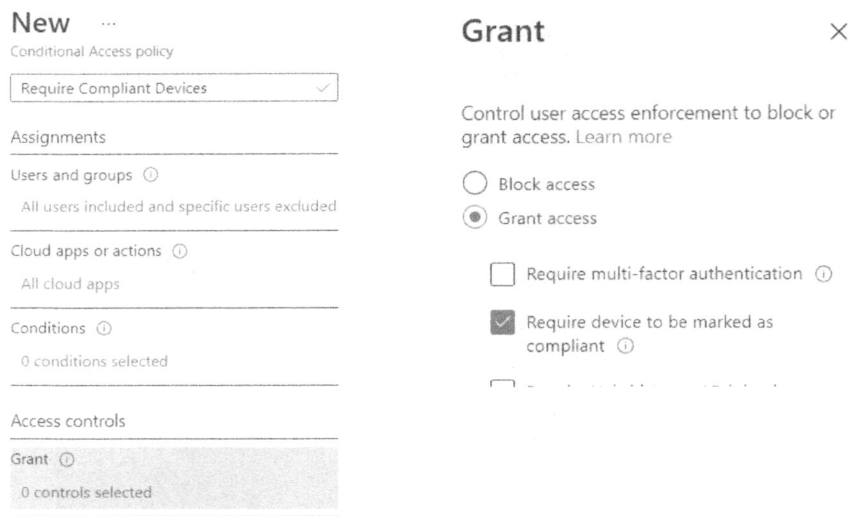

7) **Create a new Policy named "CA02 – All Users - Require MFA for Risky Sign-Ins"**

- Apply to All Users
- Exclude your Admin account ("This is known as a 'Break Glass' Account") so that if you make a mistake, you don't lock yourself out.
- Apply to All Cloud Applications
- Change the Conditions to Sign-in risk > (select both Medium and High checkboxes)
- Under Access Controls > Grant, select the "Require multi-factor authentication"

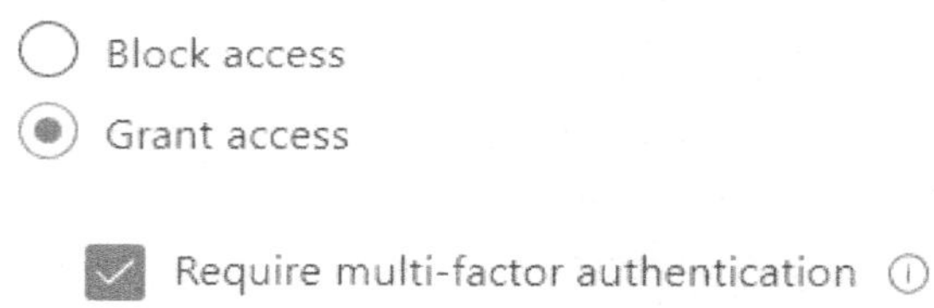

TIP: By only prompting users for MFA when there is a risk detected (impossible travel, new device type, etc) then we avoid desensitizing users to the MFA prompts (the "Rubber Stamping" syndrome that sets in) Patriot has investigated multiple cases where employees pushed "Approve" on the MFA Push Notification without realizing they were letting an attacker sign in!

---

8) **Create a new Policy named "CA03 – All Users - Require Password Change for Leaked Creds"**

- Apply to All Users

- Exclude your Admin account ("This is known as a 'Break Glass' Account") so that if you make a mistake, you don't lock yourself out.
- Apply to All Cloud Applications
- Change the Conditions to User risk > (select the High checkbox)

  TIP: When the User Risk has reached High, the user's password has either been found on the dark web, or there is enough aggregate sign-in risk or behaviors to indicate with a high degree of confidence that the user's account has been compromised.

  - Under Access Controls > Grant, select Require Password change

When the user's password has been changed, it will invalidate all previously granted session tokens

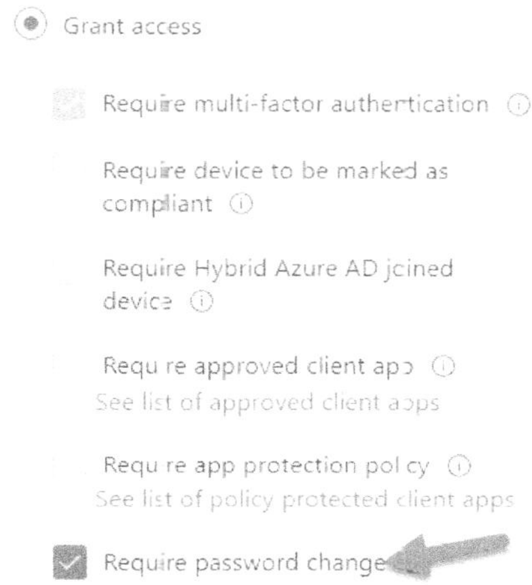

TIP #1: In a high-security environment, you might select Block so that you can coordinate with the user to change their password, especially if you have not enabled SSPR with password write-back in your tenant. The user's account will remain in a blocked state until the credentials have been reset so that the user risk is reduced.

TIP #2: In a high-security environment, if you permit a password change, you might consider adding an additional conditional access policy that restricts SSPR registration to Intune compliant PCs only, so that you are preventing the hacker from changing the password.

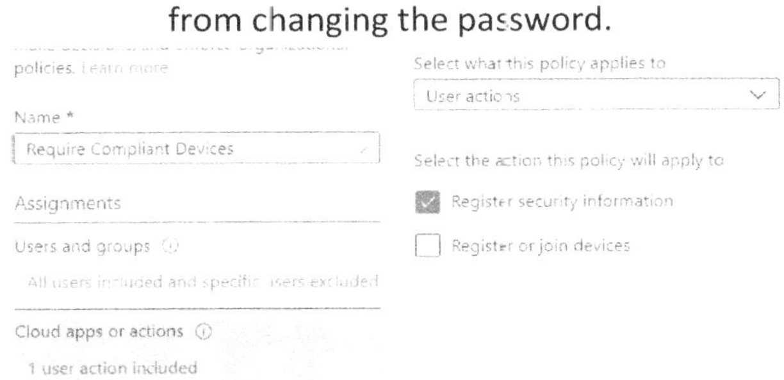

9) **Create a new Policy named "CA04 – All Users - Require Compliant App for BYOD Users"**
   - Apply to All Users
   - Exclude your Admin account ("This is known as a 'Break Glass' Account") so that if you make a mistake, you don't lock yourself out.
   - Apply to All Cloud Applications
   - Change the Conditions to only select Android and iOS
     - Under Access Controls > Grant, select "Require Approved client app" and "Require app protection policy"

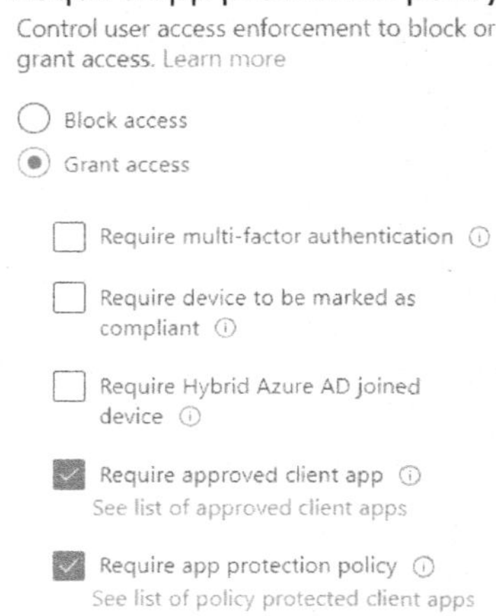

This will effectively block ActiveSync mobile connections to Exchange Online (Unless there has been a prior oAuth Grant to iOS, which seems to override these conditional access policies).

10) **Create a new Policy named "CA05 – All Users – Block Legacy Authentication"**
   - Apply to All Users
   - Exclude your Admin account ("This is known as a 'Break Glass' Account") so that if you make a mistake, you don't lock yourself out.
   - Apply to All Cloud Applications
     - Change the Conditions to only select Client App -> Legacy Auth

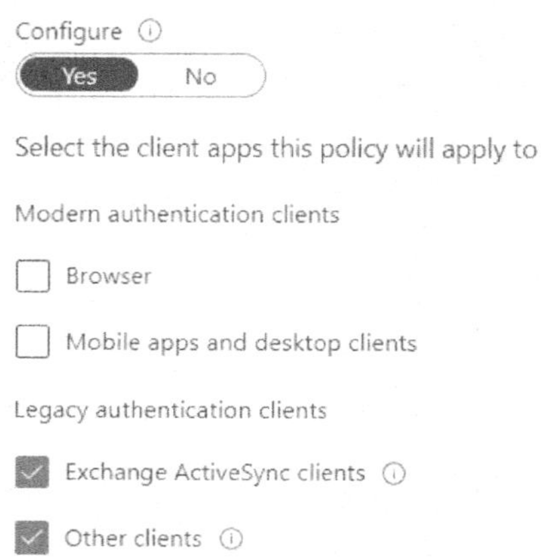

- Under Access Controls > select Block

Zero Trust Summary
The result of these policies: Only Intune Compliance PCs and Macs can connect, otherwise BYOD mobile devices can connect if they are using a compliant application managed by Intune App Protection. Users will only receive an MFA prompt if there is a risk to their sign-in. Users will be required to change their password (or be blocked) if their password has been leaked.
See the Appendix for additional config that is highly recommended for production environments but could not be simulated in this lab environment (If computers have malware on them, they will be unable to connect because their Intune compliance state will be marked as non-compliant).

Lab 2 – Email Security

We follow up securing the Identity with securing email. Once MFA policies are configured as we did in Lab 1, identities are protected from phishing campaigns and brute force attacks. Now, the next most common avenue for Ransomware to enter an environment is from email attachments.

So, we want to now show you how to configure Exchange Online Protection and Defender for Office 365 to make sure that email attachments that contain threats are blocked.

Block Executable Attachments

By default, Microsoft's EOP "common attachments filter" is disabled, which means that it does not block executables, scripts, or other file types associated with malware campaigns. This filter should be enabled, and additional file types should be added to the default list.

Navigate to https://security.microsoft.com/securitypoliciesandrules > Threat Policies > Anti-malware and enable the common attachments filter.

When you enable the policy, it will block the following 10 file types:

.ace,.ani,.app,.docm,.exe,.jar,.reg.,.scr,.vbe,.vbs.

TIP: The graphical interface allows you to select from close to 100 additional file types to block. You can also add your own custom file types using the set-malwareFilterPolicy Exchange Online PowerShell cmdlet.

Detonate Email Attachments

MDO Safe Attachments[126] is designed to block malicious attachments based on behavior observed in a sandbox. After EOP scans attachments for known malware, they are opened in parallel against a series of *Windows* sandboxes running in Microsoft's cloud data centers operating with a mix of Windows operating systems and Office versions.

The sandbox is quite sophisticated. For example, if malware attempts to check if it is running in a sandbox, it is seen as suspicious because why would a Microsoft Office or PDF attachment care what the recent file count registry value is? By default, 50% of the detonations take less than one minute, and you can view the exact mail delay latency with the new Mail Latency Report here: https://security.microsoft.com/mailLatencyReport

It's important to understand that Safe Attachments only detonates files in Windows, and therefore it won't detect exploit behavior in non-Windows computers such as macOS, Linux, Android, or iOS.

We recommend configuring MDO Safe Attachments for **Block.** The "Dynamic Delivery" option was originally created when delays in scanning resulted in customer complaints and its purpose was to allow the message to be received while the scanning was performed on the back-end.

Navigate to https://security.microsoft.com/securitypoliciesandrules > Threat Policies > Safe Attachments

Create a new Safe Attachments Policy as shown below (apply it to your (tenant).onmicrosoft.com domain). In a production deployment you would deploy it to all your custom domains as well.

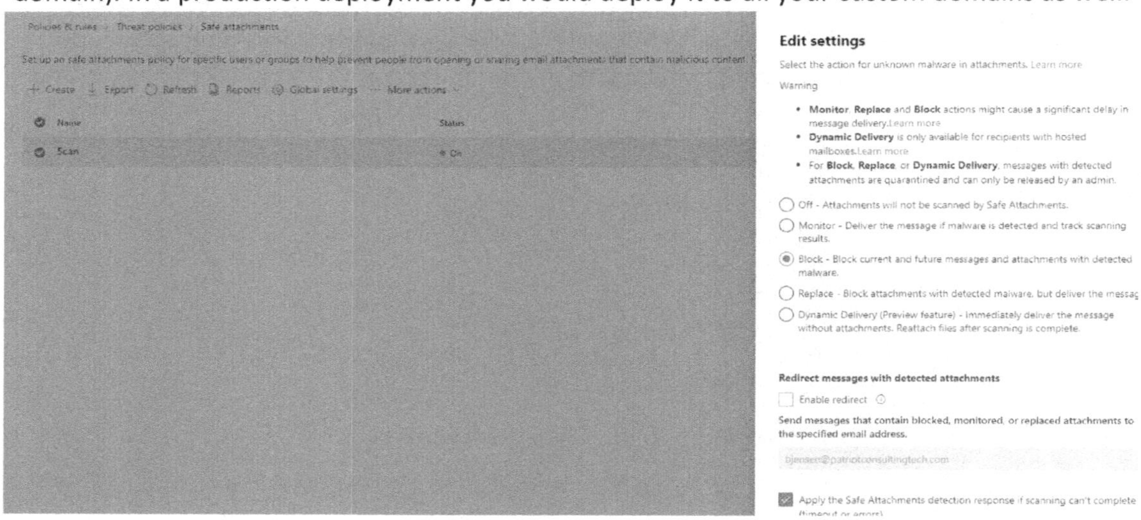

[126] https://docs.microsoft.com/en-us/microsoft-365/security/office-365-security/safe-attachments?view=o365-worldwide

Detonate Email Hyperlinks

MDO Safe Links are designed to block malicious hyperlinks, either at the time of click or at the time of delivery (this is newer).

Navigate to https://security.microsoft.com/securitypoliciesandrules > Threat Policies > Safe Links

Create a new Safe Links Policy as shown below (apply it to your (tenant).onmicrosoft.com domain). In a production deployment, you would deploy it to all your custom domains as well

Configure Safe Links as shown here:

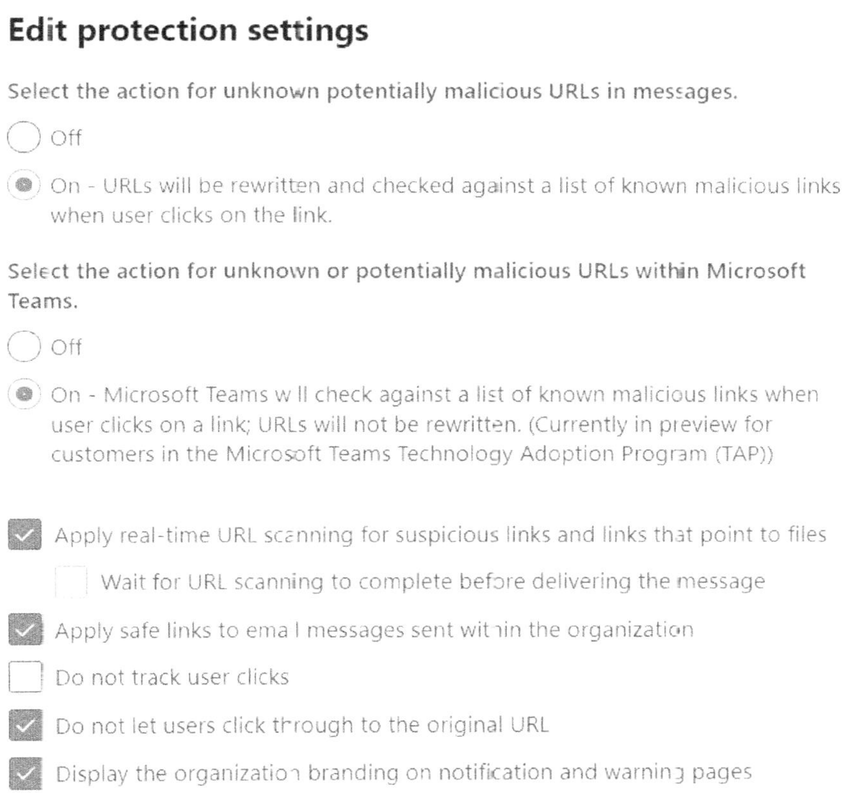

Verify Hyperlink inspection: Email your Jane Doe Test account with a hyperlink pointing to http://spamlink.contoso.com and then browse to OWA with that test account – it should result in a block page.

Block Impersonated Emails

Anti-impersonation can also detect misspelled domain names, which is another tactic that hackers use to increase the effectiveness of their spear-phishing campaigns.

Blocked by Anti-Impersonation

Misspelled domain name blocked by Anti-Impersonation

From: "Jack Johnson" <jack.johnson@conttoso.com>
Sent: Monday, October 21, 2021 9:53 AM
To: (Unsuspecting End-User – Probably in Accounting Department) <AccountingClerk@contoso.com>
Subject: RE: Invoice Payment

Navigate to https://security.microsoft.com/securitypoliciesandrules > Threat Policies > Anti-Phishing

Create a new Anti-Phishing Policy. Walk through the wizard and apply it to your (tenant).onmicrosoft.com domain. In a production deployment, you would deploy it to all your custom domains as well, and you would expand the protection beyond the Jane Doe User.

Phishing threshold & protection

Phishing threshold
2 - Aggressive

Impersonated user protection
- On for 4 user(s)

Impersonated domain protection
- On for owned domains
- On for 3 custom domain(s)

Trusted impersonated senders and domains
- On for 0 domain(s) and 12 sender(s)

Mailbox intelligence
- On

Mailbox intelligence for impersonations
- On

Spoof intelligence
- On

Edit protection settings

Actions

If message is detected as an impersonated user
Quarantine the message
DefaultFullAccessPolicy

If message is detected as an impersonated domain
Quarantine the message
DefaultFullAccessPolicy

If Mailbox Intelligence detects an impersonated user
Quarantine the message
DefaultFullAccessPolicy

If message is detected as spoof
Quarantine the message
DefaultFullAccessPolicy

First contact safety tip
- On

User impersonation safety tip
- On

Domain impersonation safety tip
- On

Unusual characters safety tip
- On

Unauthenticated senders symbol (?) for spoof
- On

Show "via" tag
- On

Email Security Best Practice Analyzer

Microsoft had previously provided the Office 365 Advanced Threat Protection Recommended Configuration Analyzer[127] which is a PowerShell Script that scans email security configuration and makes best practice recommendations. This has been replaced by an easier-to-use web interface, which offers automation to apply the recommendations. It also monitors configuration change drift history.

Try it here: https://security.microsoft.com/configurationAnalyzer

Advanced Transport Rules

There are several custom transport rules that you can consider for improving email security protection. The following two are examples of how to reduce the risk of ransomware attachments coming in through email.

Quarantine password-protected attachments

By default, EOP's anti-malware and MDO Safe Attachments cannot scan password-protected attachments unless the password is found in the body of the same email. If the password is found in the body of the email, then Microsoft will use that to decrypt the attachment and scan it for threats. To be safe, it is best to block password-protected attachments since they cannot be scanned for threats.

You can configure these in your lab, or you can skip them.

---

127 https://github.com/cammurray/orca

Quarantine hyperlinks containing IP addresses

By default, MDO SafeLinks does not scan hyperlinks with IP addresses. Therefore, it's important to prevent links from being sent that contain IP addresses. ETR can use a regular expression to search for this pattern: *(?i)http(s?):\/\/(?:[0-9]{1,3}\.){3}[0-9]{1,3}*

You can configure these in your lab or you can skip them.

Lab 3 – Windows 10 Security

We follow up security email with Windows 10 security. Why? Before an attacker can attack your on-premises Domain Controller, they first must "hop" from a workstation to the DC. Therefore, hardening the workstations will at best halt the attack, or at worst, slow it down while you are able to get alerts so you can then respond and evict the intruder.

Endpoint Detection and Response (EDR)

EDR allows us to detect suspicious activity on the endpoint since zero-day vulnerabilities could be exploited which would normally evade traditional Endpoint Protection (EPP) solutions that rely only on signature-based protection.

Since Microsoft's Defender for Endpoint is tightly integrated with Intune, it's easy and straightforward to onboard Windows 10.

Step 1) Sign into Security.microsoft.com > Settings > Endpoints > Settings > Advanced Features > Toggle the Microsoft Intune Connection to ON

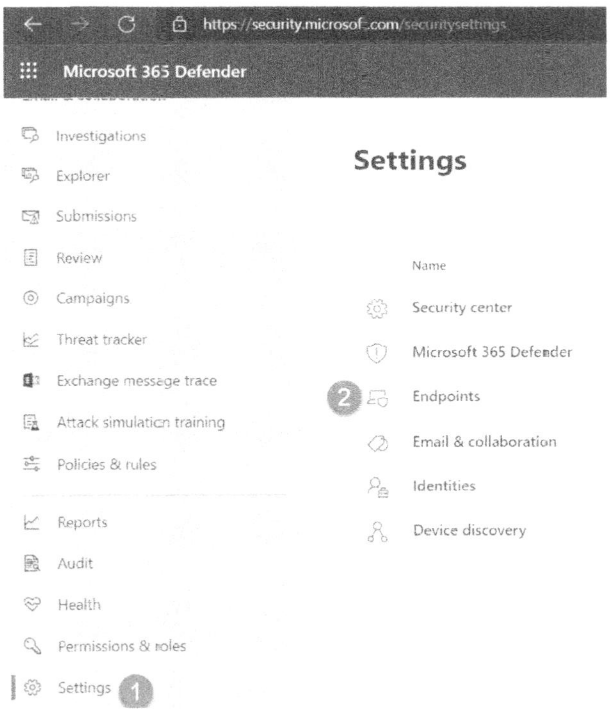

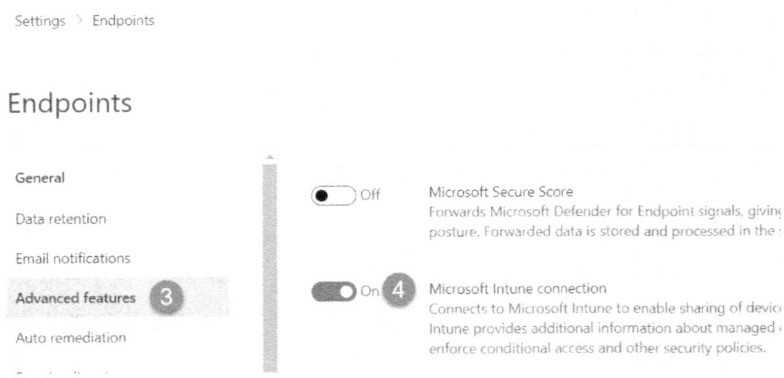

Step 2) Toggle ALL other Advanced Features to ON except for “Restrict correlation to within scoped device groups” (<- leave that one off, and all others should be set to ON)

Documentation: [Microsoft Defender for Endpoint documentation | Microsoft Docs]()

Step 3) Don’t forget to click Save Preferences!!

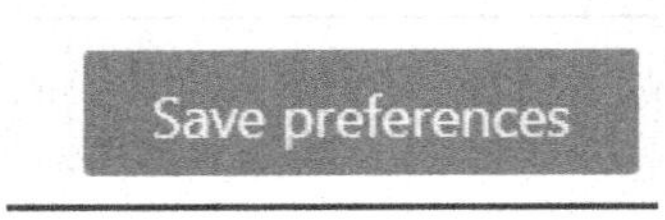

Step 4) Browse to Endpoint.Microsoft.com > Endpoint Security > Microsoft Defender for Endpoint > and toggle ALL the options to “ON” > then click SAVE

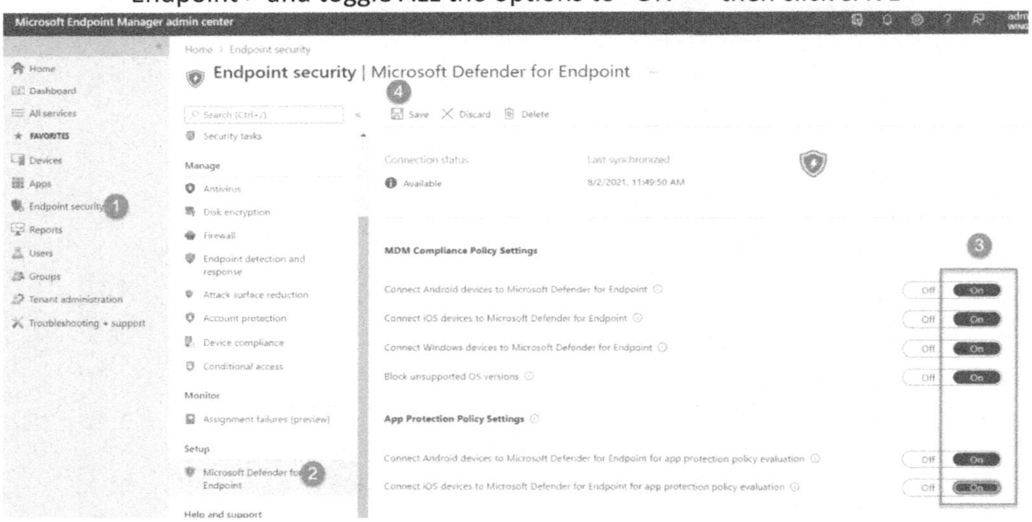

After clicking SAVE verify that the Connection Status now shows as Enabled

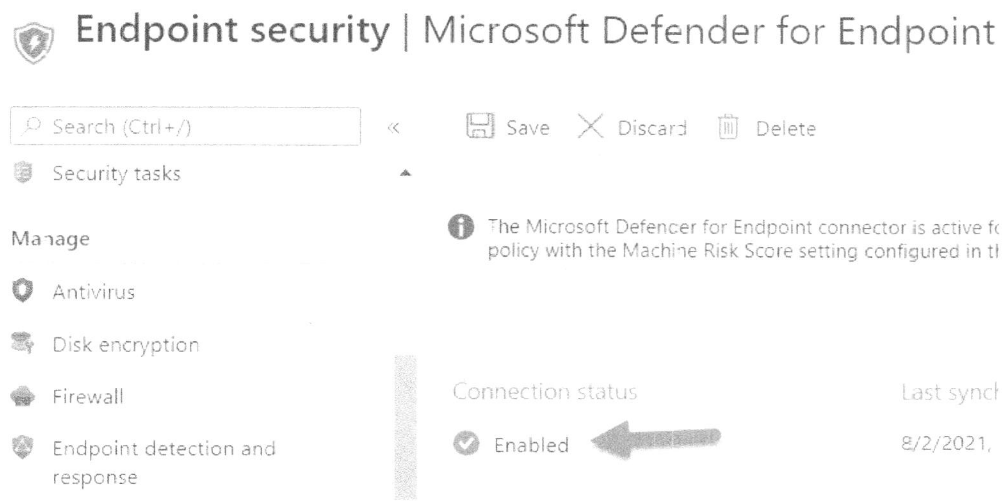

To observe your enrolled Devices in the MDE EDR Console, browse to Security.Microsoft.com and select Device Inventory under the Endpoints Section from the left navigation.

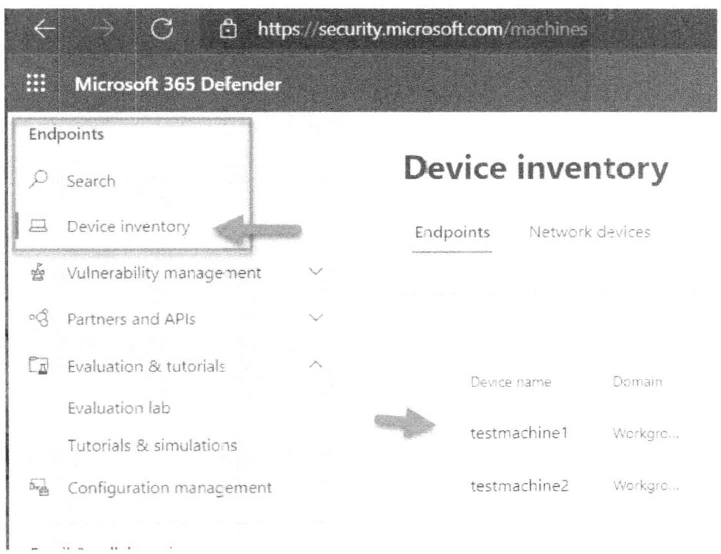

Microsoft Defender Firewall

We need to put shields up on the networking stack by enabling Microsoft Defender Firewall. This prevents machines on the network that have been infected with ransomware from spreading laterally.

Step 1) Browse to Endpoint.Microsoft.com > Click Endpoint Security > Firewall > Create Policy

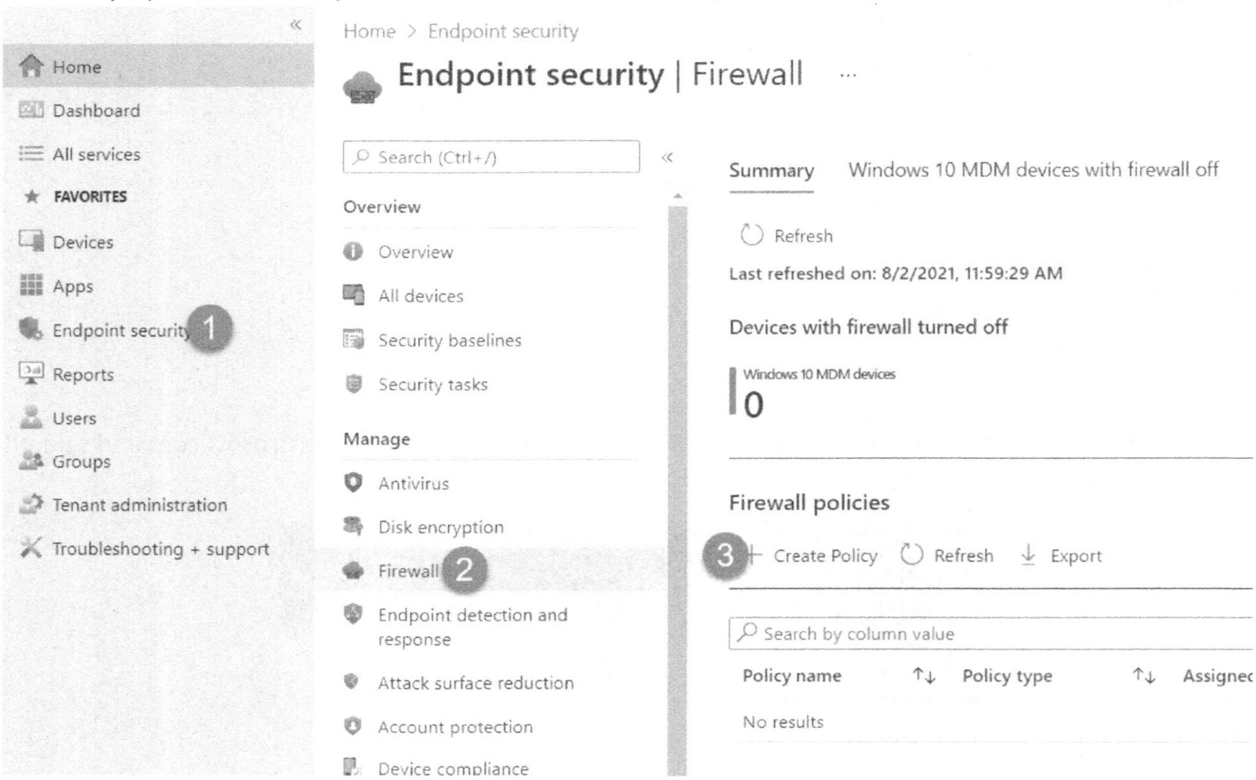

Step 2) Select Windows 10 and Later > Defender Firewall as shown below > Create

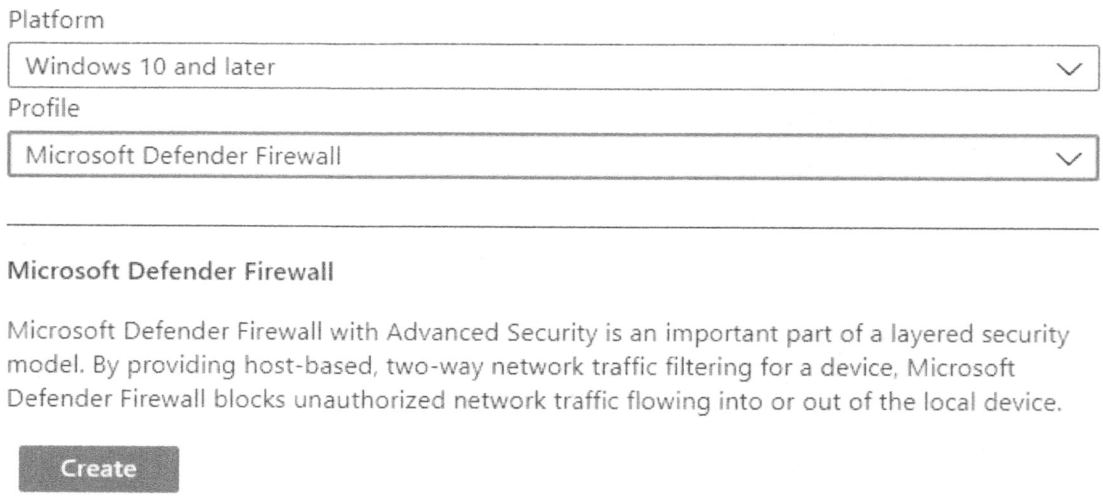

Step 3) Name the Policy, ex: "Enable Windows 10 Firewall" > NEXT > Scroll down to the bottom three

settings:

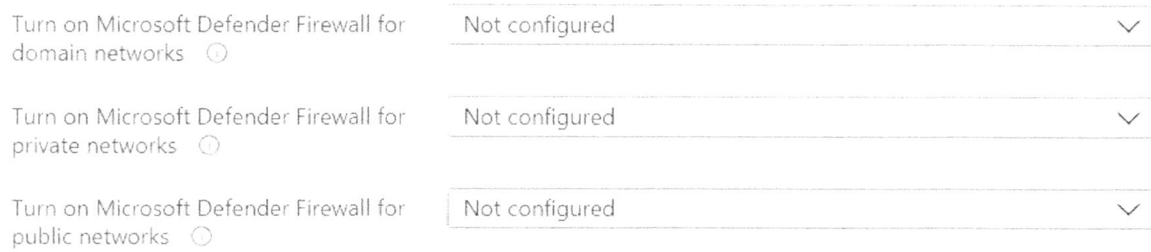

Change all three profiles to match these same three settings shown below:

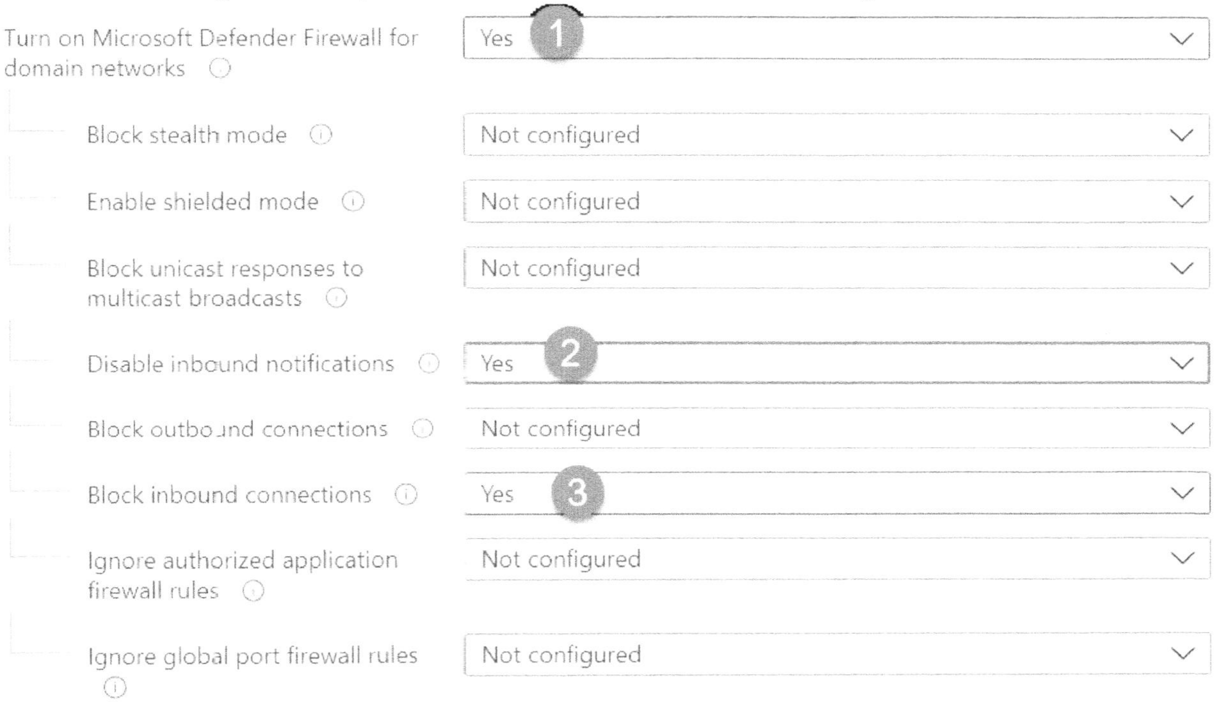

Click Next > on Assignments Tab, click Add Groups and find Lab Users then add and then click NEXT

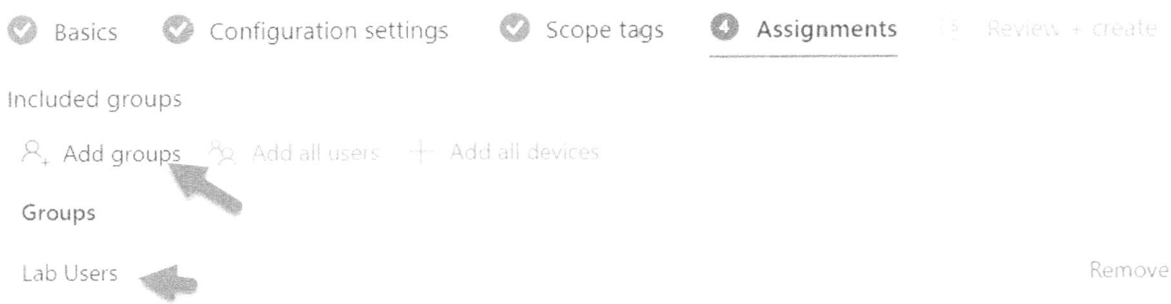

On Step 5 click CREATE

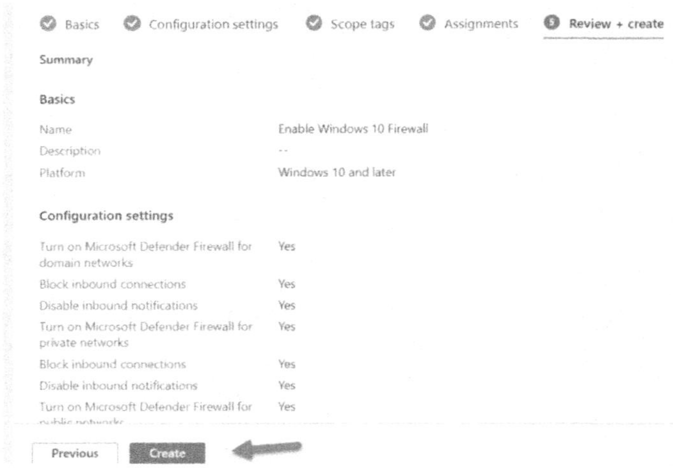

Documentation: [Windows Defender Firewall with Advanced Security (Windows 10) - Windows security | Microsoft Docs]

Tamper Protection

What good is your security solution if it can be disabled by the attacker? This is one of the most important things you can do to protect your endpoint! This should have been enabled in the previous step, but this is where you can find this important setting. This is the Global ON/OFF. If you need to allow some machines to disable their AV, then you would have to disable this Global Setting and deploy Tamper Protection via Intune Policy, scope to just the machine to enable it.

Step 1) Sign into Security.microsoft.com > Settings > Endpoints > Settings > Advanced Features > Toggle Tamper Protection to ON

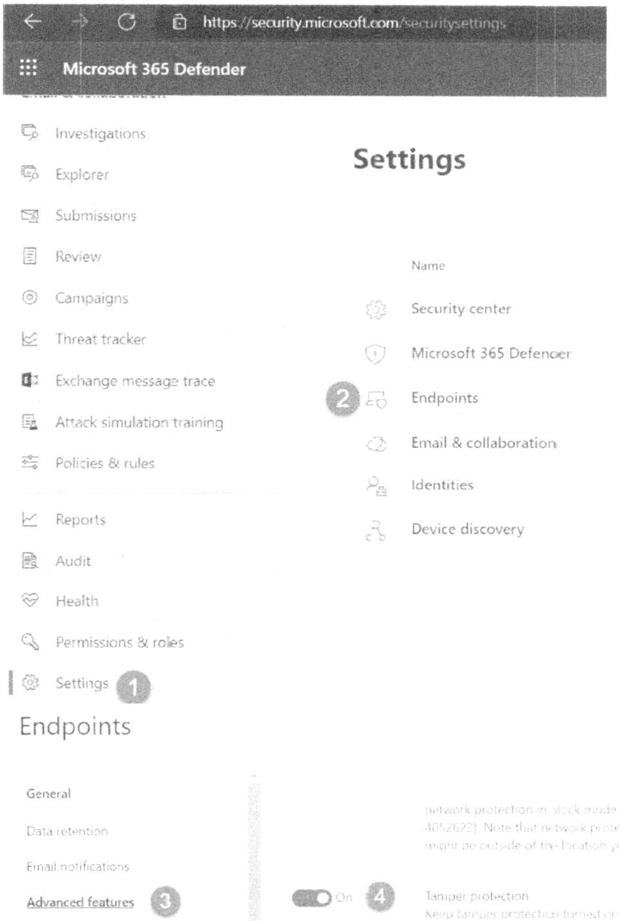

Documentation: [Protect security settings with tamper protection | Microsoft Docs]

Verify Tamper Protection

1. **In PowerShell, run get-MpComputerStatus and see if "IsTamperProtected" is set to True**

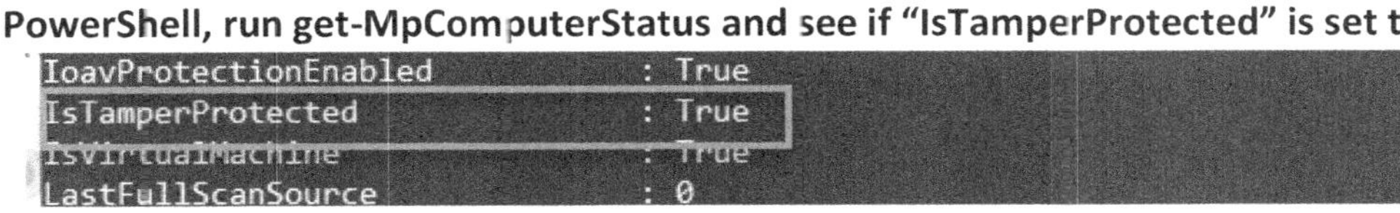

2. **In the Windows Security Center, navigate to Virus & Threat Protection > Manage Settings > Scroll down to Tamper Protection**

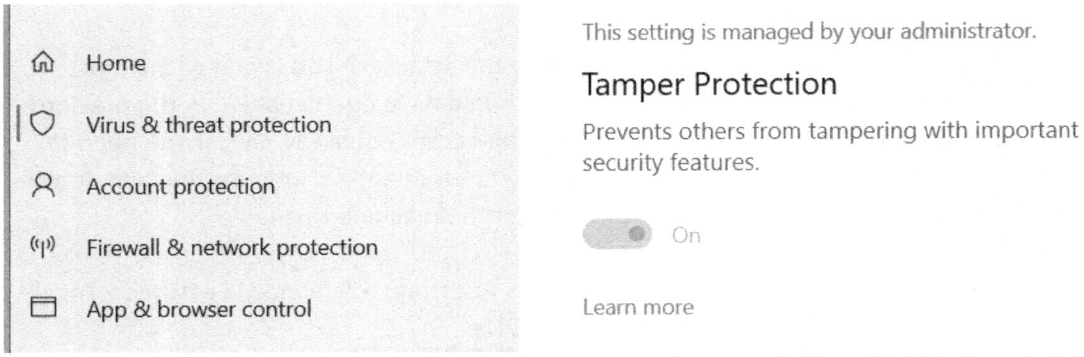

3. Try to disable real-time protection using PowerShell and notice how it fails

Option 1) in CMD, try sc stop WinDefend

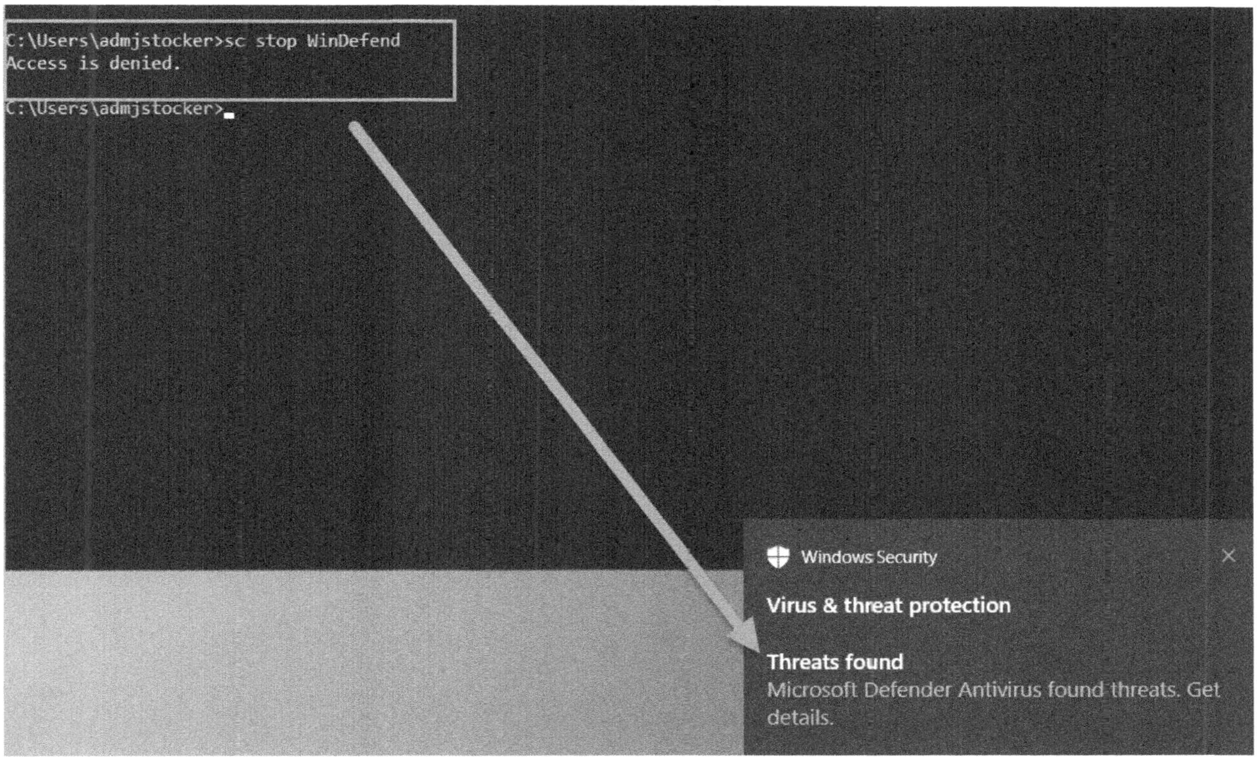

Option 2) in PowerShell try to disable real-time protection

Set-MpPreference -DisableRealtimeMonitoring $true

(then check the status to see if it is disabled. It should remain $false if Tamper Protection is working)

get-MpPreference | fl DisableRealtimeMonitoring

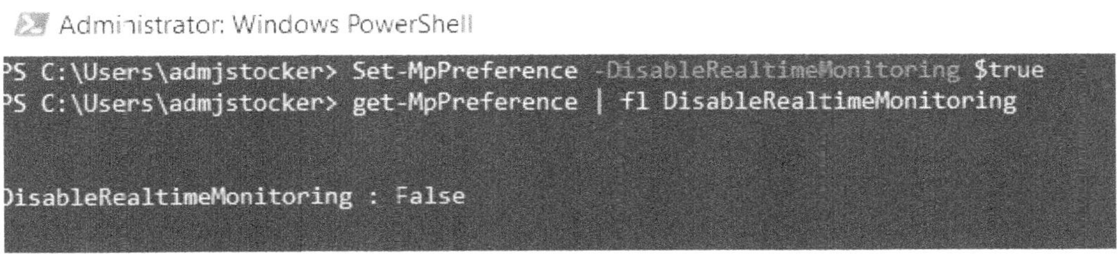

Option 3) Registry

This will fail to work if Tamper Protection is enabled. After reboot, the registry key is deleted.

Option 4) Group Policy

Computer Configuration –> Administrative Templates –> Windows Components –> Microsoft Defender Antivirus (older versions might say Windows Defender Antivirus)

From the right-hand pane, Search for Turn Off Microsoft Defender Antivirus and open and select Enable

This will fail to work if Tamper Protection is enabled. After a reboot, the policy is reverted to "Not Configured"

Troubleshooting Tamper Protection

- **If for some reason the global setting is not enabling Tamper Protection you can force it on specific computers using Intune as follows:**

Navigate to Intune Device Profiles

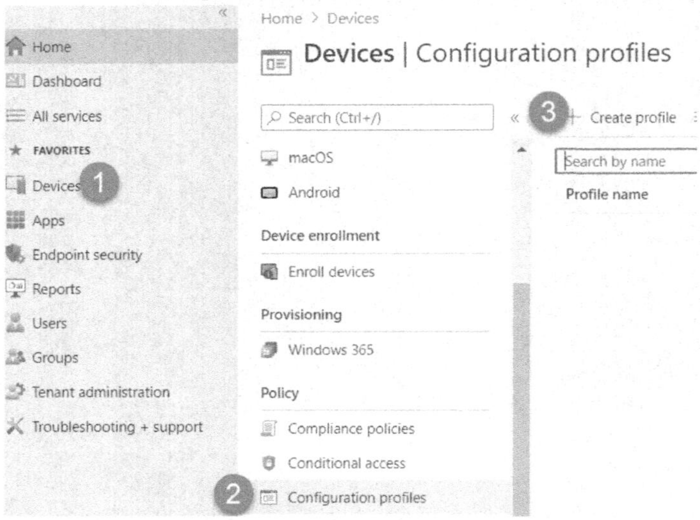

- **Create a profile that includes the following settings:**
- **Platform: Windows 10 and later**
- **ProfileType: Endpoint protection**
- **Settings > Windows Defender Security Center > Tamper Protection**
- **Assign to the Lab Users Group**

EDR Block Mode

When turned on, Microsoft Defender for Endpoint leverages behavioral blocking and containment capabilities by blocking malicious artifacts or behaviors observed through post-breach endpoint detection and response (EDR) capabilities.

TIP: Some customers enable this when they want to keep a 3rd party EPP/AV solution as primary and run Defender AV in passive mode, while then using EDR in Block Mode.

Microsoft recommends leaving EDR in Block mode at all times, even when Defender is the Primary EPP/AV Solution.

Step 1) Sign into Security.microsoft.com > Settings > Endpoints > Settings > Advanced Features > Toggle EDR Block Mode to ON

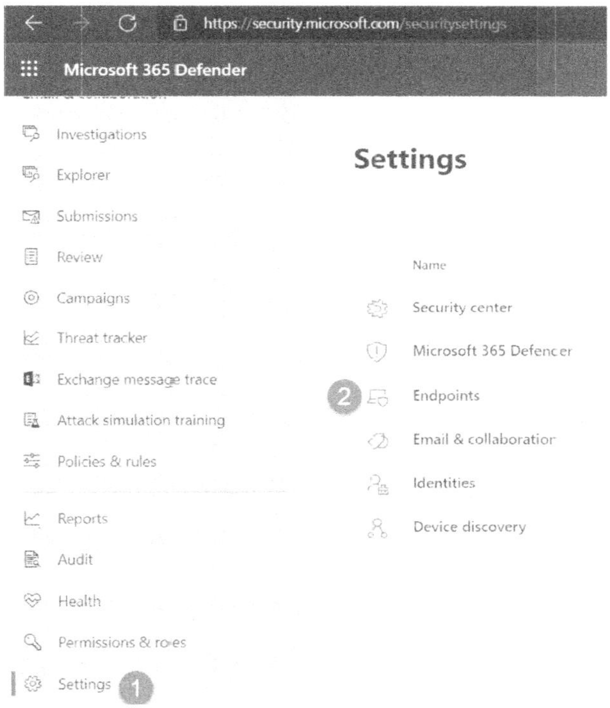

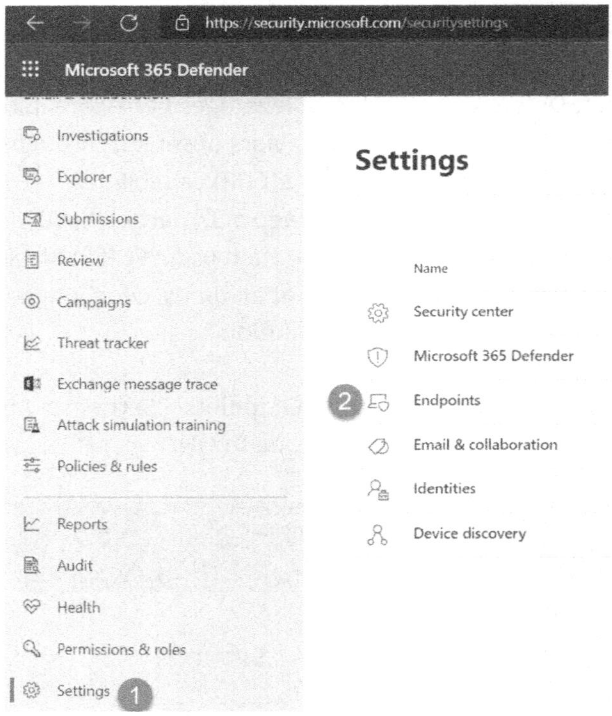

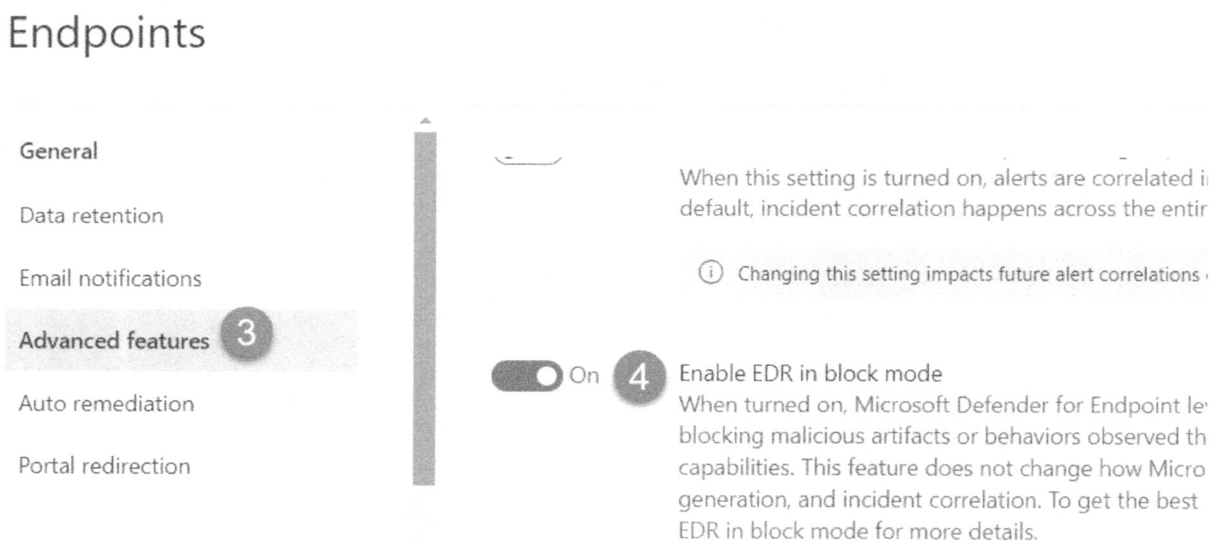

Documentation: https://docs.microsoft.com/en-us/microsoft-365/security/defender-endpoint/edr-in-block-mode?view=o365-worldwide

Block at First Sight

Once the EDR solution is deployed, the next step is to turn on one of the most powerful features that Microsoft Defender for Endpoint offers, known as Block at first sight.

Step 1) Browse to Endpoint.Microsoft.com > Click Endpoint Security > Endpoint Detection and Response > Click Create Policy

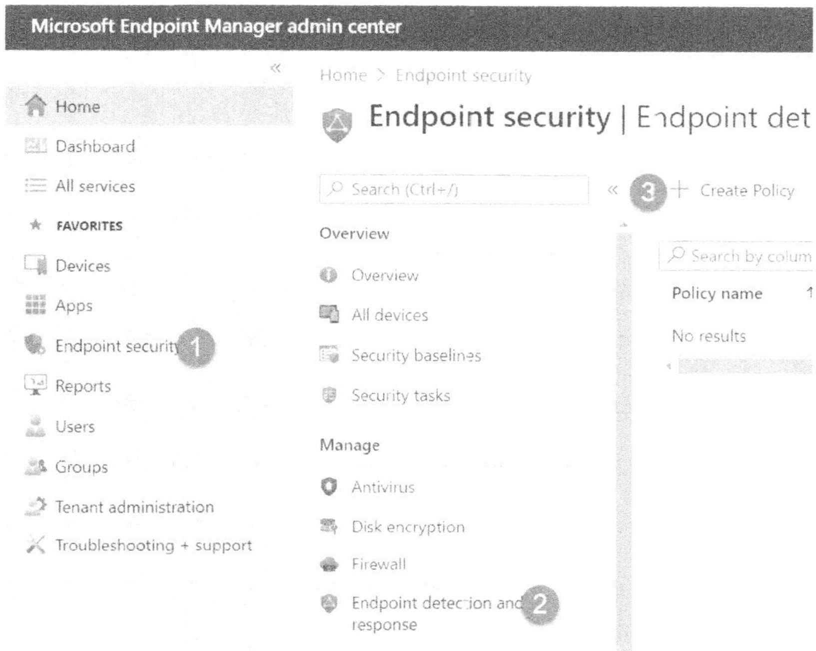

Choose Windows 10 and later, and Endpoint Detection and Response as shown below > Click CREATE

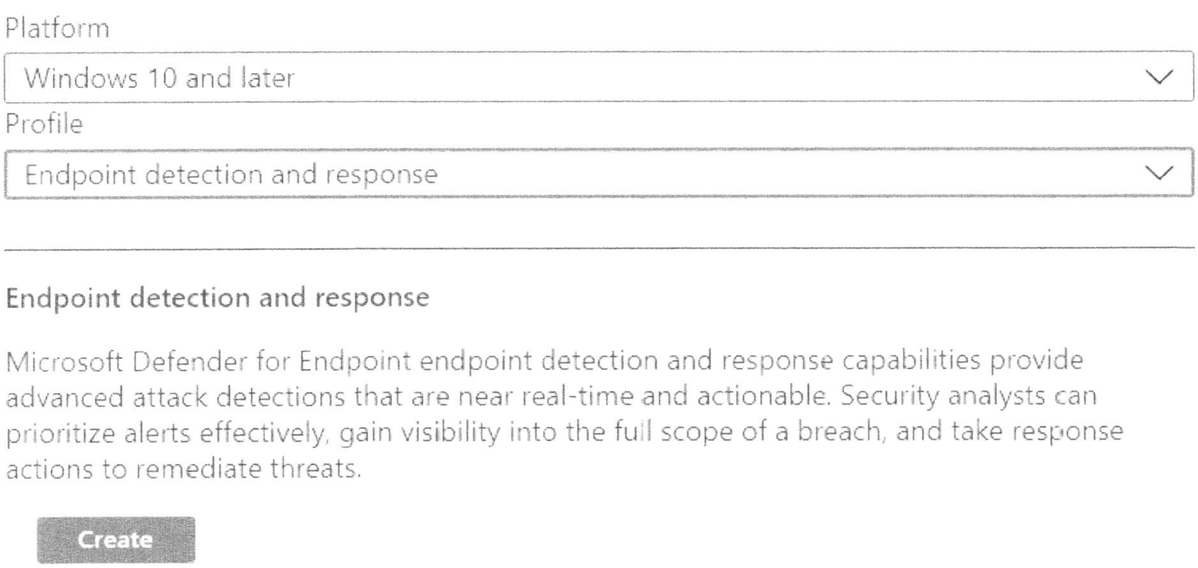

In Step 1 Basics, give it a name such as "Windows 10 EDR Policy" then click NEXT

In Step 2 Configuration Settings, toggle both options to Yes and then click Next

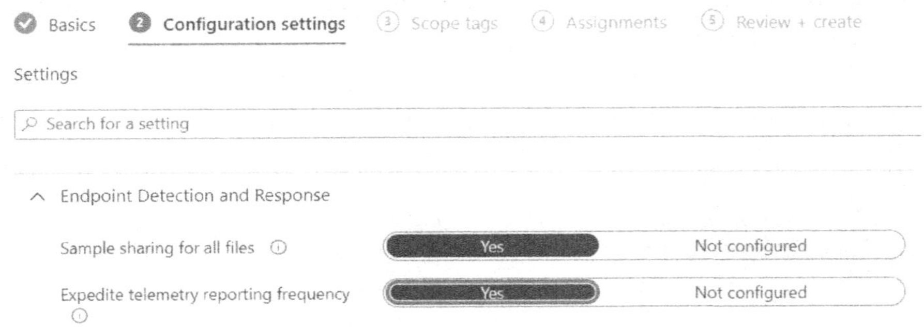

Click Next again (skip scope tags) then Click "Add Groups" in the Assignment to Add the "Lab Users" Group, then click Create to create the policy.

Step 2) The next step is to configure the AV settings so that the Machine Learning Models in the cloud can have at least 50 seconds to scan a newly encountered script or executable.

Browse back to Endpoint Security then click Antivirus > Create Policy

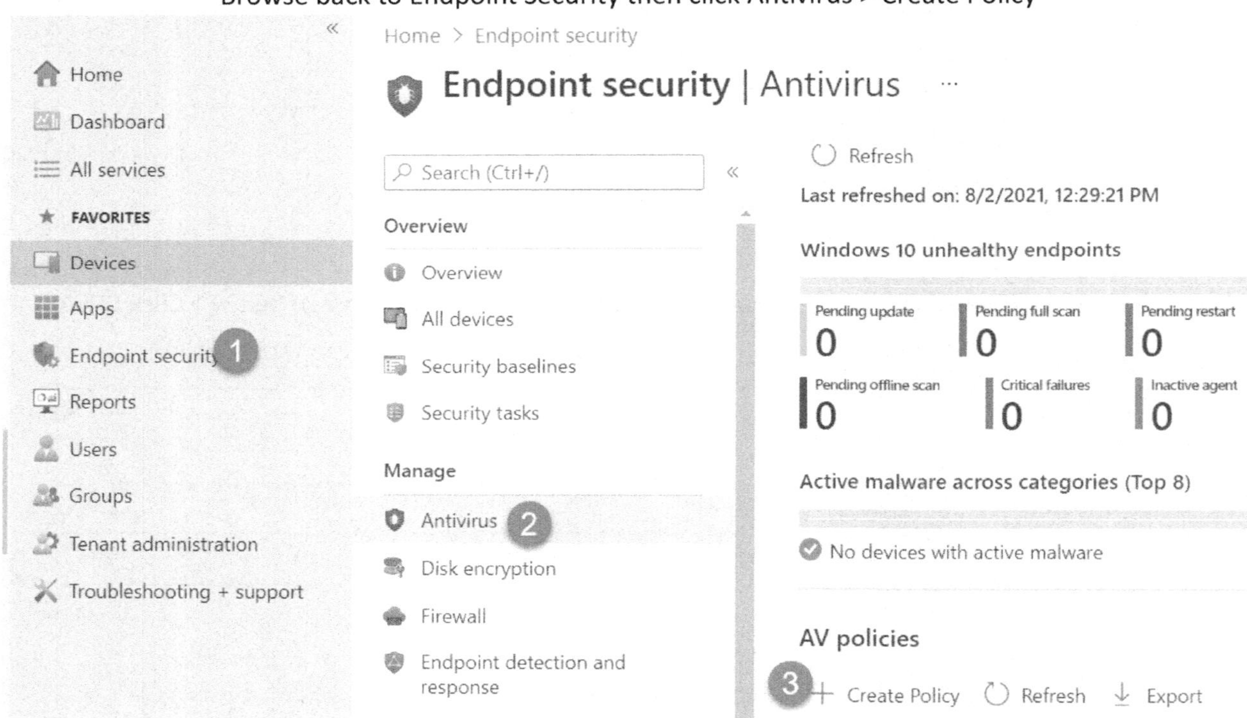

Select Windows 10 and later, and Microsoft Defender Antivirus as shown below then click CREATE

Platform

Windows 10 and later

Profile

Microsoft Defender Antivirus

Microsoft Defender Antivirus

Windows Defender Antivirus is the next-generation protection component of Microsoft Defender for Endpoint. Next-generation protection brings together machine learning, big-data analysis, in-depth threat resistance research, and cloud infrastructure to protect devices in your enterprise organization.

Name the Policy such as "Windows 10 AV Settings" then click Next

Configure the Cloud Protection settings as shown below:

Cloud protection

Setting	Value
Turn on cloud-delivered protection	Yes
Cloud-delivered protection level	High plus
Defender Cloud Extended Timeout In Seconds	50

Highly recommended: Consider **disabling Local Admin Merge**, since any local AV exclusion would prevent Defender from scanning those files. Hint: In the recent Kaseya security event, application vendors requesting exclusions allowed malware authors to hide their malware in those exclusion directories, so use these sparingly and only when applications don't function with AV. Obviously, this would lengthen your testing period since you would have to test all your applications that normally want to be excluded from AV to make sure they function.

Microsoft Defender Antivirus Exclusions

Setting	Value
Disable local admin merge	Yes
Defender Processes to exclude	0 items
File extensions to exclude from scans and real-time protection	0 items
Defender Files And Folders To Exclude	0 items

Most of the following settings are enabled by default by the client, but by configuring them by Policy, we prevent the user from disabling these settings:

Real-time protection

Setting	Value
Turn on real-time protection	Yes
Enable on access protection	Yes
Monitoring for incoming and outgoing files	Monitor all files
Turn on behavior monitoring	Yes
Turn on intrusion prevention	Yes
Enable network protection	Enable
Scan all downloaded files and attachments	Yes
Scan scripts that are used in Microsoft browsers	Yes

In Remediation leave the first text box empty, which will not remove quarantined files, and then change the other two settings as shown below:

Review the Scan settings (these are preferences, and they vary client by client, so we are going to leave the default here but you may want to limit CPU utilization to 10% during scheduled scans since the default is 50%.

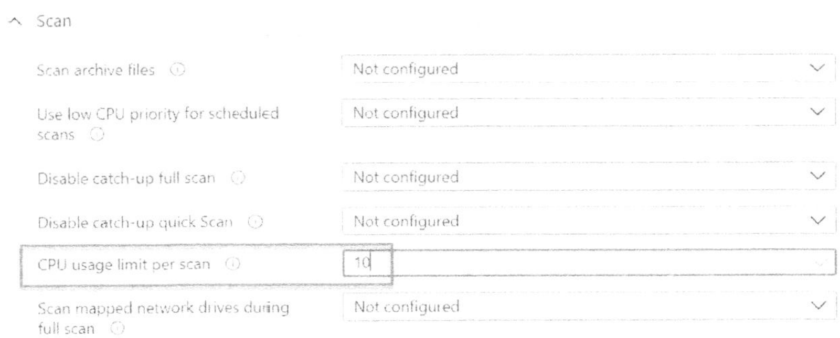

Consider increasing the frequency of Definition updates to every 2 hours (the default is 8). What's really cool about the way Defender works, is that if you encounter polymorphic threats that change faster than the 2-hour interval, the 'block at first site' feature we previously configured will cause any new executable encountered to be detonated in the cloud for threats.

In a production environment, you may want to adjust the 'fallback order' so that if the internal WSUS or SCCM is not available, the client will fall back to get definition updates over the internet from Microsoft (this is the default behavior) but you can adjust it as shown. In this lab, we'll leave it to defaults.

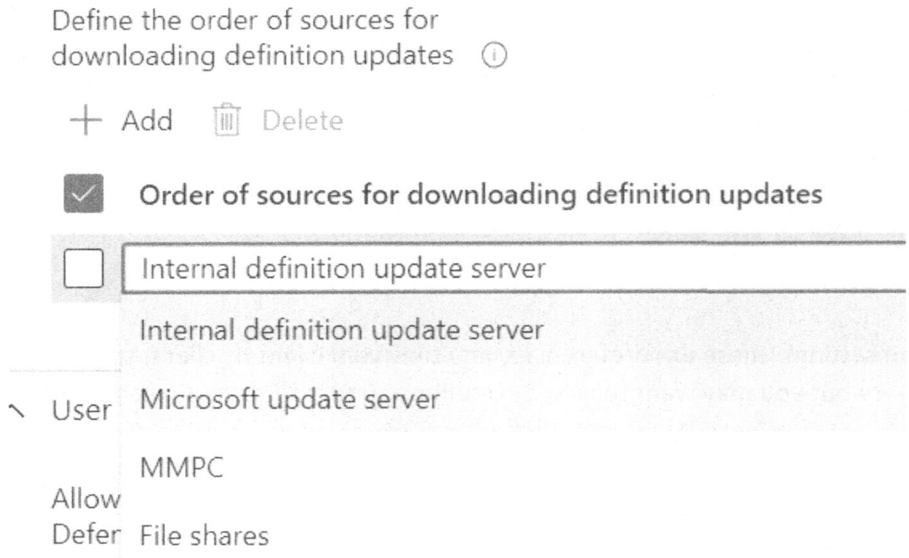

Click Next, then in the Assignments, apply to the Lab Users. Click Next, then Create

Documentation: Enable block at first sight to detect malware in seconds | Microsoft Docs

Controlled Folder Access

By preventing executables and scripts from touching the files on your computer, we can reduce the risk that ransomware can encrypt those files. Controlled Folder Access is a Windows 10 feature that can protect your most sensitive files like "My Documents" or the "Desktop" folder.

GUIDANCE: We recommend enabling this sparingly, on 'Privileged Access Workstations' or IT Administrators and High-Value Targets. We recommend enabling this locally at first so that you can allow users to add exclusions during the testing phase, as there are lots of applications like NotePad++ that your users will likely want to access their local documents.

In the Local Security Center (Taskbar) find the Windows Security icon

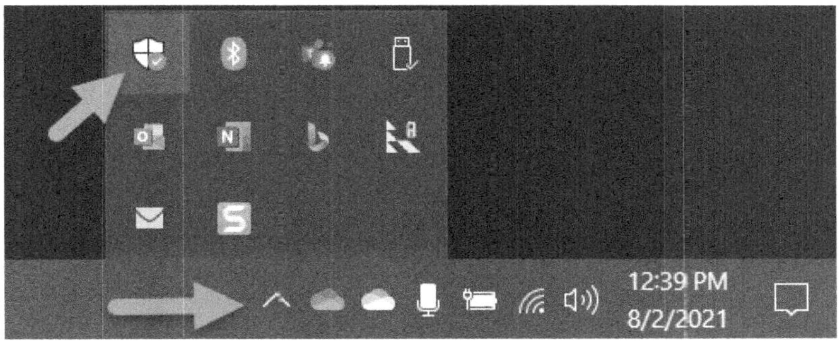

Click Virus and Threat Protection > Manage Ransomware Protection

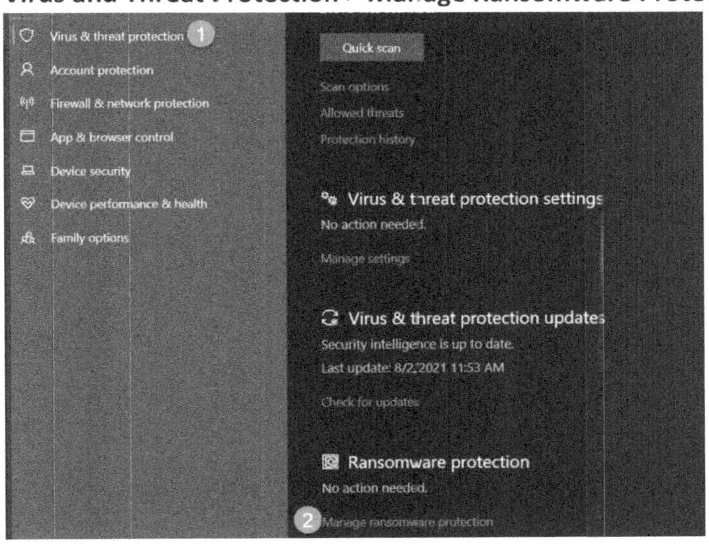

Toggle CFA to ON, then add folders you want to protect such as your Desktop Folder. Finally, add a few applications that you use regularly such as NotePad++ (as an example)

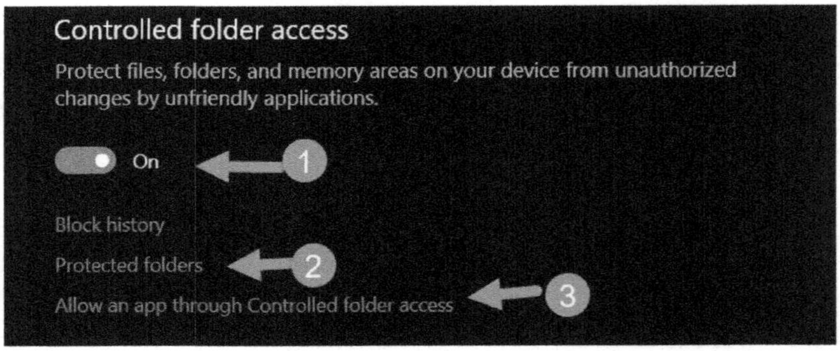

Documentation: Protect important folders from ransomware from encrypting your files with controlled folder access | Microsoft Docs

Verify Controlled Folder Access

Download Malware Simulator from Github (here) The password to unzip the file is malwaresimulator

Sample Syntax: MalwareSimulator.exe -localsystem -evidence

Attack Surface Reduction (ASR)

What if we could prevent Office and Adobe from spawning child processes like CMD.exe or Powershell.exe? That is what ASR rules can do.

Step 1) Browse to Endpoint.microsoft.com > Click on Endpoint Security > Click Attack Surface Reduction > Create Policy

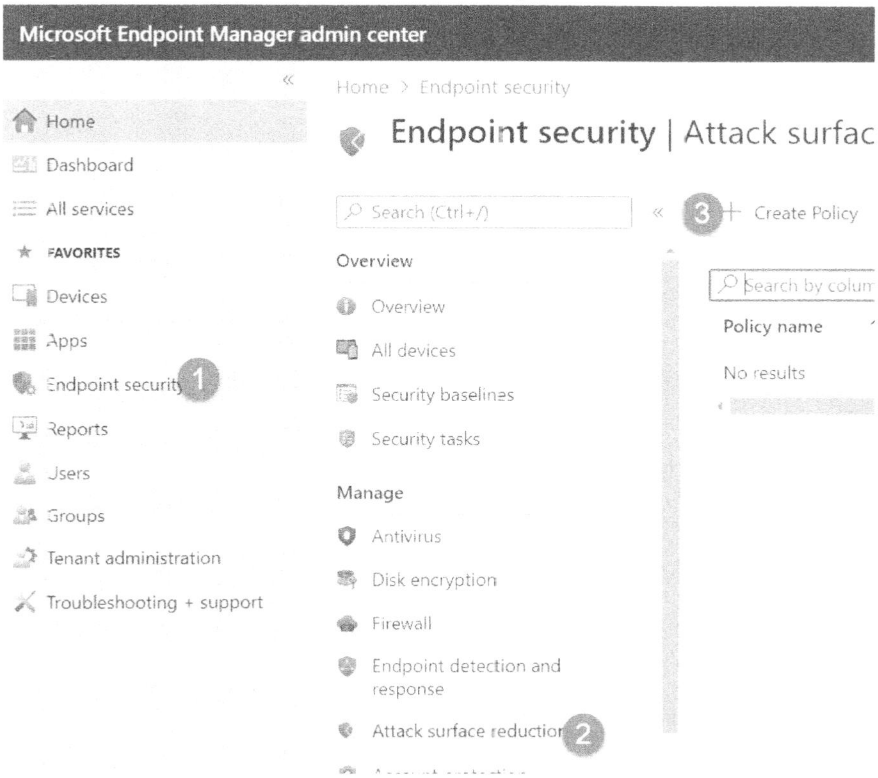

Fill out the selections for Windows 10 and Later > Attack Surface Reduction rules as shown below then click Create

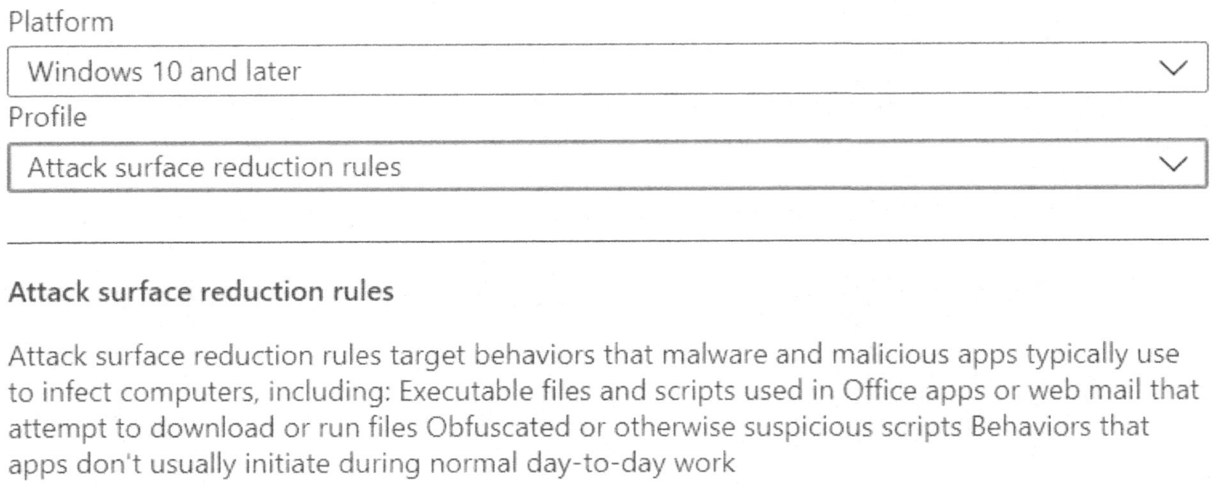

Enter a policy name such as Windows 10 ASR Rules then click Next

Modify each ASR rule as shown below.

Attack Surface Reduction Rules

Block persistence through WMI event subscription	Block
Block credential stealing from the Windows local security authority subsystem (lsass.exe)	Warn
Block Adobe Reader from creating child processes	Enable
Block Office applications from injecting code into other processes	Block
Block Office applications from creating executable content	Block
Block all Office applications from creating child processes	Disable
Block Win32 API calls from Office macro	Disable
Block Office communication apps from creating child processes	Enable
Block execution of potentially obfuscated scripts (js/vbs/ps)	Block
Block JavaScript or VBScript from launching downloaded executable content	Block
Block process creations originating from PSExec and WMI commands	Block
Block untrusted and unsigned processes that run from USB	Block
Block executable files from running unless they meet a prevalence, age, or trusted list criteria	Warn
Block executable content download from email and webmail clients	Block
Use advanced protection against ransomware	Enable
Enable folder protection	Not configured

In the next section, you would add any exclusions. The first two are for Controlled Folder Access, which we did not enable centrally/globally on purpose. This is the policy we discussed earlier deploying as a local policy first. If you decide to then push it out centrally, this is the policy you would modify:

Setting	Value
Enable folder protection	Not configured

The 3rd option is used for excluding items from the ASR rules, whereas the first two are for adding protected folders for Controlled Folder Access and excluding executables from Controlled Folder Access.

Click Next, Assign to Lab Users, then Create.

Documentation: Use attack surface reduction rules to prevent malware infection | Microsoft Docs

Verify Attack Surface Reduction

Download ASR_Analyzer_v2.2.ps1 **and** ASR_Rules_PoSh_GUI.ps1

Sample File 1
https://demo.wd.microsoft.com/Content/TestFile_Block_Office_applications_from_creating_executable_content_3B576869-A4EC-4529-8536-B80A7769E899.docm

Sample File 2
https://demo.wd.microsoft.com/Content/TestFile_OfficeChildProcess_D4F940AB-401B-4EFC-AADC-AD5F3C50688A.docm

Malicious Macros

90% of the malware that enters an organization is said to be some form of Office Macro.

The challenge most organizations face is that some of their departments use Macros for legitimate use (Finance/Accounting Departments).

So how can we block just malicious Macros? We also discussed Attack Surface Reduction rules, which are very effective. Microsoft also offers the "Safe Documents" feature which relies upon virtualization-based security.
But what about when you don't control the endpoint, for whatever reason? You wouldn't be able to deploy ASR or Safe Documents.

For unmanaged endpoints, you can still disable macros in untrusted documents (such as those downloaded from the internet or received via email attachment) using Config.Office.com comes into play, or "Policies for Office Apps." Any edition of Microsoft Apps for Enterprise (formerly known as Office 365 Professional Plus) will download a policy every time the application launches. So, any user who has registered their version of Office with their corporate credential will be protected by the policies created.

To get started Browse to Config.Office.com > Click Sign-IN

On the left navigation, expand Customization > Click "Policy Management" then click Create

Enter a name such as "Office Security Policy"
Select the Group Type: "This policy configuration applies to users"

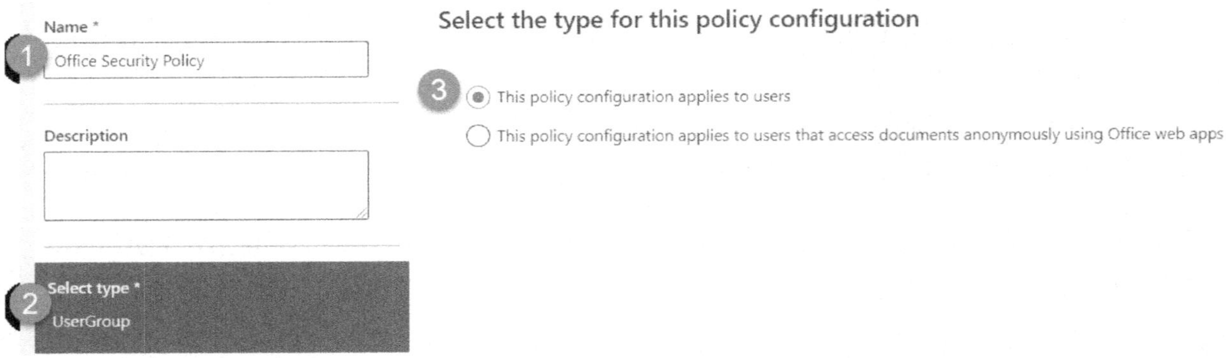

Select the "Lab Users Group"

Click "Configure Policies"

- Disable Trust Bar Notification for unsigned application add-ins and block them
- Disable all Trust Bar notifications for security issues
- VBA Macro Notification Settings: Enable with "Disable without Notification"
- Disable VBA for Office applications
- Block macros from running in Office files from the Internet

When done, click "Create"

TIP: In a production environment, you could enable two additional settings to avoid blocking legitimate Macros:

- Allow Trusted Locations on the network
    - Lockdown the NTFS and/or Share Permissions to only allow authorized users (admins?) from adding Macros to this path (Ask each Department to provide Macros for review)

- Trusted Location #1 (through #20)
    - This is where you can specify the network path of where the authorized Macros can run from

Note: In a production environment, we recommend not pre-configuring policies until after you have allowed "Security Advisor" to look at user telemetry. We'll skip this in the lab since there is no prior user data for the Security Advisor to analyze. But for documentation purposes, here is how you would enable Security Advisor:

Click on "Recommendations turned off"

Click: "Turn on Security Policy Advisor"

The policy advisor will look at user behavior over the previous 14 to 84 days and make recommendations that include guidance on how much the user impacted change would be. This is incredible! This avoids enabling a policy that would disrupt user productivity.
To learn more, see the Documentation here: Overview of Security Policy Advisor for Microsoft 365 Apps for enterprise - Deploy Office | Microsoft Docs

Network Protection

Network protection must be enabled for several technologies that depend on it to work. Patriot once observed a ransomware attack that could have been prevented if Network Protection was enabled. In the customer environment, we saw the MDE log detect that the endpoint was downloading files from a suspicious IP address. However, the client had network protection in Audit only mode, so it did not block the connection.

This was configured in an earlier step when the Defender AV policy was configured. We just want to call it out here again since this setting is so important!

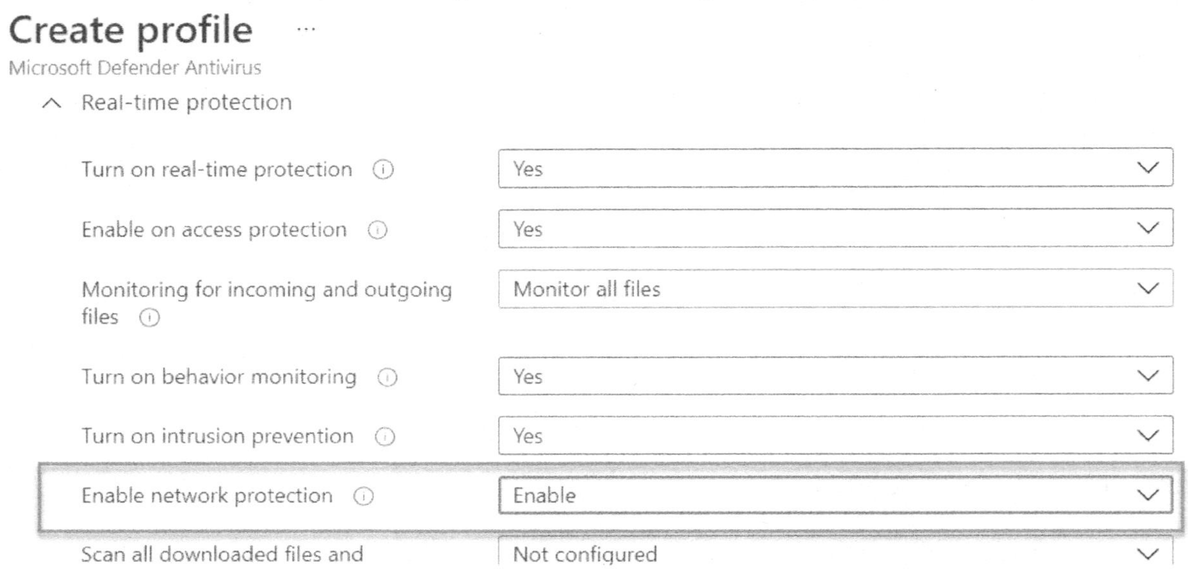

Documentation: Use network protection to help prevent connections to bad sites | Microsoft Docs

Hunting for Threats

Once you have hardened Identity, Email, and Desktop, the next step is to hunt for intrusions, because you should always assume breach. A recent informal survey on Twitter revealed that > 50% of security professionals believe their network has already been breached. You cannot respond to an attack until you have detected the breach. You can't detect a breach unless you are hunting for one.

Microsoft's Advanced Hunting is surfaced in Microsoft Defender (Security.Microsoft.com) and Azure Sentinel. The two main differences between the two products are duration and sources.

Feature	Microsoft Defender	Azure Sentinel
Log Duration	30 Days	>30 Days (As much as you need)
Log Sources	Microsoft Defender Products and MCAS	Anything including generic sources

Regardless of whether you hunt for intrusion using a SIEM like Azure Sentinel or Microsoft Defender, both rely upon the same query language: Kusto Query Language (KQL).

The security analyst executes KQL queries against a cloud-based repository containing all events from the endpoint registry, file system, network events, process launches, as well as vulnerable software installed on the endpoint that is mapped to the CVE database of global vulnerabilities. So, you can write a query that says "show me the endpoints that are vulnerable to CVE-2020XYZ like vulnerable Adobe Acrobat, and then show me if those machines are suddenly modifying the registry or communicating with external IP, or launching obfuscated PowerShell or WMI". The KQL schema can also query against Emails and Attachments in Exchange Online so you can write a query that says, "for this given attachment or subject or MessageID, show me if the attachment was opened on which workstations and what exactly happened after that."

Sample KQL Query – Hunt for SeriousSam (aka Hive Nightmare)

On your VM (TargetMachine1) Simulate the threat activity by querying the SAM folder:

icacls c:\windows\system32\config\SAM

Then hunt for that command line using these KQL queries in the Advanced Hunting Interface https://security.microsoft.com/advanced-hunting

```
#Query1 - Looking for recon activity
DeviceProcessEvents
| where ProcessCommandLine has_all("icacls","config\\sam")
#Query2 - Looking for people attempting to exploit with VSS Shadow Copy
DeviceProcessEvents
| where ProcessCommandLine has_all("HarddiskVolumeShadowCopy","config\\sam")
```

GitHub Repo for additional hunting queries

https://github.com/microsoft/Microsoft-365-Defender-Hunting-Queries

Appendix I Microsoft Security Baselines

The Security Baselines in Microsoft Endpoint Manager were carefully chosen by Microsoft to include top recommendations for protecting the endpoint. Since older protocols like SMB and NTLM are disabled by the baseline, we recommend carefully testing them before applying to production endpoints. According to Microsoft's documentation, the Defender for Endpoint baseline is for physical devices and is not virtual machines (VMs) or VDI endpoints. They caution that certain baseline settings can impact remote interactive sessions in virtualized environments.

Appendix II Protecting Remote Access against Ransomware Threats

This lab experience protects cloud-only organizations. What if you are Hybrid and still have on-premises AD or VPN to protect against ransomware? The recent Colonial Pipeline incident revealed how an unprotected VPN with weak passwords can lead to a ransomware incident.

- Apply security updates/patches to all internet-facing equipment, especially VPN products. The issue with most VPN products is they don't perform posture checking to make sure that the devices that connect are corporate-owned or meet minimum system requirements such as device risk level (posture checking). Also, most VPNs do not implement the principle of least privilege (users can browse to the entire flat network). Microsoft offers several alternatives to replace these older remote access solutions.
    - Microsoft Zero Trust Alternatives to VPN
        - Azure AD App Proxy (included in Azure AD P1 License)
            - Benefits: True Zero Trust, only presents the applications that the employee needs to access. Integrates with Conditional Access, so you can force MFA and even posture check using Intune compliance policy. You can also protect or encrypt downloads using Microsoft Cloud App Security.
        - Microsoft Cloud App Security
            - This CASB solution can sit in the middle between the remote employee and the SaaS application, or the internal application published through Azure AD App Proxy.
        - Azure Virtual Desktop (formerly known as Windows Virtual Desktop)
            - This is a great solution for granting access to vendors or contractors since you wouldn't trust their equipment to connect to your internal network. Great fit for organizations that implement a BYOD policy where employees are allowed to use their own personal laptops/desktops.
        - Cloud PC (for sale beginning August 2nd, 2021, in Windows 365 SKU)

            - Same benefits as Azure Virtual Desktop, but comes pre-installed with Intune and Microsoft Defender, for a flat monthly price. Lower administration overhead compared to Azure Virtual Desktop.
        - Secure Hybrid Access with Authentication Partners such as F5, Citrix, Zscaler, and more.
            - These solutions use Azure AD Conditional Access as a front-end, to secure access to internal applications that may be using legacy protocols
- Implement MFA on any internet-facing remote access solution
    - Microsoft Solutions for integrating MFA with VPN:
        - Azure MFA can integrate with VPN or VDI
            - SAML
                - Cisco ASA
                - Palo Alto
            - RADIUS
                - Microsoft NPS Server

Appendix III – Additional Zero Trust Policies for Production Environments

In an ideal Zero Trust configuration, we would prevent personal machines or hackers' machines from enrolling into Intune, as that would circumvent the device authentication. However, in this lab environment, we didn't configure enrollment restriction since you are likely connecting from your home computers.

Here are the additional policies we would normally recommend for an ideal Zero Trust Configuration

1) Create a new Policy named "CA06 – All Users – Block Intune Enrollment from External IP ranges"

   Why is this policy being created?
   - If a hacker has the username and password, they can enroll a device into Intune to satisfy the conditional access claim. This eliminates the benefit of device-based authentication.
     - Another risk is if an end-user enrolls their home machine into Intune, this might take IT management beyond what the organization is prepared to support
   - Solution: In a production environment, you would create a CA policy to prevent Intune Enrollment from external IP ranges.
   - Considerations:
     - When this policy is in place, a remote user on VPN can enroll into Intune if their VPN configuration is set to 'force tunnel' and not 'split tunnel', and therefore this policy assumes that you have somehow restricted your VPN to only work with company-owned devices.

   - Step 1) Create a Named Location "Authorized Intune Enrollment Locations"
     - Add the IP v4 subnet range "1.1.1.1/32"
       (We won't be enabling this policy for reasons described below, but we want you to get the practice of creating the policy as a reference for what you would do in production).
   - Step 2) Create the Policy with the Cloud App set to "Intune Enrollment"
   - Step 3) Set the Condition to exclude Location: Named location created in Step 1
   - Step 4) Set the Grant Policy to "Block"
   - Step 5) Set the Policy to 'ON' and click Save.

2) Modify the Intune Compliance Policy to require Devices to be at or under a device risk level

- Browse to Endpoint.microsoft.com > Endpoint Security > Compliance Policies or copy and paste this URL into your InPrivate browser window: https://endpoint.microsoft.com/#blade/Microsoft_Intune_DeviceSettings/DevicesComplianceMenu/policies
    - Modify the Compliance Policy

- Modify the bottom policy, Microsoft Defender for Endpoint, to require the device to be at or under the machine risk score of Medium

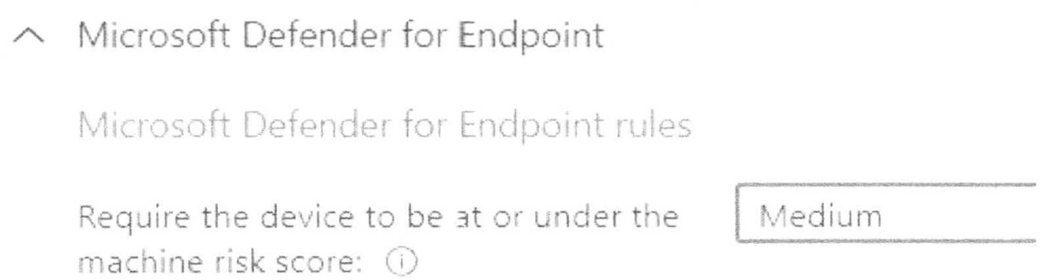

Note: In a lab environment, we are working with an AAD Registered VM, and we are not signing in to it with an AAD or Hybrid Domain Join credential, and therefore the MDE risk score will not be associated with the user and the compliance policy.

Need Help?

Need Professional Consulting to help deploy M365 for your organization? Contact our sales team for a complimentary consultation to discuss your unique project needs and objectives at Hello@PatriotConsultingTech.com

How you can help solve the Cybersecurity Staffing Problem

There are 3.5 million unfilled cybersecurity jobs in the world today and 58% of Chief Information Security Officers expect the problem to worsen[128]. This means that businesses are struggling to fight cybercrime because there are not enough skilled professionals to fill the ranks.

This is the topic of my podcast "Cybersecurity 101 with Larry and Joe"[129] which began when my friend Lawrence "Larry" Lishey asked me how he could transition from his job as a warehouse manager to his dream role in cybersecurity. The idea for the podcast was to record our conversations so that others who had the same goal as Larry may benefit from his experiences. My hope is this book will be another aid for Larry and others like him, so we can all help solve the cybersecurity staffing problem together.

We need more bridge builders and fewer gatekeepers in cybersecurity because we all had to get our start somewhere. I encourage you to blog, mentor, coach, teach and share your knowledge with others.

Thank you for reading my book. If it helped you, please share this link on Social Media: http://bit.ly/OrderSecurityBook

[128] https://cybersecurityventures.com/jobs/

[129] You can follow Larry's journey to a cybersecurity career on iTunes or Spotify at http://bit.ly/CyberSecurity101Podcast or the Web at https://cybersecurity101.podbean.com/

Made in the USA
Las Vegas, NV
06 March 2022

45112472R00098